Janez Juhant,
Bojan Žalec (eds.)

Reconciliation

Theologie Ost – West

Europäische Perspektiven

herausgegeben von

Prof. Dr. Janez Juhant
(Universität Ljubljana)
und Prof. Dr. Albert Franz
(Universität Dresden)

Band 16

LIT

RECONCILIATION

The Way of Healing and Growth

edited by

Janez Juhant and Bojan Žalec

LIT

Cover Picture: Alenka Doblekar, Photomontage
Copyright: Anka Doblekar

Gedruckt auf alterungsbeständigem Werkdruckpapier entsprechend
ANSI Z3948 DIN ISO 9706

Bibliographic information published by the Deutsche Nationalbibliothek
The Deutsche Nationalbibliothek lists this publication in the Deutsche Nationalbibliografie; detailed bibliographic data are available in the Internet at http://dnb.d-nb.de.

ISBN 978-3-643-90202-3

A catalogue record for this book is available from the British Library

Klosbachstr. 107
CH-8032 Zürich
Tel. +41 (0) 44-251 75 05
Fax +41 (0) 44-251 75 06
e-Mail: zuerich@lit-verlag.ch
http://www.lit-verlag.ch

LIT VERLAG Dr. W. Hopf
Berlin 2012
Fresnostr. 2
D-48159 Münster
Tel. +49 (0) 2 51-620 320
Fax +49 (0) 2 51-23 19 72
e-Mail: lit@lit-verlag.de
http://www.lit-verlag.de

Distribution:
In Germany: LIT Verlag Fresnostr. 2, D-48159 Münster
Tel. +49 (0) 2 51-620 32 22, Fax +49 (0) 2 51-922 60 99, e-mail: vertrieb@lit-verlag.de
In Austria: Medienlogistik Pichler-ÖBZ, e-mail: mlo@medien-logistik.at
In Switzerland: B + M Buch- und Medienvertrieb, e-mail: order@buch-medien.ch
In the UK: Global Book Marketing, e-mail: mo@centralbooks.com

Acknowledgments

We thank to all persons who contributed to the appearing of the book. Our special thanks go to: the reviewers, Professor Matjaž Potrč and Professor Dean Komel, both from Faculty of Arts, University of Ljubljana; to Samo Grčman for the layout; to Valerija Japelj, who helped by the final corrections of the book; last, but not least, to all the authors of the book.

Our special thanks go to Slovenian Book Agency, which financially supported the appearing of the book.

Janez Juhant and Bojan Žalec, the editors
Ljubljana, July 2012

CONTENTS

PHILOSOPHY AND ART

CHURCH, MINISTRY AND RELATIONAL THEOLOGY

INTRODUCTION

The motivation for the book and its aims

The distant and the recent history of humanity in large amount consist of clashes, conflicts, wars, violence etc. The same is true on more individual and personal level. Yet, on the other hand, the life of quality, development and flourishing of persons and of society is possible only in the contexts that are not poisoned with fear, hate, distrust, resentment and other negative factors that block empathy, compassion, dialogue, solidarity and cooperation. To cultivate the conditions characterized by the last mentioned positive attributes, and taking into account constant arising of afore mentioned negative phenomena in any place and time inhabited by humans (growing to extremes in particular cases) it is plane that forgiveness and reconciliation are necessary moments of every successful human development, either individual or social or even global. Hence, the importance of reconciliation is enormous. However, its cultivation is alas quite often almost at the edge of human capabilities.

The central goal of this book is to contribute to the answer about the possible ways of realization of reconciliation, particularly in our times of globalization and of spreading of the instrumentalist reason. The knowledge gathered on it should help individuals and groups in their efforts for forgiveness and reconciliation with each other and to promote dialogue among (especially quarreled) societal groups. Taking into account the nature and central meaning of reconciliation for a human life of quality it is not surprising that it can be successfully and integrally considered only through dialogue between different approaches and scientific disciplines. This is the reason for the decision that such a variety of approaches will adorn our book.

For future from history

Unger claims that reconciliation is a difficult process yet it is indispensible for perspective society. The prerequisite for reconciliation is tolerance, "the virtue of living together". Additionally he stresses the following conditions or positive factors of reconciliation: recognition that life has the highest value; justice: "Justice is an excellent and human basis ensuring coexsistence, freedom of people and therefore peace"; a cultivation of dialogue. Reconciliation is important as a positive factor for actually united Europe. He ends by establishing that after all reconciliation depends on us and on our living in truth.

Trontelj observes that the past of humankind abounds with injustice and violence, often committed against large numbers of innocent people. Most of the victims were caught against their will between sides in various conflicts, which did not solve any of the problems that served as proclaimed reasons for war. During the intervals of peace, many became victims of paranoid measures put in place for the security of the state. On European soil, World War II and the three totalitarian systems are the darkest examples. The European Union was created in order to avoid similar senseless destruction, atrocities and suffering in the future. However, our fading memories of the horrible abuses may no longer guarantee the culture of peace, collaboration and democracy needed to avert the risk of repeated cycles of war and violence. Honest and passionate learning from history may be one of the few ways to avoid future disasters. On the other hand, enforced forgetting would be an enormous moral mistake with long-term, potentially severe consequences for society.

Biblical foundations and education

Krašovec argues that the Hebrew Bible is a message of forgiveness and reconciliation and that they have the highest priority in God's relationship to humanity, higher than punishment. God is much more God of mercy than God of strict justice. This supremacy is made possible only by the victory of the absolute monotheism over the effect of polytheism. God is by his essence God of forgiveness, forgiveness is a supreme mark of his goodness. An attainment of reconciliation and of unity is the true purpose of activities of God and humanity. Given that all non-righteous people are members of community Kraševec stresses the importance of the role of a minority of the righteous and their suffering.

Gerjolj considers the conflict between Esau and Jacob and their reconciliation as an example where we can learn and discern several levels or stages of reconciliation and the relations between them. He distinguishes ten stages ranging from the reconciliation out of love (matrimonial or partner reconciliation) to the honest, responsible and with God connected life which is the last and the highest level of reconciliation. Especially important and crucial is the stage of reconciliation with oneself. Gerjolj claims that the process of solving of the conflict between Esau and Jacob can serve as a special learning model which is relevant and useful in many actual situations and distresses where humans long for solution.

Măcelaru argues that the story of the Tower of Babel (Genesis 11) aims at promoting peaceful cohabitation in spite of cultural differences. He concludes "that reconciliation is an idea deeply rooted in the world and thought of the Old Testament. It includes that provisions for the restoration of Israel's fellowship with God and its manifestations at the social level are multiple and highly encouraged. As such, both the vertical and the horizontal dimension identified in the New Testament usage of the term are available in the Old Testament theology as well."

Victims

Juhant reminds us that according to *Charta of human rights* all people should be integrated in a universal moral community. Every moral which excludes some persons or groups is not moralistic in accordance with the *Charta*. All racist and ideological images of man have been a forgery of people in order to sacrifice them. The consequences have been suffering and sacrifice of nations like Armenians, Ukrainians, Jews, Bosnians, Slovene and other class-enemies, Christians, and other mass victims. Because "the essential is against life", we can say that the modern life is against the essence of man, because it deals mostly with his immediateness and austerities. Still today we are witnesses of mass-victims and unfinished processes of reconciliation. Those campaigns are covered by media and other mechanisms. We can paraphrase Girard: the old myths have been replaced by new (modern) ones. Because man is a limited being ("original sin"), we are all involved in victimisation and burdened with guilty. The Slovene revolutionary case is a horrible example of the implementation of modern machineries of victimisation. The processes of reconciliation here and over the world are going slowly and the "birth of humanism" and of empathy remains still an important task of moral consciousness of Slovenes and of whole humane race.

The main frame of **Palaver's** reflection on forgiveness is Girard's theory of violence. Palaver considers the danger of using the status and suffering of victims for further violence. In preventing such an instrumentalization forgiveness is of crucial importance. In this sense he understands forgiveness as a precondition of reconciliation. As an example of being defeated by temptation of turning a concern for victims into aggression he alleges crusades. Also modern terrorism can be understood in this way. Palaver supports and complements his views also by reference to works of Charles Taylor (powerful cachet of victimhood) and also Vamik Volkan (egoism of victimization). He stresses the importance of acknowledgment of our own impurity and weakness ("we are all to blame" (Dostoyevsky)) to avoid falling in the dangerous cult of a victim and scapegoating. This leads us to the topic of the original sin. Indeed, Palaver's thesis is that we can find a connection between forgiveness and proper attitude to a victim and a perpetrator "at the heart of Abrahamic revelation". He concludes with the political outlook we may derive from Taylor's work. Regarding the modern situation he states:"We are today so much in need of forgiveness that we should encourage all religious and world views to develop it as strongly as possible".

Strehovec applies Girard's theory to the situation in Slovenia. He concludes: "The theory of mimetic violence of Rene Girard could be one of many possible interpretations of Slovenian recent history and violence. The reconnection of the mimetic violence and the founding murder with the Slovenian history, mass killings, independence, and present initiatives for national reconciliation could be the starting point to overcome the historical divisions and to build the culture of dialogue, peace and unity. The divinization of innocent victims, the identification of justice and righteousness in Slovenian past are important preconditions for establishing symbolic places where the name of every innocent victim will be remembered and the righteousness as a virtue will be celebrated. Every civilized society should reveal the historical truth from the perspective of justice, overcome the frameworks of past violence, and embrace the truth and symbols which reunite, heal and finally give it hope and prosperity."

Philosophy and art

Žalec analyses the concept of reconciliation. He tries to shell out the conditions of reconciliation. His analysis involves the investigation of the connections between justice, punishment, inner motivation and transformation, reparation of relationships and forgiveness. Inner motivation for establishment of positive relationship and internal transformation of the parties involved in reconciliation are necessary conditions of true reconciliation. The author gives the following definition of reconciliation: Reconciliation is achieved when the harm done by injustice to positive relationship between individuals or groups is repaired or compensated in such a way that it no more hinders the establishing of positive relationship. Regarding justice he concludes that justice is an essential part of the process of reconciliation. On the other hand reconciliation is a positive factor, background or even a condition of (future) justice. Reconciliation is a relative, manifold (differentiate) and transitive concept. It is not true that forgiveness is a necessary condition of reconciliation as such.

Klun deals with the Levinas' understanding of the uniqueness of an individual person (of his/her irreducible singularity) and his/her (ethical) meaning. This uniqueness lies in the person's relationship to the Other. The true individuality of a person and his/her ethical greatness cannot be grasped and evaluated by the history or an impersonal reason. Rather it is founded on person's relationships to the Other, on his/her unique responsibility to the Other. The Other calls me and thus individuates me, assigns me with unique obligations, duties, vocation, responsibility, gives me an infinite meaning (I am called without any limit and thus subjected to an infinite responsibility) and thus makes me transcendent. An individual person as an irreducible singularity is born only through a unique call of the Other. On this background Klun explains also Levinas' understanding of (proper) time, messianism and the possibility of the meaning of suffering and deaths (of innocents).

According to **Jamnik** reconciliation does not imply forgetting about past events, rather it has to do with internal liberation which manifests itself in forgiveness, mutual respect and sincere wish to create new relations. Reconciliation is a sign of internal strength, freedom and courage, but most of all it is the work of God (Bl. John Paul II). Thus - according to Jamnik - the human perspective of reconciliation complements the theological perspective. Every human being in this world, in all its fragility, is in need of forgiveness. This need presents itself in his humility to sincerely accept the forgiveness of both his fellow humans and God. At the same time, every human being is expected to exercise forgiveness, as this is the only way to stop the vicious circle of vengeance and hatred. Pace Jamnik reconciliation happens on both personal and structural levels. If the latter are unfair, it is impossible to achieve a new quality of relations within a society.

Avsenik Nabergoj compares narrative from the Old Testament Joseph of Egypt with Shakespeare's play *The Tempest*. She finds important similarities between the two. In the second part of the article she briefly comments some modern philosophical texts on forgiveness (Hampton, Griswold, Konstan) and establishes "that purely rational philosophical arguments are not sufficient when it comes to most important points to observe".

Strahovnik analyses and compares the emotions of shame and guilt and lists and explains the differences between them. He argues that we should understand shame as an emotional response to the violation of humanity or neglect of it in the other. This breach is also the criterion of its adequacy. At the end he stresses the importance of the proper understanding of moral emotions and of truthfulness for national reconciliation.

Paganini deals with the question how reconciliation can enrich media ethics. She investigates the possibilities of minimal common media morality and application of minimalist ethics - in particular of principlism and its principles (autonomy, beneficiance, nonmaleficience, justice) - to the field of media. She claims that reconciliation could give orientation to media ethics and form the background for understanding and discussing of principles of media ethics.

Church, ministry and relational theology

Constantineanu examines the paradigm shift which Apostle Paul makes vis-a-vis the classical understanding of reconciliation and the radical novelty he brings to the concept. He concludes: "Paul's vision of reconciliation was radically shaped by, and grounded in, the story of Christ: a world of new possibilities and radical innovations is opened up now "in Christ", with serious implications for all those living within this new reality. We have seen that there is in Paul's theology an understanding of reconciliation that is linked to a vision of reality that transcends the natural possibilities and which offers a different set of values from those of this world, and produces different results. This vision inspired him throughout his life and ministry and gave him the impetus to be constantly engaged in *reconciling practices /.../* It was the same vision worked out in Paul's life that offered an incentive for his congregations to think and act likewise and, indeed, it also inspires us to continue to build on that vision".

Guggenberger's paper has three parts. He starts with the introduction of Dietrich Bonhoffer's thesis that Church is the place where guilt is acknowledged. In the second part he explains the meaning of this statement and reasons for it. He claims that forgiveness and confession of guilt are necessary conditions of reconciliation. At the end he reflects on the chances and duties of churches in the reconciliation process and points out "[t]hat it is of enormous importance - not only to the church itself - that the Christian community asks forgiveness in public".

Prüller-Jagenteufell is following Dietrich Bonhoffer in his consideration of penultimate forms of forgiveness and reconciliation that Bonhoffer named "scarring over" of guilt. They are needed for the creation of a peaceful society. It is a task of politics and of the churches to pursue the goal of their realization. A responsible action in the penultimate reality is pace Bonhoffer a preparation for Christ. Its counterpart is a restrainer by which the restraining power - which sets limits to the evil - is realized in the penultimate reality. A restrainer is used by God to protect the world from disintegration, to protect His creation for the ultimate salvation.

Scaring over of guilt is an analogy of reconciliation - which is a matter of ultimate reality - in the penultimate reality. There are profound differences between the two which Prüller-Jagenteufell points to. At the end of the paper he draws some consequences from his consideration of the scaring over of guilt for our present situation and for the resolving of political conflicts. He explains three steps that such a resolving should involve: articulation of the truth, building of a transitional justice and finding the ways to heal.

Oprean deals with the idea of the Church as God's reconciliation agency. In order to fulfill this task the Church must avoid not only the vertical reduction of reconciliation to a relationship of individual to God (individualism) but also its horizontal reduction (egocentrism) by way of limitations of reconciliation only to "us" (captivity of reconciliation as only internal practice of the Church). Only so the Church can perform her threefold ministry (education of faith, social care of love, and prophetic ministry). "Reconciliation is God's initiative toward humankind. To reduce reconciliation /.../ means actually to deny God's eternal plan of reconciliation, powerfully displayed and reveled in Christ event."

Osredkar claims that forgiveness is on one hand a renunciation of one's self, but exactly this renunciation means the continuation of the life of the forgiving person on the other hand. The frame of his reflection is the relational theology. According to it, to live means to be in a relationship. A man who forgives accepts his imperfection and recognizes his dependence on the other. Forgiveness is an undeserved gift. This gift is a continuation of a relationship. As such it is a continuation of life for both, the subject and the other.

Religion, culture, history and society

Ocvirk`s thesis is that the opinion that Christians and Muslims can improve their relationship on the virtue that they both respect Jesus is ill founded because the image and meaning of Jesus in their narratives is quite different. Ocvirk stresses especially Suni Islam as problematic from the point of view of modern free and democratic society. The way to reconciliation is not the stressing of similarities but rather the respect of uniqueness and particularity. In the process of cultivation of such a respect knowledge based on reason and (humanities and social) science plays an important role.

Mester investigates the ways and concrete examples of the creation of narrative identities based on political reconciliation (either based on cultural memory or rooted in the taboo of public speech). The theoretical frame of the reference of his essay is constituted by the works of Nietzsche, Jan Assmann, Harald Weinrich and also Robin G. Collingwood.

Kovács paper is intended as a draft of the study of the Hungarian collective and political mentality in the 20th century. He leans on the work of the Hungarian political thinker István Bibó. Kovács` starting point is the situation in Hungary after the First World War when Hungary was left without one third of its prior territory. This situation was characterized by the feeling of defeat (Kovacs claims that Hungarian culture emerged after the First World War was, borrowing the term of Wolfgang Schivelbusch, the culture of defeat) and there was the need for many-layered reconciliation (of the past and present times etc.). But unfortunately reconciliation did not take place. The reality was rather quite opposite. Two sides dominated the political scene at that time: westernizers on one side and the Hungarian populists on the other. The tension between the two sides was very intense. Additionally political hysteria (which always starts out from a traumatic historical experience in the life of a community), myths (neurotic fictions), suppression and forgetting of the past have taken place. The adaptation to the new situation was just partly successful; in many respects it was a failure. This can be said also for the following Hungarian history (including terror against Jews and coping with the communist past) up until the present days when the concurrence of victims (Chaumont) takes place. Kovacs concludes: 1. Hungary is today in the state of a permanent cold civil war; 2. For reconciliation a delicate balance of recollection, forgetting and a common set of basic values accepted by the whole national community is needed. 3. Those preconditions are missing in Hungary.

Dežman's essay brings many data about the communist revolution in Slovenia. They form the evidence of the criminal nature of the revolution. Dežman claims that reconciliation (in Slovenia) is a dynamic process which consists of detabooisation of many half-truths and lies of Titoistic ideology and of intense public and political facing with the criminal heritage of the totalitarian regimes. He adds that "reconciliation is not wordless and senseless pacification, it is a painful and long-term process of individual and social change". He concludes that the agents of Titoistic regime in Slovenia probably will not be punished. However, we should not accept their version of the history.

In July 1990 a big reconciliation ceremony happened at mass grave Kočevski Rog in Slovenian woods. After the democratic turn many people expected that the mass killings in Slovenia and the mass graves will be investigated. But this expectation was not realized, establishes **Ferenc**. Events that happened immediately after the Word War II are one of the most traumatic in the Slovenian history. Yet twenty years after the mentioned reconciliation ceremony and the change of the regime we observe that the graves of the war losers and some civilians even 66 years after the end of the war are still not properly arranged. For majority it is not known where their bodies lie and they were not buried in decent and human manner. In Slovenia there is an agreement only on the principal level that everyone who lost his life in the war or because of the war has the right to his name and his grave. On the other hand in the regard of many practical questions there is no sufficient consensus to arrange the matters properly. Even the reproaches that the past should be left alone because it supposedly does not concern young generations are unfortunately accepted by many Slovenians. Ferenc concludes that all thoughts about reconciliation and unity of Slovenian people will be in vain if a lack of concrete action of executive power will continue and that as a nation we are for decades confronted with the challenge to overpass this burden of the past that is pushing us to the ground.

Kleyman deals with the origins of grassroots authoritarianism in Russia. In the 20th century there was a rapid urban growth in Russia which caused an identity crisis. Combined with a totalitarian ideology it resulted in the grassroots authoritarianism which is characterized by intolerance to any form of (O)otherness. In the post-Soviet era the rapid social capitalization was not accompanied by reconciliation and coping with the totalitarian past. So the grassroots authoritarianism survived. It is an important factor of the shaping of the contemporary official ideology and policies. Violence is not only a Russian problem. It is rather a universal problem of the world. According to Kleyman the important factor of violence - partly because it causes the feeling of loosing of identity- is urbanization. The solution is maybe in the realization of the motto of unity in diversity. This realization is however hardly possible without cultivation of a reverence for life (Schweitzer). This reverence is at the same time the starting point of reconciliation worldwide.

Bahovec deals with the role of culture and community in reconciliation processes. He believes that a genuine reconciliation process should integrate all aspects of human life. Without this reconciliation cannot reach the deep level of human life needed for genuine co-existence and the more profound cooperation of previously conflicting people, groups and cultures. He devotes special attention to the clarification of the Ubuntu (Southern African) way of reconciliation. He reminds us on the truth pointed out by Jovan Jukić that the war in the territory of ex-Yugoslavia was a war of centuries of unresolved memories. This explains the fact that in the first phase of that war the symbolic cultural objects, mosques and churches, were destroyed with great intensity. The destruction of culture was an integral part of the efforts to create an ethnically monolithic society. He concludes: "The African concept of Ubuntu reminds us that in a reconciliation process the whole society and its cultures should be included".

Trauma and divorce

Kompan Erzar & Erzar consider the importance of liberation from trauma. They stress "that a traumatic experience is primarily defined by our internal responses to it". They list and explain its conditions and needed steps and the obstacles for living a trauma behind. They especially concentrate on the Slovene situation marked by mass killings after the Second World War. However, also the rest of Europe is not much better off regarding healing of post-war traumas: "it may be that we all lack a model of how to get out of black-and-white historiography and how to set up a convincing and effective treatment of trauma." The example of Slovene writer Boris Pahor - who is relatively widely read in Europe - can be seen as an evidence for this thesis.

Simonič points out the importance of empathy to hear the other, his/her suffering and pain. By recognizing that our enemy suffers we recognize that he/she is a human being. This is the beginning of the process of forgiving and maybe also of reconciliation. It is also the moment of liberation from trauma since we recognize that it does not really control our love.

Slatinek claims that gospel considers forgiveness as the most important way for reaching reconciliation among people, especially in the case of conflict among spouses. Forgiveness and reconciliation are long and difficult processes. Gospel is of the crucial importance in helping the quarrelling spouses to realize them. He points out also the importance of penance regarding the other's (spouse) guilt ("Reconciliation is possible if the innocent spouse is willing to suffer and atone for the guilt of his/her spouse") and of awareness of one's own imperfection in order to reach marital reconciliation. In general he stresses the importance of gospel and fidelity to Christ, of rediscovering of the grace of following Christ (Benedict XVI). "Only fidelity to what God once and for all realized in the crucified and resurrected Jesus Christ will inspire (Christian) spouses to forgive and reconcile."

Janez Juhant and Bojan Žalec, the editors

FOR FUTURE FROM HISTORY

RECONCILIATION: THE PREREQUISITE FOR THE FUTURE IN EUROPE

Felix Unger, Salzburg

Reconciliation is a very difficult endeavour indeed, but an indispensable tool for our society with look to the future. Many problems in our society occur and exist due to different views and different attitudes starting mostly with a lack of discussion leading from aggression up to war. The tragedy is war, where many people are killed, wounded, resulting in harm in their souls too. Reconciliation is becoming much more difficult for the relatives of killed people, for survivors and victims. Sometimes we see a lot of aggression which are nurtured by religions additionally too.

Our Academy had the noble task gathering in the nineties of the last century all the 8 Academies of Former Yugoslavia together. On the Balkans remained many problems unsolved. The conflicts exist over centuries. At the end of the 20th century the clamp of the former Yugoslavia was lost and the unsolved problems started to be lived out. This has been done in such a severity what we have all experienced recently. As result I have seen young people severely wounded in hospitals of Belgrade and Zagreb. The pictures I can not forget anymore and are stimulating me to fight for peace.

There are many harms set in Europe after the Second World War too. It is very difficult to overcome the harm of the wounded souls of the families, mostly the trauma is heritated to the next generation. But a mightful prerequisite for reconciliation is tolerance, the virtue of living together. Tolerance is a part of our value system and mainly based on the individual readiness to stand up for the dignity of any man – very difficult indeed. In reality reconciliation based on tolerance requires skills in education too. It's necessary to involve all issues of conflicts in Pros and Contras. So it is necessary to activate tolerance involving the whole cascade of the virtues. To speak together is a main task – easy and difficult.

We have to be aware that man lives in a balance of the virtues and that man is in his essence an entity of soul, spirit and body (Fig. 1). For the future it has to be recognized that life has the highest value. In living together, in administration and in all governmental levels all we have to consider “Justitia Fundamentum Gentium”. Justice is an excellent and human basis ensuring coexistence, freedom of people and therefore peace (Fig. 2).

In future we have to discuss all conflicting items in our society even when it’s very hard and try to understand why an explosion started. Members of my family have been victims in two corners of Europe, in Slovakia and in Slovenia. I have learned to find a basis how to overcome the injustice and to create the soil for peace in future. Everything has to be discussed for our future, for collaboration leading to a peaceful coexistence in mutual and fair exchange of different views.

From the gospel we learned a very good parable: Jesus told us: When a Roman asks you to go with him one mile, go with him a second mile. Because the first mile was a duty, the second mile is voluntarily. This is the key for starting to discuss,to speak, and a new vision arises.

Reconciliation is a very very difficult task and is very personal after many traumas to the souls. It depends on the scars which have been set in the soul. To avoid future mutual insulations, we should try hard bringing a new basis for co-existence for a mutual life in peace. The virtue would be the tolerance within the frame of the values (Fig. 3).

Additionally reconciliation is a contribution to a real united Europe. There are many areas of conflicts unsolved in Europe. As example it is time to overcome the “Beneš Decrees”- with an apology - like Willy Brandt did it in Poland or Pope John Paul II. in Rome. Unsolved perpetual problems will bother any free communication. The list of unsolved problems is long, but just behind our doors. They deserve reconciliation. Otherwise we are endangered by a new nationalism, which is contradictory to a united Europe and finally to what we dream from peace. We have in our hearts the power to overcome the past. Vaclav Havel brought light to the darkness in the rigid political system. Our children deserve the proper soil for the basis of developing in freedom. The historical past has to be discussed fairly, on the basis of the Jesus: “The truth will make you free”.

Reconciliation depends on us totally.

Fig. 1

Education

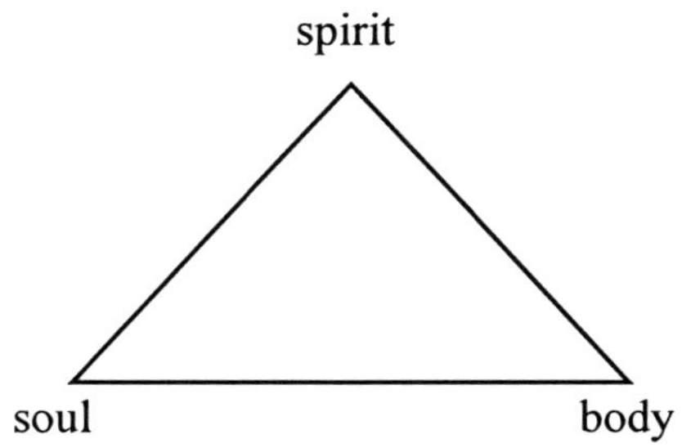

Acting: a balance of the values and virtues

Fig. 2

Values

- Life
- Acting as known in the virtues
  "JUSTITIA FUNDAMENTUM GENTIUM"
- Education

Fig. 3

Tolerance: The Virtue of Living Together

1\.
Tolerance is the individual readiness to stand up for the dignity of any other human being.

2\.
Tolerance is a part of a value system that emphasizes human dignity.

3.
Tolerance requires a person's ability to understand other people and to respect different behaviour.

4.
Tolerance is based on a self-confident point of view.

5.
Tolerance serves as a protector of dignity and freedom of each human being within his or her own cultural environment.

6.
The guaranty and continuing development of **tolerance** should be considered our common duty and the fundamental element of any education.

ON THE DUTY TO LEARN FROM HISTORY

Jože Trontelj, Ljubljana

Introduction

We sometimes hear that history should be left to historians. Many would disagree. Finding historical facts and interpreting them scientifically is certainly a job for experts. On the other hand, it would be preposterous to claim that we should also leave to historians ethical judgement of historical events, decisions and the behaviour of key historical personalities, especially those from the recent past, whose ethical standards are more or less known to us. On the contrary, understanding history should help us understand our present situation and our alternatives in the future. Responsible behaviour should be based on this understanding. Acceptable ethical reasoning cannot exist without proper awareness of the good and bad experience accumulated throughout history.

Europe, with the Near and Middle East, was the cradle of today's Western civilisation. The last two or three millennia, which is as far back as our historians can see, have been full of bloody conflicts, cruel wars, revolutions and violence of all kinds. But with time, Europe has also grown a culture of law and order, peace and tolerance, a spirit of collaboration and concern for fellow human beings in need. That culture contains examples of truly compassionate care, inspiring unreserved respect. Christianity doubtlessly played a crucial role in these developments, although it was itself often terribly misused.

Horror as cultural heritage

The Europe of today may be more sensitive to values and ethics than most of the rest of the world. I think we know some of the reasons: the recent horrible history of both World Wars and the gruesome experience of inhumane totalitarian regimes of the twentieth century, which brought systematic violations of human rights, disregard of moral codes and neglect of values combined with a reckless hunger for power that took millions of human lives and caused severe suffering of tremendous numbers of people of many nations. This was particularly painful as it followed a period of peace, relative welfare, fine culture, reasonable security and some degree of democracy.

The horror of those days, years and decades has become deeply embedded in the European history of the past century. It has become a dreadful experience, a nightmare for hundreds of millions of Europeans. It has become part of both the European and Slovenian *cultural heritage*. Talking of massive human rights violation as part of a cultural heritage may sound pathological. But that is precisely what it is. Europe lived in a culture of violence, destruction and killing. Few nations can claim to have had nothing to do with the intentional, cruel inflicting of pain and suffering. Few could claim to be guilt-free.

The order in the name of the people to kill

In Slovenia, particularly tragic events took place during the months following the end of World War II, when tens of thousands of prisoners of war, including civilians, were sent to their death. These extrajudicial killings were committed by the new state leadership as an act of vengeance of shocking dimensions. Needless to say, a large majority of the unfortunate victims could not have been guilty of acts deserving capital punishment, not even by the standards of those days, when people's hearts were hardened by the four years of cruel war. The order to kill tens of thousands of defenceless persons, men, women and adolescents, and the carrying out of that order in an organised, cold-blooded, cruel campaign *"in the name of the people"*, was a *crime against humanity* of huge proportions.

During those days, one of the smallest European nations, numbering less than 2 million, lost between 14,500 and 19,000 young men and women to barbaric extrajudicial killings, committed illegally and in secrecy on the order of the post-war leadership. In addition, tens of thousands of non-Slovenian disarmed prisoners of war and refugees were put to death on the soil of this same country during the same period and in the same way.

The years after the crime against humanity

This crime was then followed by decades of human rights violations. These gradually took on a less brutal character and affected progressively smaller numbers of citizens. However, they still inflicted considerable painful discrimination, injustice, suffering and fear. After Yugoslavia broke away from the Soviet bloc, the authorities somewhat relaxed the previous strict regime, although they still tightened the screws on their real and imaginary opponents, especially the few publicly denounced dissidents. Many people enjoyed relative freedom and prosperity.

The strict silence and secrecy in which the post-war killings were kept for decades, associated with the systematic build-up of President Tito's personality cult, tight media control, carefully performed mass indoctrination and brainwashing, have helped create and maintain an illusion of justice and democracy. In the background, however, there remained an awareness of restricted freedom of speech, undercover activity of secret police informants and a suspicion that many thousands of citizens had files in secrete archives, ready to be used for the purposes of discrimination and repression.

Nevertheless, in the final years of the 2nd Yugoslavia there was an increasingly relaxed system with features of self-management, although there was no real democracy. Nowadays, many citizens favourably remember that period, since it permitted a relatively comfortable, although not particularly wealthy lifestyle, with low unemployment rates and a seemingly secure future.

The culture of selective blindness

In the light of these memories and reasoning, many people wish to forget the dark sides of the Titoistic period. In fact, they tend to be annoyed by discoveries of the hundreds of hidden mass graves scattered throughout Slovenia, and newly publicised evidence of atrocities committed during the post-war period, when the new authorities were already in total control. Many of our contemporaries exhibit a kind of selective blindness, excusing abuses of the newly installed authorities led by the Communist Party, who ignored their duty to protect legal order and the safety of citizens, for which they were responsible, but instead chose to commit a colossal crime against them.

Many of their victims were young people who had been, since early in the war, summoned into military units, originally self-organised for the protection of the rural population against the violence of the communist revolutionaries. Later on, these poorly-armed and untrained units unfortunately came under the control of the occupator's armed forces and were misused against the liberation movement. Many of these young people were recruited against their will, having no free choice. One out of ten was a girl or a young woman. Some of the victims of the post-war extrajudicial killings had not been involved in any conflict, but were just considered *potential opponents* in the future; hence they were eliminated as a preventative measure. The term *cleansing* was used in the orders of mass murders.

Stop "bone counting!"

The gruesome details of the crimes committed by the authorities *"In the name of the people"* are increasingly coming to light, to the embarrassment of people who still indiscriminately esteem both the heroic resistance, which deserves respect, and the communist revolution, which abused the resistance and humiliated patriotic sentiments during the post-war period. The reaction of public opinion as well as the opinion of leaders is mixed. We often hear demands that the painful part of the past should finally be forgotten, the sooner the better, allowing people to devote their undivided attention to problems of today and tomorrow. Such voices also come from high positions in society. Not many realise that this is inappropriate, misplaced advice. In fact, it is a call that we should turn away from ethics, away from fundamental values, such as the right to justice, the duty to respect human dignity and the sanctity of life. We hear derogatory remarks about *"bone counting",* referring to the uncovering and investigating of the hidden mass graves of men and women killed by the secret order of the authorities in 1945 and 1946.

A surprisingly large proportion of the older generation rejects any suggestion that they may need to review their own image of the moral integrity of the communist leadership and its role in the post-war history of Yugoslavia. The so-called *revision of history*, an obviously legitimate undertaking, has become a derogatory, sarcastic, scornful phrase. This attitude towards new discoveries about our past was best seen on the recent occasion when the Office of the Mayor of Ljubljana decided to name a new street after Tito. This gave rise to protests, and finally an old lady, herself a victim of the previous regime, submitted an appeal to the Constitutional Court to determine whether the Mayor's decree was in fact in breach of the Constitution, as it represents an insult to the human dignity of those who suffered injustice under Tito's rule.

No to Tito's alley!

The Court unanimously decided that the decree on the new naming of a street after Tito must be cancelled, since it is in disagreement with the constitutional principle of the respect for human dignity. The decree has symbolic significance, *"since... to name a street after Tito today can be understood as an act of acknowledgement and acceptance of the former undemocratic regime, and that can have no place in today's time and space."* The purpose of the Constitutional Court was not to judge Tito's personality and actions, nor to assess the historical facts and circumstances, but only to consider the symbolic significance of Tito's name. That symbol and the values associated with it were deemed to be *incompatible with fundamental constitutional values such as human dignity, freedom, democracy and the rule of law.* Using that symbol by the authorities as a name for public places would mean that they accept another perception of values and identify themselves with that perception.

When is state violence acceptable?

It was both interesting and sobering to see and hear the comments that made their way into the media. On the one hand, many surviving victims felt relieved, having received long overdue moral satisfaction. On the other hand, an astonishing number of people stepped forward and expressed their disapproval of the verdict, often in an emotional and indignant way. It was especially painful to read comments that revealed a shocking insensitivity towards the ultimate injustice committed indiscriminately against thousands upon thousands of our fellow citizens. This *moral blindness* gives rise to concern. Should we become involved in another serious conflict in the near future, what can we and our children expect if such people come to power? Next time when a crisis erupts, what kind of behaviour can we expect from our neighbours who think that violence is acceptable, as long as it serves a purpose chosen by those in charge? Should we even be ready for something like the mass slaughter of the Srebrenica Bosnians or Vukovar Croats less than two decades ago? Recently one of the commentators in the Serbian media remarked that the siege of Vukovar had been a mistake; other cities should have been attacked (!). Among the people who justify the mass post-war murders in Slovenia are our colleagues, our superiors, our elected politicians, our neighbours. Among these, and this is my greatest disappointment, I even find fine intellectuals who have made important contributions to our science and culture.

Can persistence of such wide differences in opinion regarding the place of fundamental values in society allow *reconciliation*? How could we reduce the gap in the first place? Would it be possible to reach agreement on an absolute ethical minimum, below which nobody would be allowed to go, regardless of the circumstances? That would naturally exclude tolerance for the worst massive human rights violation, such as the post-war killings. My personal experience with such attempts is not encouraging. Childhood education leaves deep impressions, which cannot be easily changed. They tend to become an integral part of the personality. Any attempt at correction of the old erroneous convictions instilled at a young age is met with resistance, regardless of how irrational that resistance may be. Moreover, the distorted moral attitudes are often transmitted to the next generation, so that the 50-year-old, post-war value system will not die with the last participants in the war and the post-war events. We actually see similar developments in several European countries.

Appeal for empathy and compassion

In fact, indoctrination of several generations of young people in the belief that violence may be justified when used in a higher interest was the last massive crime of the totalitarian systems of the past century in Europe. We will have to live a long time yet with that indoctrination. The only way out seems to be an honest presentation of facts, combined with training of emotional intelligence and education in empathy. In the light of what has just been said, not much success can be expected after the end of childhood and adolescence.

On the other hand, there are many people without such strongly held beliefs. These can be more easily made aware of the indispensable value of truth and of the huge significance of duty to respect human rights. Attempts at reconciliation should best be addressed to that part of society. Therefore, let me end my talk with an appeal aimed at *these* people:

Do read from history. But when you come across tragic events, such as mass crimes of the post-war Yugoslav authorities, try to find unbiased sources. Read with sensitivity for human dignity, because denial of dignity was the first step in the chain of brutalities inflicted upon the victims – the chain that was to end with their murder. Read with compassion for the innocent victims who were forced down the path of martyrdom leading to their death, for compassion was denied to them and was replaced by sadistic tortures. Remember that each of these victims was a human being, with his or her own life and family, loves and fears, talents and potentials, with a place in society. Imagine having your brothers, sisters, parents, children among those victims. Imagine the horror and pain of their martyrdom. Admit the likelihood that some of those on the defeated side were guilty. However, remember that the civilised world has abolished the death penalty, even for the worst crimes. And that in civilised society, revenge has been replaced by justice. Guilt must be proved before justice takes place. And the accused must have a chance to defend himself.

Do not believe that massacres were simply an inevitable event, a result of the workings of history. This would relieve the perpetrators of their responsibility. Do not let your empathy be blunted by prejudice, ideology and unfair generalised accusations. Many of those can even be found in history books. Accepting biased views of alleged, unproven collective guilt may irreversibly harm one's own perception of the need for truth and justice, one's own sense of values. Moral blind-

ness is not only regrettable. It is dangerous. Think of the future of our children and grandchildren.

Do not forget!

In fact, nations with a traumatic past like ours have an important moral obligation. The memory of the dreadful deviation of the 20th century must not be lost. The mass murders of our compatriots well after the dawn of peace in spring 1945 turned our country into a land of horror. This appeared as a warning that the horrors of war would soon be replaced with terrors of the totalitarian system. The shocking disappointment following great expectations of freedom and a new, just order must be taken as a strong historical lesson. The victims must be given a respectful place in our national memory. To this day, that duty has not yet been served. The victims are still being denied their last human rights: the right to a decent burial, the right to an apology and the right to a respectful memory. If we choose to keep their arbitrary label of national traitors, or simply push them out of our conscious awareness, we will commit a final, great crime against them.

It would mean discarding their last message, a message of huge ethical significance: a plea for confession and apology on the one hand, and a promise of forgiveness and reconciliation on the other. That message does not call for *forgetting*. This nation needs a catharsis. Refusing it and remaining insensitive to the extreme human rights violation would mean choosing to ignore massive guilt, choosing to neglect the most basic human sentiments, abandoning compassion, leaving the crime against humanity committed *in the name of the people* as an undeserved stigma on our children and grandchildren and accepting the nurture of serious social pathology.

In short, enforced forgetting would be an enormous moral mistake with long-term, potentially severe consequences for society. The moral burden would be passed from the generation that committed the crime to the next, and from that to the next. This simply must not happen.

BIBLICAL FOUNDATIONS AND EDUCATION

BIBLICAL FOUNDATIONS OF RECONCILIATION

Jože Krašovec, Ljubljana

Forgiveness is essentially an aspect of the intimate relationship between God and the chosen people. It is not surprising, therefore, that the most profound statements on forgiveness are found in the context of the covenant relation. For God to show forgiveness usually presupposes a confession of guilt and repentance. Paradoxically, it is possible for God's willingness to forgive to exceed Israel's capacity for repentance and atonement for sins. The Bible indicates that even a grievous apostasy does not rule out forgiveness and reconciliation. The obvious and unequivocal manner of referring to the issue of forgiveness or mercy is by using the kind of language that involves naming the appropriate concepts (cf. roots such as *nś', slh, kpr, rhm, etc.*). There are, however, many other ways of expressing the message of forgiveness. It is, for instance, sometimes the case that, although there is no direct reference, the conclusion can be drawn that extenuating circumstances play an important role. If they explain why punishment is less severe than might have been expected, there are probably good grounds for discerning at least an element of forgiveness or mercy (cf. the role of seduction in Gen 3). In this article the treatment of biblical concept of forgiveness is limited to the Old Testament.

1. Biblical Passages Focused on Forgiveness and Reconciliation

One of the most important passages dealing with divine mercy and forgiveness is the narrative of the golden calf and renewal of the covenant in Exod 32–34. (Krašovec 1999: 84–109) Making and the worship of the golden calf is the gravest case of Israel's apostasy. Such a sin could not remain unpunished. But after repeated intercessions for mercy by Moses and because of evident repentance of the people, God was willing to forgive and to renew the covenant with Israel. In this connection God himself recited the confession formula (34:6–7) which clearly shows that God is by his essence much more a God of mercy than of strict justice. The importance of this formula is attested by the fact that it appears, in slight variations, in several important texts (Exod 20:5–6 = Deut 5:9–10; Num

14:18; Deut 7:9–10; Jer 32:18). The message of renewal is very important also in Lev 26:40–45 and Deut 30:1–10 as a promise for those who return to God after they have been punished for their disobedience to the Law.

The prophet Hosea is unique in his depiction of the contrast between the passion of anger that surges spontaneously in the wake of grievous disappointment suffered by one who has been deceived, and the deeper, higher love that calls for forgiveness and reconciliation under the new covenant relationship (cf. 2:18–25). The first part of the book of Hosea (chs. 1–3) is also unique in its intertwining of plot with allegory – i.e., of anthropology with theology – so that the obligatory nature of following in the footsteps of the Lord is made obvious. (Krašovec 1999: 406–427) The unusual story of the prophet's life serves as an illustration of the relationship between God and the chosen people; the divine insistence on preparing an unfaithful wife for a renewed covenant implies rejection of divorce. Punishment may be unavoidable, but it has a strictly pedagogical role that is motivated by burgeoning love. In spite of the shift towards reconciliation, we must not overlook the fact that the estranged wife returned to her first husband only after a disappointment that was inevitable, given that she tried to console herself with other men for the loss of her first love. Reconciliation is only possible after purification in the desert (cf. 2:16).

The prophecies of Jeremiah and Ezekiel imply the denial of the people's capacity to repent and of the possibility of being forgiven in the conditions then obtaining. Forgiveness becomes, therefore, a promise projected into an unforeseeable future. Jeremiah and the Deuteronomistic editors of his prophecies continually echo God's lamentation that the chosen people are rejecting the Lord and turning to idolatry, which is why their threats of punishment are often linked to appeals for a return, so that God might have reason to be gracious. Their warnings and conditional promises apparently failed to produce results in the present, so that mercy and forgiveness became glimmering hope for the future. When the people were humiliated and had partially atoned their guilt, God addressed them in emollient language. In the celebrated oracle in 31:31–34 the forgiving of Israel's guilt is taken as the source and proof of the making of a new covenant.

Ezekiel's understanding of the relation between the requirements of punishment and the reasons for mercy is at its clearest in his presentation of the history of Israel's rebellion (20:1–44) and in God's promise that Israel will be created anew (36:16–38). Punishment invariably follows in the wake of specific guilt on the part of specific offenders, whereas divine leniency in general may express itself by God's act of punishing a sinner more mildly than he or she actually deserves; only the obdurate are condemned to death. It follows that it is crucial to distinguish between individuals, groups, and the chosen people as a whole. In the final analysis, God's promise of mercy "for the sake of his name" (20:9, 14, 22, 44) aims primarily to secure the ultimate survival of Israel. The same applies to other parts of the Hebrew Bible (cf. 1 Sam 12:22; Isa 48:9; Jer 14:7, 21; Ps 25:11; 79:9; 106:8; 109:21). Such an assurance would be, however, without solid foundation if it were not based on the principle of Creation, and if the fundamental promise of divine mercy as expressed in the famous pledge to Noah (Gen 8:21; 9:8–16) were not valid for mankind as a whole. (Krašovec 1999: 463–483)

The themes of God's mercy and forgiveness play an important part in some other exilic and post-exilic prophetic literature. Mention may be made first of Deutero-Isaiah (Isa 40:1–11; 48:1–11; 54:1–10). In this part the personality of the fourth Servant Song of God appears as the one who bore the sin of the people and healed them through his voluntarily accepted suffering (Isa 52:13–53:12). Within the Apocalypse of Isaiah (Isa 24:1–27:13) we find the announcement that the guilt of Jacob will be expiated by exile (27:9). Of special interest is the idea that God shows mercy also to heathen peoples. In Isa 19:6–25 healing is promised to the Egyptians within the surprising announcement of their conversion to God of Israel (cf. especially v. 22). According to the Book of Jonah the penitent Ninivites were saved, because they responded to Jonah's preach of punishment with penitence.

From the nature of prayer as the highest and the profoundest manifestation of Israel's religion, it follows that the themes of divine mercy and forgiveness assume a striking prominence in the book of Psalms. There are two main reasons for this fact. First, prayer is an expression of the most personal relationship to God implying consciousness of God's absoluteness and holiness on the one hand and of human limitations on the other. In Ps 78:39, for instance, the psalmist points to the one of the fundamental reasons for manifestation of God's mercy towards Israel: "He remembered that they were but flesh, a wind that passes and comes not again." In 103:14 a similar statement is found: "For he knows our frame; he remembers that we are dust." God cannot deal with frail mortals by deploying absolute power.

The sublime nature of divine mercy and forgiveness is most often expressed in short, often formulaic passages within larger structures in a variety of literary genres that reflect a variety of sentiments, experiences and beliefs: in individual or communal laments, hymnic praises of the divine character and deeds, historical accounts, and wisdom writing. Their role as a universal expression of this divine quality is underlined by their occurrence within the whole of the Bible. Catastrophic situations such as illness, persecution by enemies, and exile unavoidably help awaken the sense for intrinsic causal connections operating between with the state of mind and the fate of the suffering people. An awareness of limits is the surest way of teaching the people that, in the final analysis, God alone can save them. They are the most effective means of moving them to humble supplication in the face of their God.

In three psalms (51, 78, 106) the entire structure is based on the belief in God's mercy and forgiveness. It is natural that in the penitential psalms proclamation of divine mercy and supplication for God's healing intervention occupies the central place. This holds especially true of Ps 51, which occupies the most prominent place among the penitential psalms. The suppliant of Ps 51 stands before the mirror of his inherent sinfulness and the knowledge of divine holiness. In the first main part (vv. 3–11) the psalmist prays for forgiveness of his guilt, in the second one (vv. 12–19) for his inner renewal – in the sense of an imminent re-creation – and for a new relationship with God. He sinks so profoundly in the sublime nature of God's holiness and mercy that his confession and prayer display an eschatological orientation.

Psalms 78 and 106 are characteristic as historical recitations of Israel's sin. Their antithetical structure brings into focus the characters of God and of the people. God was always gracious and merciful, Israel was constantly faithless and rebellious. Despite Israel's constant unfaithfulness God remembered the covenant and forgave the people, after having resolved to reject and to destroy them. The first act of election is considered as the reason for a new election, providing new ground of hope. It seems that God can never totally reject the whole body of the chosen people. But this conclusion can withstand only within the more fundamental reason for God's leniency: the Creator cannot abandon the created world in its totality. The two psalms reflect the belief that divine promise and election are unconditional in relation to the whole body of divine Creation and the chosen people, but conditional in relation to particular groups or individuals. (Krašovec 1999: 590–634)

2. Theological Presuppositions of Forgiveness and Reconciliation

In establishing the true relationship between punishment and forgiveness the most important fact is that in the Hebrew Bible it is the message of forgiveness and reconciliation, conceived of as the supreme rule and goal of God's relationship with his people, that eventually prevails despite Israel's rebellious attitudes. This is understandable only in the light of the reciprocity of all the basic Hebrew theological presuppositions. The supremacy of forgiveness and reconciliation over the imperatives of punishment was made possible only by the victory of absolute monotheism over the effects of polytheism. Monotheistic theology is responsible for the characteristic properties of the Hebrew understanding of punishment and forgiveness. The discussion on retribution has so far shown that the perception and interpretation of punishment essentially depend on our understanding of the link between the physical-material and personal-spiritual realms. In all religions based on cosmological and collectivistic social foundations the understanding of punishment is very simple. It is essentially reduced to the operation of the law of causality: bad actions automatically and inevitably produce bad consequences. It is easy to grasp that the destructive results of wrongdoing can affect not only the wrongdoer but others also. In this sense it is justifiable to speak of collective punishment or retribution. Naturally, this is not a pathway to forgiveness, nor does it touch on anything characteristic of interpersonal relationships. No wonder, then, that cosmological cultures and religions tend to fatalism and a collectivistic view of humankind. The depth dimensions of the human being remain essentially untouched.

In contrast to the surrounding cosmological ancient cultures, the Hebrew religion which is based on belief in God as Person is chiefly interested in looking into the depth, in divine intervention in the human soul, in God's guidance dispensed through charismatic leaders who have absolute trust in him, in an interpersonal relationship between God and his people, and in community among souls. Accordingly, the currency of their thought and expression is rich in such fundamental anthropological, theological and ethical semantic coinage as covenant, faithfulness, righteousness, and love. The prophets are no less sensitive to the laws of the physical world than the sages and magicians of surrounding cultures. On the contrary, since they are seized by the desire to save their people, to lead them to a genuine relationship with their God and their fellow men, they have unusual moral and practical insight and so are capable of seeing most clearly shortcomings in relation to the universal moral order. Their great achievement is to hold in correct balance and perspective the interior and exterior worlds. Their vision of realities is so total that they can never judge the physical world in separation from the spiritual one, or vice versa. And especially striking is their consciousness that God can work in the world both directly and indirectly. He can intervene with miracles, influence human events through direct address with oracles, or bring his plans into being through secondary causes.

God's absoluteness and his demand for unfaltering loyalty, and human fluctuation between desperate rebellion and hopeful expectation inevitably create extreme tensions and oppositions. What may seem compatible in a cosmic and collectivistic social context is totally unacceptable in a covenant relationship between an infinite personal God and a limited humanity. Instead of purely rational accounts of God's absoluteness we find many analogies and symbols that play an important part in expressing the relation between a personal God and his people both in concord and discord. There is a rich use of analogy between visible and invisible, material and spiritual, infinite and limited, universal and particular or individual. Transcendent realities are most often expressed in metaphorical or anthropomorphic terms. Theological and moral demands imply complete polarization between the concepts of bad and good, obduracy and contrition, anger and compassion.

The central message of the Hebrew Bible is that forgiveness and reconciliation have the highest priority in the hierarchy of God's attitude to humankind – much higher than punishment and that the attainment of reconciliation and of unity is revealed to be the true purpose of God's and humankind's activity. Divine forgiveness transcends all the limitations of humankind and persists in spite of the rebellion of human beings and Israel. The primacy of forgiveness can only be understood in the light of the reciprocity of all the basic Hebrew theological presuppositions. It was the ascendancy of monotheism which permitted forgiveness to come to be as the hallmark of God's attitude to human beings. On Old Testament foundations is built the whole of theology of reconciliation of the New Testament. (Krašovec 1999: 767–783)

Biblical foundations of forgiveness have continued to play a central role across the whole range of philosophical thought, from Augustine, to most modern theologians, philosophers and writers. The interest of poetic portrayal of the human sin, repentance, and forgiveness from the personal perspective is timeless. The issues of reward, punishment and forgiveness are central not only to philosophy but also to literature.[1]

Conclusion

To conclude, it must be emphasized that God is willing to forgive whenever humans are penitent. Since God is never faithless himself, he is never under an obligation to exculpate those who are disloyal. But in the final analysis, he does pardon "for the sake of his name" (cf. 1 Sam 12:22; Isa 48:9; Jer 14:7, 21; Ezek 20:9, 14, 22, 44; Ps 25:11; 79:9; 106:8; 109:21), i.e., out of faithfulness to his own essence; he cannot abandon his creation (cf. Ps 143:11). In 1 Sam 12:22 Samuel assures the people: "The Lord will not cast away his people, for his great name's sake, because it has pleased the Lord to make you a people for himself." Since God is absolutely righteous humans may ask for forgiveness but have no right

1 The way of representation of forgiveness in literature became one of central concerns of Irena Avsenik Nabergoj; see References.

whatsoever to demand it either for themselves or for others (cf. Gen 18:16–33); forgiveness is the supreme mark of God's goodness. Given that no human being is righteous, and that all are members of the community, it is natural to expect willingness, or even a sense of obligation to atone for one's own sins and for those of others. The natural bonds in the community and especially the theological covenant justify and even call for mediation for the condemned through supplication and atonement. In this context the extremely important role of the minority of righteous and their suffering becomes especially clear.

References

Avsenik Nabergoj, I. 2006. Pomen kazni in odpuščanja v Svetem pismu (The Meaning of Punishment and Forgiveness in the Bible). In: *Bogoslovni vestnik/ Theological Quarterly* 66/4, pp. 471–483.

Avsenik Nabergoj, I. 2008. *Mirror of Reality and Dreams : Stories and Confessions by Ivan Cankar*. Frankfurt am Main [etc.]: Peter Lang.

Avsenik Nabergoj, I. 2009. *Longing, Weakness and Temptation : From Myth to Artistic Creations*. Newcastle upon Tyne: Cambridge Scholars Publishing, XII.

Krašovec, J. 1999. *Reward, Punishment, and Forgiveness: The Thinking and Beliefs of Ancient Israel in the Loght of Greek and Modern Views*. Leiden / Boston / Köln: E. J. Brill.

EDUCATION FOR RECONCILIATION ON THE EXAMPLE OF CONFLICT BETWEEN ESAU AND JACOB

Stanko Gerjolj, Ljubljana

On the example of solving the conflict between the brothers Esau and Jacob we recognize reconciliation as a unique stage learning model that is relevant and useful for many contemporary situations and distresses, where a man "longs" for solutions.

According to the biblical story Jacob and Esau have been in a dispute in fact already in the prenatal period. Furthermore, they were born as twins in a conflict family, in which each of the parents assimilates one child (Gen 25,22–28). The dispute deepens until the Jacob's "forced" leaving from home (Gen 27,41–45).

When Jacob gets married, he experiences a new unpleasant surprise already during the wedding night, as he wakes up with a completely changed bride. Since despite unpleasant changes he accepts and becomes fond of her, we are able to understand this noble act as a beginning of the reconciliation process (Gen 29,20–30). Then, his efforts for reconciliation continue and end with his realization that he is capable of independent life and caring handling with his family. In terms of "pedagogical model" we are able to recognize ten development stages in the reconciliation process with Brother Esau:

1. **Reconciliation of love – matrimonial or partner reconciliation** is Jacob's first and fundamental experience of reconciliation. In the moment, when he was, out of love towards his wife, capable of accepting Rachel and also grow fond of her as Lea (Jacob's wifes can be interpreted as one person with several faces), he felt that he is capable of reconciliation. He overcame fore judgements and also accepted her shadow sides of life. Namely, he realized that ugly Lea, once she is accepted by him and after he starts serving her again, gradually turns into a beautiful Rachel, he once knew before the wedding. So, after he reconciled with Lea and accepted her without hesitation, he again had a beautiful and charming wife he always wanted to have. At the same time he discovered that reconciliation trains a man for ability to form stable and lasting relations. Matrimonial reconciliation or reconciliation between husband and wife is the cornerstone to learn of reconciliation as a way of life, which successfully regulates also the wider habitat.

2. **Reconciliation at the rational or contract level** is the next step in reconciliation. It is taken by Jacob in his relation to his father in law, Laban. Stimulated and encouraged with the first and the fundamental positive experience

of reconciliation Jacob tries to rectify his wider habitat, which also includes his relation with his father in law. He is aware that reconciliation with his father in law, Laban, has a different role compared to matrimonial reconciliation of love he feels towards his wife. Although his father in law in his current life helped him a lot and gave him his daughter for wife, he cannot compare himself with the wife in terms of emotional connection (Hartley 2000, 272–273). Thus, arranging the relationship with father in law has a different connotation, but is nevertheless very important, since their conflict would burden relations in Jacob's family.

Relations between daughter-in-law and mother-in-law and son-in-law and father-in-law are rarely positively and emotionally intensive. Jacob finds that this only is not necessary, but may even be harmful, as it is the ability of distancing emotional attachment to the generation of parents the one that strengthens the sense of belonging to a new collective identity (Kille 1995, 49). It is important that this relationship is formally and "contractually" arranged, that competences are clearly delineated and divided, that in this relationship everyone knows their rights and duties, that he agrees with his status and accepts it and that interrelationships are relevant and transparent (Gen 31,45 – 32,1).

3. Visualization of reconciliation is necessary and important, when it comes to solving a complex and emotionally intense conflict. At this stage it is already dealing directly with the conflict between the brothers. The desire for reconciliation leads him in his father's house (Gen 21,3). Jacob left "and returned to his hometown" (Gen 32,1b), which means that he plans his reconciliation in place, where the conflict has occurred.

He begins to prepare for this step immediately after reconciliation with Laban. We know how time consuming and difficult arranging relationships between brothers and sisters can be if they are not arranged regularly, and – as in Jacob's and Esau's example – tensions become so deep and painful to interrupt all communication. In such cases the first feelings of success in solving conflicts are usually experienced outside the nuclear family, often within relations, in which we entered already as adults. Furthermore, we observe, how disputes in adults life may pull us in similar situations from the nuclear family, which also disturb us in resolving the current conflicts. Thus, reliving traumatic events from childhood additionally motivate us to undertake a path of "general mental cleansing".

Jacob was certainly additionally encouraged to this by reconciliation of love and successful completion of arranging the conflict relation Jacob had with his father-in-law. Compared with Laban, the conflict between two brothers is about a stronger, blood and emotional connection. Jacob feels the weight and complexity of this step; therefore, he wishes to prepare himself properly for it. The experience that he has gained in the period of twenty years, as has elapsed since his leaving from home, changed him a lot. He became a self-confident husband and father, while forming himself into a careful and conciliatory man. In the conflict with his wife Jacob, however, fails to pay special attention to visualization, as the situation surprised him, while at the same time in the common existence he cannot withdraw from the relation and afford greater emotional distance and waiting for a solution. In relation to Esau, it is about a known, quite a bit outdated, but for both of them painful conflict that requires a correct strategy of the reconciliation process. Because he feels how the conciliatory meeting with his brother goes beyond his abilities, he, at the bottom of his soul, is becoming more open to divine inspirations. Thus, in the sentiment communication, he experiences a meeting with God's deputies, who – like in a dream on the stairs and a ladder – makes such a strong impression on him that this place is given a new name – Mahanájim (Gen 32,2–3).

Probably the whole drama of visualization with the brother, which at this level may be imbued with fear, takes place at the unconscious level (Cohen 1995, 111). It is evident that in his interior he empathically visualized one of the variants of the meeting, in which he experiences Esau as an existential threat. In doing so, despite the lengthy and thorough preparation the events are overtaking him (Hartley 2000, 281), which further enhances his internal tension and drama. After "twenty years" of consolidation in a conflict and hostile attitude, not only will face two "brothers", but two "encampments". So, everyone will come with their own "army" of arguments and prejudices, which they won in a long time of uncommunicative burial in the "shelter".

But visualization of further steps of reconciliation meeting with Esau illustrates how much Jacob has changed since he left home. Although he was recently a sharp and tough negotiator with Laban, he completely changes his attitude in relationship to his brother. When in his imagination he sends negotiators to Esau, there is no trace left of a "big brother, who is fighting for birth right and domination" and in doing that even cheats and deceives. On the contrary, in his subconscious, he is steps in front of his brother as a "servant in front of his Lord" (Gen 32,5–7).

When – still in the form of inner experience or visualization of the meeting – Jacob becomes more and more afraid, he also divides his people and property into two encampments in order to protect at least one (Gen 32,8–9). He is particularly frightened, when negotiators return with completely different messages than he expected: "He is coming towards you alone and four hundred men with him" (Gen 32,7).

If we interpret the story as Jacob's internal, subconscious happening, than Esau does not represent the actual "physical" brother, but brother that wakes up and speaks in Jacob. In this case it is about Jacob's "other side", about his mirror image. Jacob is intimidated by himself or by Esau in him. More specifically, we can imagine that he has become accustomed to the role in personal history of Esau and cannot imagine forgiving a man, who would have caused similar pain to him, as did Jacob. In Esau's circumstances he would thus go after a man, such as Jacob, with an army, because, given the experience he would be convinced that he has prepared a new snare for him. Esau's dimension in Jacob is thus not yet entirely convinced that Jacob has really so changed as told by his negotiators.

In the fear and uncertainty of that, how this path of reconciliation that he has taken will turn out, Jacob recourses to God and actually for the first time actively and consciously prays (Gen 32,10–14). When he is turning to God in distress, he admits his smallness and weakness, and at the same time also reinforces the power of God's goodness. However, we cannot detect any sinful dimension of life. He actually does not ask for forgiveness but only to be resolved from his distress.

In accordance with the concept of prayer Jacob gets a new inspiration, which still does not exceed the anthropological dimension of communication and remains trapped in a pragmatic immanence. He is willing to give up a part of his wealth and give it away as present and thus bribe Esau or "calm his down" (Gen 32,21). Although he continues to expose his changes, servant attitude in relation to Esau, is a gift that he carefully sends in front of himself, still a sign of fear before the meeting and a form of avoiding of redemptive confrontation with conflict (Gen 32,22). For a greater risk and a purified viewing the truth in its eyes he must continue to work on himself and to learn not only to forgive others but especially itself. Before reconciliation with his brother he thus requires reconciliation with itself.

4. Reconciliation with itself is the following and the most difficult level and is one of the constituent, actually key elements of the reconciliation process. It was probably Jacob's visualization, which led to recognition about the necessity of this action. Without reconciliation with itself Jacob would not have been capable of any changes that are needed for further steps.

Jacob is slowly revealing the roots of fear of Esau. Thus, he has not been sleeping for the second night now. The first night he spent in fear and prayer (Gen 32,10–14), whereas the second one will – after he has been preparing presents for his brother all day long – be even more difficult. Namely, he still has to face the famous fight with God, which can be seen as an internal, mental event (Bucher 1992, 9–11). This is Jacob's reconciliation with himself, where in the depth of the soul we are dramatically experiencing the dynamics of acceptance and rejection (Kille 1995, 43).

Jacob is carrying out reconciliation with himself in front of the river Jabok, which in this example plays a role of a key moment for own transformation, which allows passage to "the other side", where we see an opportunity for a new start (Höfer 1993, 138).

Given the fact that drama takes place in the darkness of the night, the Bible intuitively suggests Jacob's passing to subconscious (Kille 1995, 49), where he is taken by prayer and meditation (Hartley 2000, 283). At the conscious level, he has probably done much to resolve the conflict with his brother. However, the Bible is challenging him, in fact forcing him to "push off to the deep", enter in to the subconscious and also "here" overcomes and integrates dimensions, which he was unable to accept until now.

Preparation for the meeting with his brother awakes dilemmas in him, which are so demanding that they are perceived as fighting with God. In fact, they enhance, as fear or funk, because it firstly fights only with "some man", then with God (Gen 32,25–30). Namely, a dilemma arises in him, what about the past that is different than known by the family and fundamentally different than he himself admitted so far. Hereby Jacob existentially feels that without accepting the genuine and complete past, no matter how sinful and obscene it is, there is no way to the future.

For "some men" that turn into an angel or even God, thus hides his sinful past or shadow side of personality (Loder 1998, 302). This is seen strong as God and Jacob is afraid that he will be defeated and destroyed. He is afraid to take off the mask and to spoil the false image, with which he has been successful is protecting the environment. However, during the fights, he is becoming more and more aware that without accepting and recognizing sins and mistakes there is no forgiveness and changes. Personal growth is necessarily associated with accepting and integrating own shadows (Corey 1995, 9), only then we are able to process and change them (Cloud, Townsend 2001, 318).

Jacob must the truth about the past first tell himself and later also to his family. This will hurt him and "sprain his hip" (Gen 32,26). In the eyes of his family members he will no longer be faultless and perfect, but wounded, vulnerable and crippled. His image will strongly "limp". But despite that he is still struggling, all night, until the morning dawn or until he senses a clearer view in the future. Only then the past passes off and announces that it will give up, saying: "Let me go, for dawn is already rising!" (Gen 32,27). Jacob methodically raises the awareness of his shadow side of life and wants to keep it for so long that he receives a blessing on the basis of new knowledge (Kille 1995, 51). Only after he knowingly accepts and integrates it and learns from it and in the form of transformation receives the first fruits, Jacob as a new man – Israel – blessed and relaxed breaths (Hartley 2000, 284, Kille 1995, 50). Finally, he dares to be before himself, before God and before family such, as he really is: Jacob, who is changing and becoming Israel. Similarly as in reconciliation of love, when Lea turns into Rachel, also discovers in him that love infused with unconditional acceptance and respect, changes the face.

5. Transparency of reconciliation with itself is necessary in particular that in personal changes we are confident and convincing, while at the same time we sensitize the environment with this step, which supports us in our efforts for quality interpersonal relations. Jacob thus sensitized his family in such way it became fully sympathetic with him since it empathically adopted "his" conflict. From now on, Jacob's entire family, unconditionally, even for the price of life, supports him in all further reconciliation steps and actions.

6. Personal reconciliation on the emotional level is after reconciliation with itself the second key step in this learning process. Reconciliation builds on personal and emotional signs. It is however not required that every reconciliation leads to hugging and crying, but requires an opportunistic sign, which emotionally moves us and thus exceeds the pragmatism and "playing reconciliation". Reconciliation signs deepen sincere personal communication.

When Jacob approaches his brother he, in accordance with recognitions and feelings from the past regarding Esau's behaviour, feels extremely insecure (Hartley 2000, 288). When he perceives Esau, he realized his strength has not reduced and remained the same as reported about by the first reconciliation negotiators (Gen 32,7). However, since the first visualization Jacob's confidence and willingness to take risks significantly increased. He is perhaps strengthened by mental wounds that he gained in the aforementioned fight with God. Namely, from the moment, he listened to them and accepted them, became fond of them and started caring for them, they became his teacher. Despite vulnerability he is overcoming fear more easily while at the same time increasingly recognizes, which attitudes and what kind of behaviour most suits the context of the overall situation. In contrast to visualization, when in fear of Esau he divides "people and property" in two encampments (Gen 32,8–9), this time, he is willing to risk it all. In visualizations he is still allowing the possibility of defeat and escape with "less pain", while after reconciliation he goes on "all or nothing".

His courage is otherwise not reflected in the audacious manifestation of power, as he is already continuously and humbly bowing to Esau already on the way and is acting significantly different, as he announced in his childhood and adolescent years and differently, as known by his closest ones until Jacob. In this attitude Esau recognizes his brother as a changed and different man. This brave, strong and convincing attitude disarms until then angry and fundamentally aggressive brother in humility and thus excitingly positively addresses that anger, aggression and power leaves behind and runs towards him like a child, hugs him and outs arms around him as it is searching for support in him.

In the embrace all the current roles of both have weirdly mixed up. Jacob fought all his life for not being obliged to kneel before his brother, and now he does not stop to do that. He never wanted to serve him and now, he is voluntarily and with inner persuasiveness approaching as a humble and faithful servant. In this child's attitude – in the site of conflicts, disputes and deceptions – Esau kisses Jacob and they "cry" (Gen 33,4).

Reconciliation at personal, in particular emotional level is achieved. However, we know from our experience that despite even a very strong emotional discharge and experiencing a long-term and with hatred imbued conflicts are not solved and that reconciliation requires a sequel. Thinking itself about conflict past and its reliving could trigger a new conflict and accumulated hatred will arise again.

7. **Collective or community reconciliation** is very welcome, and in resolving complex conflicts even a necessary stage. With a seven times bow Jacob confessed sin and asked for forgiveness not only himself, but was this done by his entire family. Although each conflict is about personal responsibility, it is collective reconciliation that reflects the high level of changed communication of a "sinner" giving the reconciliation happening necessary relevance. Collective request for forgiveness does not mean collective sin and confession, but reflects unconditional acceptance of a "sinner" and love for him. Children and women use this collective gesture (Gen 33,5–7) to announce that Jacob confessed, processed and accepted his past, and he, with all his burdening, is also loved by women and children (Hartley 2000, 288).

8. **Giving away gifts** is the third key element of reconciliation and assumes the role of a visible "monument", which protects us from repeating the past as well as from unnecessary burdening with it.

At the level of visualization Jacob prepares his gift initially out of fear of his brother and with the intention to come closer to him and win his heart through gifts, although before "fight with God" also bribing was not unfamiliar to him. In the course of further preparation for the meeting he is increasingly realizing, how serious concern reconciliation is. Doing so, he is probably very happy of his intuition, as gift, he previously prepared, can now be placed in different context and may be used in the reconciliation process using more sense than it may have been its original purpose.

Esau's avoidance probably exceeds the usual rejection of gifts due to "decency", although habits were apparently quite stubborn at that time (Hartley 2000, 289). Even more surprising is Jacob's persistence, because he did not only offer gifts to his brother, but "imposed" them on him (Gen 33,8–11).

Jacob believes that reconciliation requires termination and a victim, which represents a sign of a true affection. Recognition of a sin and request for forgiveness may be found in the gift. His personal and collective bowing confirms that he is not looking mitigating circumstances and excuses for his sin but wishes to cooperate in resolving the conflict without setting any conditions. This generous cooperation in the reconciliation process, in which he is not dealing only with his sin, but without reproaches empathically participates even in the feelings of his brother (Cloud, Townsend 2001, 314), introduces him in further forming of a solid, responsible and independent personality.

If our decisions, steps and actions have disrupted the relationship we have with our closest ones and may have caused damage and pain, we later try to arrange this relation one more time, and cannot take reconciliation steps "empty hatred and empty handed". As a customer asking for forgiveness and approaching reconciliation with gifts, we say we do not wish to take that step in a hurry and carelessly, but have thought about it, prepared our self for it and have actually carried it out through the preparation of the gift.

Esau was probably less prepared for reconciliation than Jacob, who is surprised by it over and over again. He was surprised, and immediately convinced and "won" by his brother's humility, and probably also by solidarity radiated by Jacob's family. He was also surprised about the gift, but not necessarily impressed. He was probably promptly aware even without a thorough preparation that acceptance of a gift also brings responsibility. If Jacob and Esau reconciled without a gift than both sides could enter the reconciliation process half-hearted and "play it". Jacob surpassed such temptations, while Esau not yet completely. In case of a "fictional reconciliation" it would come to a simulated and simply quasi-forgiveness. Thus, Esau would use every smallest tension and list all sins out to his brother, also those, which he himself allegedly forgave. By accepting the gift and by Jacob on every such attempt reminding him of a gift, which symbolizes a confirmation that their past has been cleared up. For Esau and for every one of us in similar circumstances accepting the reconciliation gift requires an actual reconciliation. Reconciliation gift takes away all the capital from us that we have accumulated during the unresolved and conflict past.

In addition to denunciation of complaints from the past Esau, by accepting the gift, lets Jacob know that as a brother he is again as valuable, important and necessary to him that he will let him give presents. By accepting the gift we once again accept a man, who for years we could put up with or see, as a "gift" that enriches us.

9. Sovereignty and independence is a sign of surpassing the emotional level and is in fact already a fruit of reconciliation, even though the process is not fully completed yet. However, this is the first feeling that says how successful was reconciliation and what we learned from it.

Mutual closeness brought by reconciliation, cannot be enjoyed by Esau. Therefore, he wishes to form together with his brother a common future and finally come to life as a single community, actually as one family. At the same time he is still acting very protectively in relation toward his brother. Jacob is in these moments more sober and more rational than his brother and is aware of the risk of new conflicts. As a grown man and father he has many experiences now and knows that excessive and indeterminate closeness threatens independence and sovereignty and almost necessarily leads in new tensions. Therefore he communicates his wishes and ideas of their mutual relations in the future in a polite and respectful way (Gen 33,15–17). He wishes to live with him in good, and at the same time so distant relations, which will not endanger the family as an independent, sovereign and indivisible intimate habitat. At this level Jacob has grown up and knows, what it means to "belong" and at the same time "be independent" (Cohen 1998, 127). Belonging and independence became compatible and complementary categories, which he can quickly and confidently institutionalise.

10. Fair, responsible and God related life is the last and the highest level of reconciliation.

When Jacob comes to Sukkoth, his new habitat, he firstly takes care for the family and arranges a safe home for it.

When as a teenager he dreamt of a future, he was so taken over by that experience that he placed a monument there and promised God to give him a tithe (Gen 28,22). Even than he concludes that he will strive for an honest life and strengthen his consciousness, that the fruits of his work are not only the result of his diligence, but also God's gift. This conclusion, marked with a monument, has despite the deficiencies and falls led him to a moment, when he senses that his teenage dreams have been realised. This, his home becomes a sacred place, where he places an altar that summarises the role of stairs or ladder from the teenage dreams. On the altar God is coming into his home and his family. From this moment on, God is "home" in his place.

Bible playfully and provocatively remarks that Jacob came healthy into the new habitat. In this way he incidentally warns that he was ill once. He takes us in the time of his struggles and fights with God or with his own shadow past, in fact with himself. Capacity for forgiveness, which led him to reconciliation and integration with himself, with his brother and environment, has placed him on his healthy feet again (Sperry, Giblin 1996, 526). Here, the entire story unambiguously indicates that reconciliation with himself and with God represents a prerequisite for reconciliation with fellow man (Hartley 2000, 290). Reconciliation with God actually itself leads us in reconciliation with the loved ones. Thus any reconciliation is at the same time a redemptive act (Höfer 1993, 140). It is no wonder that in the fullness of life he forgets his lameness and heals in a moment and again starts living.

References

Bucher, A. A. 1992. *Bibel-Psychologie: Psychologische Zugänge zu biblischen Texten.* Stuttgart – Berlin – Köln: W. Kohlhammer.

Cloud, H. & Townsend, J. 2001. *How People Grow: What the Bible Reveals about Personal Growth.* Grand Rapids – Michigan: Zondervan.

Cohen, N. J. 1995. *Self, Struggle & Change: Family Conflict Stories in Genesis and Their Healing Insights for Our Lives.* Woodstock: Jewish Lights Publishing.

Corey, M. A. 1995. *Job, Jonah, and the Unconscious: A Psychological Interpretation of Evil and Spiritual Growth in the Old Testament.* Lanham – New York – London: University Press of America.

Hartley, E. J. 2000. *New International Biblical Commentary: Genesis.* Peabody, Massachusetts & United Kingdom: Hendrickson Publishers, Paternoster Press.

Höfer, A. 1993. *Gottes Wege mit den Menschen: Ein gestaltpädagogisches Bibelwerkbuch.* München: Don Bosco Verlag.

Kille, A. L. 1995. Jacob – A Study in Individuation. In: David L. Miller (ed.). *Jung and the Interpretation of the Bible.* New York: Continuum, pp. 40–54.

Loder, E. J. 1998. *The Logic of the Spirit: Human Development in Theological Perspective.* San Francisco: Jossey-Bass Publishers.

Sperry, L. & Giblin, P. 1996. Marital and Family Therapy with Religious Persons. In: Shafranske, P. E (ed.). *Religion and the Clinical Practice of Psychology.* Washington DC: American Psychology Association, pp. 511–532.

Sveto pismo Stare in Nove zaveze: Slovenski standardni prevod iz izvirnih jezikov. 1997. Ljubljana: Svetopisemska družba Slovenije.

BABEL FROM TEXT TO SYMBOL: POSSIBILITIES OF RECONCILIATION IN THE HEBREW BIBLE

Marcel V. Măcelaru, Osijek

There is somewhat of a consensus among biblical scholars that "reconciliation" is a New Testament concept. Though the term itself appears seldomly in Paul[1] and only once outside the Pauline corpus,[2] the idea of reconciliation occupies a central place in New Testament theology.[3] It implies the overcoming of an enmity between two or more parties and its applications are thoroughly encompassing.

Admittedly, New Testament commentators (e.g., Taylor, 1942; Ridderbos, 1975; Marshall, 1978) have traditionally explained reconciliation only in vertical terms, whereby God's enmity towards humanity, that is, his wrath, and mankind's enmity towards God, that is, our sin, rebellion, indifference and disobedience, are resolved through Christ's sacrifice. However, more recently Constantineanu (2009; 2010) has argued successfully that there is also a social dimension in Paul's use of the concept, thereby showing that reconciliation is the operative antidote to the breakdown of all relationships, either divine-human or human-human.

* * *

Although the word "reconciliation" does not appear in the Old Testament,[4] one should not think that the notion and practice of reconciliation was unknown in Ancient Israel. In fact, there are scholars who have argued that, although using a Greek term, Paul relies for the meaning of "reconciliation" on Old Testament teachings (e.g. Stuhlmaker, 1979; Beale, 1989). Of course, the extent to which that is the case remains unclear. What *is* clear, however, is that, when allowing for

1 The actual terminology appears in Paul in Rom. 5:10–12; 11:15; 1 Cor. 7:11; 2 Cor. 5:18–20; Eph. 2:16; and Col. 1:20–23.

2 See, Matt. 5:24.

3 Concepts related semantically and theologically to "reconciliation" (e.g., forgiveness, justification, fellowship, sanctification, atonement, peace, freedom, and sonship) are employed frequently in various New Testament writings.

4 Fitzmyer (1981:164–65) and Martin (1981:104–106) have argued convincingly that the terminology employed by Paul is borrowed from Judeo-Hellenistic and Greco-Roman contexts.

conceptual parallels and thematic connotations, there are several distinct ways in which the idea of reconciliation is expressed and promoted in the Hebrew Bible.

First, regarding the divine-human relationship, the Old Testament talks about atonement through ritual sacrifice in more than one place (e.g., Lev. 8:15; 2 Chron. 29:24; Ezek. 45:15–17). A quick look at these passages reveals that such action required the shedding of animal blood and its result was the restoration of fellowship between Israel and God.

Second, under the same rubric one can include the theme of covenant, with its overtones of love and adoption (e.g. Exod. 19:1–6; Isa. 43–45) and the promise of *shalom* with its implications of restoration to wholeness (e.g. Lev. 26:6; Ps. 29:11, 147:14; Isa. 35:4–10; 60:1–22; Ezek. 34:25). These are both borderline concepts, for in both cases the accomplishment of reconciliation vertically has horizontal, that is, human-human implications as well.

Third, moving into the horizontal plane, one should note the prophetic denouncement of social injustice and the oppression of the underprivileged (e.g. Isa. 10; Amos 2:6–16). Such message, delivered within a culture functioning on the principles of honour and shame, carries within it a call to relationship restoration (Blenkinsopp, 2008:346–48). A case in point in this regard is the law of the Jubilee (Lev. 25) – although probably never observed, the fact remains that this law calls the Israelites to an ideal of forgiveness that would have been a revolutionary, unheard of, practice.

Fourth, the Old Testament contains many stories that provide worthy examples of enemies turned friends (e.g. Gen. 13; 18:16–33; 45; Prov. 25:21–22), examples of inter-ethnic marital relationships (e.g. Num. 12; Ruth 1:1–4; 4:9–10; Esth. 2.17) and laws that provide for peaceful interactions with the non-Israelite (Exod. 22:21; Lev. 19:33–34; Deut. 27:19; 31:12–13; Mal. 3:5). All these speak powerfully in favour of peaceful coexistence and reconciliation.

In light of all the above, we cannot but conclude that reconciliation is an idea deeply rooted in the world and thought of the Old Testament. It includes provisions for the restoration of Israel's fellowship with God and its manifestations at the social level are multiple and highly encouraged. As such, both the vertical and the horizontal dimension identified in the New Testament usage of the term are available in Old Testament theology as well.

This conclusion may come as a surprise to some of the readers, especially if they adhere to the view that the Old Testament is a violent book, full of conflicts and enmity and lacking forgiveness. Given the points listed in the previous section, the very opposite seems to be true. In fact, there appears to be enough relevant material in the Hebrew Bible to make the undertaking of writing an entire monograph on the topic of reconciliation in the Old Testament a tempting prospect; and although such a task cannot be accomplished here, I propose in the pages below to at least explore the possibilities of such an interpretive paradigm shift. To do so I offer the Tower of Babel story (Gen. 11:1–9), which is a pericope traditionally interpreted in terms of rebellion, enmity and dissent, as an example of what can be accomplished hermeneutically if one approaches a text having in mind the ideals of reconciliation identified above.

* * *

The story of Babel is a provocative legend, filled with irony and symbols, a story about the first human community at a time lost in the mythical past. Imagine a world where all humans live together and speak the same language, a world in which humans find their own way to God by building cities that reach heavens, a world where God walks among men and retorts to extraordinary actions – the confusing of the primeval language and the scattering of humans all over the face of the planet – in order to ensure that mankind does not accomplish what it had planned.

This plot is as dramatic as the imagery it contains is unusual. Most evidently, this is a story that escapes historical scrutiny, for no such world has ever been within our reach. Therefore it should be approached from a non-historical vantage point if our interpretation is to be faithful to the genre of the passage. In this regard I suggest that this story should be treated as an aetiology, though not a simple explanation of a *status quo*, but rather a type of moralising symbolical aetiology, that is, a story whose purpose goes beyond explaining and educating to challenging and changing the way we see and relate to the world around us.

Traditionally interpreters have seen in the story of Babel a tale about human pride and divine punishment, a tale about mankind's attempt to take control of her destiny (Aageson, 1989) and God's intervention to stop that from happening. Within this line of thought it is the human search for self-sufficiency that prompts God to intervene. Such attitude is a "sin" terrible enough to warrant a divine curse whose consequence – the inability to communicate fully – has plagued mankind for millennia. For whatever action God took at Babel, it only started as confusion of language; subsequently it led to a proliferation of cultural differences and consequently to social, racial and ethnic enmity.

This interpretive paradigm, originating with some of the church fathers (see Louth, 2001:166–70) and continued by Luther (1960:210–28) and Calvin,[5] has also prevailed in most modern commentaries (e.g. Panikkar, 1979; Wenham, 1987:232–46; Blough, 2002).[6] However, the reading of the story offered below shows that such an interpretation is not consistent with what the text actually says. I suggest that, when nuances and inferences available in the story are assessed carefully and contextually, a different meaning for the tale emerges. That is, that this is not a story about dissent and brokenness but an explanation for the multiplicity of languages and traditions existing in the world. Consequently, such an explanation offers the possibility to see cultural diversity as a positive feature of human societies. The few scholars who do not take the traditional pride–punishment approach (e.g., Anderson, 1978; Brueggemann, 1982:97–104; Hiebert, 2007) have noted various features of the text which, when brought together, provide strong arguments in support of this interpretation. These make the basis of the commentary offered below.

* * *

The first task in undertaking a fresh reading of the passage in view is to consider carefully what the story itself, that is, its content and structure, tells and does not tell about the issue at hand. In this regard, it may surprise the reader to find out that there is no mention of divine punishment in this account. The words "punishment" or "curse" do not appear in the text and God's intervention does not lead to destruction, as is the case in the earlier story of the Flood, but to the fulfilment of God's initial good purpose for mankind – the dispersion of humans over the whole face of the planet (q.v. Gen. 1:28; cf. Gen. 1:31). Thus, the idea that we are dealing here with divine punishment appears to be a typical gap-filling act on the side of the interpreters.

Moreover, the fact of the matter is that the motivation behind God's activity in the story is not explicitly given anywhere in the passage. However, the structural arrangement of the passage (cf. Wenham, 1987:235) makes v. 5 the centre of a chiasm, therefore identifying God's move of coming "down" as the climax of the

5 When discussing the action undertaken by mankind here, Calvin exclaims: "How is it that they harass and wear themselves out in vain on a difficult and laborious enterprise, unless that, like madmen, they rush impetuously against God?" (see *Calvin's Commentary on Genesis* 11:3).

6 See also the bibliography listed by Wenham 1987: 232–33.

story. This may suggest that we are dealing here with an interested deity, a god who visits with the ones he created[7] out of curiosity, and his decision to intervene is only the aftermath of this climax. This is supported by the grammar of the verse in the original Hebrew, where the verb har (to see) prefixed by the particle l is an infinitive construct that conveys purpose (cf. Wenham, 1987:234). The implication here is that the desire to see his creation rather than the intervention to disperse mankind is what animates God in the story. Therefore, interpreting God's interest as a gesture of vengeance or control is unwarranted.

Admittedly, one may riposte to the above by pointing out that God does in fact intervene in order to put a stop to the building project. However, since neither the action of building the tower nor the meaning humans assign to that action expressed in the words "let us make a name for ourselves" are seen in the passage as sinful, a divine intervention described as "curse" or "punishment" would seem at least exaggerated if not plainly unjust. Unquestionably, the idea of Babel is an error, for otherwise God's intervention would be completely unreasonable. Interpreting it as sinful, however, is yet another example of gap-filling – it is the result of inaccurately regarding the phrase "let us make a name for ourselves" as prideful. In light of Prov. 22:1 and Eccles. 7:1, where a good name is something to strive for, the humans in the story are motivated by a good objective. As such, it seems that the most we can "accuse" these people of is a desire to build and preserve their community at all costs (see v. 4b). Arguably, it is also this desire that prompts God to react; but even so, that would not be because there is something sinful about preserving the community, but because the way this was being done would have interfered with God's initial plan for mankind to multiply and fill the planet. The conclusion of the story (v. 9), which rehearses that which is accomplished, stresses that it was *from* there, that is, *from* Babel, that humans were scattered over the face of the planet. This, I believe, is a hint that the purpose of the story is not to point to yet another human failure. Rather, it is to show that the very cultural diversity resulting from the dispersal *from* Babel fulfils God's purposes for the creation.

***

7 Note the similarity between this passage and Gen. 3:8 where God walks in the Garden of Eden. Neither passage suggests a ghoulish reason for God's action.

In addition to the above it should also be mentioned that proper exegetical practice avoids isolating a text from its canonical context. If this principle is respected here, the interpretation given thus far is the most logical explanation for the place this story occupies in the book of Genesis. First, the ten chapters that precede it provide a thematic context in which the diversity of God's creation is described and lauded. Such diversity characterises God's work from the very beginning and is described by the Creator himself as "good" (q.v. Genesis 1). Similarly, the story of Noah in Genesis 6–9 is a veritable statement in favour of diversity and growth – Noah is tasked with ensuring the survival of each and every form of life God has created and in the concluding covenant humans are again commanded to multiply and fill the face of the earth. This connects well with the table of nations in Genesis 10, which bridges the story of the flood with the story of Babel and whose purpose seems evident – to present the diversification of human language and culture as the status quo. All these bring to mind the fact that in Biblical cosmogony, as well as in other Ancient Near Eastern cosmogonies, the emphasis falls on explaining the emergence of human society shaped along lines familiar to the author of the telling as the result of the act of creation – a fact which reveals the aetiological character of such stories.

Second, the teleological development of God's purposes available in the canonical material, which serves as the larger thematic context within which the story of Babel should be considered, talks about eschatological consummation in language that also cherishes cultural diversity. To give but one example, Isaiah 2:1–4 does not envision the eschaton as a return to a homogenised humanity modelled after the Babel community prior God's intervention, but as a journey towards Zion in which all nations, with their respective ethnic and cultural identities intact, partake. Thus, once again, since the culmination of God's activity in history is unity in diversity, the act of confusing the language in the plains of Shinar and the subsequent scattering over the face of the earth should be seen as a continuation of his activity as Creator, a fulfilment of divine purposes rather than as a vengeful reaction to a particular human undertaking. The story of Babel then is an aetiology explaining a state of being rather than a narrative condemning one. As everything else God did, the creation of cultural diversity is good.

* * *

Given the arguments presented thus far it would appear that gloomy conclusions about God's action and its results have no actual basis in the text. Admittedly, the story of Babel as it stands is at places ambiguous. However, a proper exegetical analysis will not proceed by filling in gaps, be these real or imaginary. Such a practice reflects an approach that does injustice to the biblical text by overlooking its artistry or by regarding its literary artefacts as leftovers from a convoluted compositional history (e.g. Gunkel, 1977:94–102). The position preferred here is to take the biblical text at its face value and to limit the interpretation to the information explicitly given in it. As the case in view shows, in doing so one may discover meanings previously ignored.

Specifically, the interpretation proposed here provides a biblical basis for promoting a positive view of cultural diversity, and by implication, it provides hermeneutically for social reconciliation. This is a message that speaks strongly against viewing cultural diversity as a negative feature of humanity. The post-exilic context, within which the story of Babel was probably heard, was characterized by ethno-centrism and religious exclusivism. Other biblical texts from that period – for instance Ezra and Nehemiah – make this quite clear. Given this, could it be that the story of Babel was promoted exactly because it sarcastically counteracted such attitudes?

Evidently, if seen in this way, the story of Babel can be a resource for believing communities to address differences constructively. Its message is one of hope. It tells us that tensions and conflicts perpetuated on the basis of racial, ethnic, gender, or other differences need not pull us apart. We are not doomed to fail in our pursuit of loving communion, for diversity is not an obstacle to, but a vehicle for, bringing the church to its desired maturity. It is what makes us a powerful witness to the world concerning God's purposes – the possibility of loving unity and understanding while at the same time celebrating the diversity inherent in God's creation.

References

Aageson, J. W. 1989. City-Building and the Benefits of Babel. In: *Christian Century* 106.17, pp. 517–18.

Anderson, B. W. 1978. Unity and Diversity in God's Creation: A Study of the Babel Story. In: *Currents in Theology and Mission* 5.2, pp. 69–81.

Beale, G. K. 1989. The Old Testament Background of Reconciliation in 2 Corinthians 5–7 and Its Bearing on the Literary Problem of 2 Corinthians 6:14–7:1. In: *New Testament Studies* 35, pp. 550–81.

Blenkinsopp, J. 2008. Reconciliation in the Middle East: A Biblical Perspective. In: *Theology Today* 65, pp. 344–55.

Blough, N. 2002. From the Tower of Babel to the Peace of Jesus Christ: Christological, Ecclesiological and Missiological Foundations for Peacemaking. In: *Mennonite Quarterly Review* 76, pp. 7–33.

Brueggemann, W. 1982. *Genesis: A Commentary for Teaching and Preaching.* Interpretation. Atlanta, John Knox.
Constantineanu, C. 2009. *Encountering the Other: Studies in Reconciliation.* Cluj-Napoca, Casa cărţii de ştiinţă.
Constantineanu, C. 2010. *The Social Significance of Reconciliation in Paul's Theology: Narrative Readings in Romans.* London, T. & T. Clark Continuum.
Fitzmyer, J. A. 1981. *To Advance the Gospel.* New York, Crossroad.
Gunkel, H. 1977. *Genesis.* Trans. Mark E. Biddle. Macon, GA, Mercer University Press.
Hiebert, T. 2007. The Tower of Babel and the Origin of the World's Cultures. In: *Journal of Biblical Literature* 126, pp. 29–58.
Louth, A., ed. 2001. *Genesis 1–11. Ancient Christian Commentary on Scripture 1.* Downers Grove, Intervarsity Press.
Marshall, I. H. 1978. The Meaning of Reconciliation. In: *Unity and Diversity in New Testament Theology: Essays in Honor of G. E. Ladd.* Edited by R. A. Guelich. Grand Rapids, Eerdmans.
Martin, R. P. 1981. *Reconciliation: A Study of Paul's Theology.* Atlanta, John Knox.
Panikkar, R. 1979. The Myth of Pluralism: The Tower of Babel – A Meditation on Non-Violence. In: *Cross Currents* 29.2, pp. 197–230.
Ridderbos, H. 1975. *Paul: An Outline of His Theology.* Grand Rapids, Eerdmans.
Stuhlmaker, P. 1979. Das Evangelium von der Versöhnung in Christus. In: *Das Evangelium von der Versöhnung in Christus.* Edited by P. Stuhlmacher and H. Class. Stuttgart, Calwer.
Taylor, V. (1942) *Forgiveness and Reconciliation: A Study in New Testament Theology.* New York, Macmilllan.
Wenham, Gordon J. 1987. *Genesis 1–15. Word Biblical Commentary 1.* Dallas, Word Books.

VICTIMS

ARE VICTIMS NECESSARY FOR THE SURVIVAL OF MANKIND

Janez Juhant, Ljubljana

A being of leisure

Man is a being of leisure, not ready for profound changes in himself and in the society. One of his (negative) properties is to persevere in his old stage and miss opportunities to change his life for better. This is the case with individuals and the society, in our own life and in the lives of others. Many opportunities for good individual and social life are lost because of this, and much more should be offered to make such changes afterwards. The changes after the First World War did not offer opportunities for self-determination of nations. Despite tens of millions of victims, the end of the Second World War brought no freedom for all. Rolf Zimmermann analyzes in his book *Moral as power* the moral side effects in the politics of the last centuries. He tests the morality of the politics in the genocide of Armenians, Jews, Chinese by Japanese, and different nations and groups by the communists. Why were these groups being murdered? Are the events like holocaust and other genocides of this historical period products of the nihilistic technical era, as Günther Anders stressed (1992, 1996; Zimmermann 2008, 92), or is this a product of the modernity with its technical equipments, which made possible such criminal enterprises, as Bauman stressed (1994,27; Zimmermann 2008,90). Against the non-differentiated thesis of Anders and Bauman, according to Rolf Zimmerman, the modernity could develop an adequate democratic structure to prevent such terrible events. This means that these deeds do not stem necessarily from the development of the modern world, but are caused by the lack of democratic culture. This means that man is not ready to adapt himself to the claims of human life's essence. Especially the European continental man is a man of a system, of authority and of the framework, in contrast the Anglo-Saxon is much more concrete from experience.

The continental framework's ways of thinking tend to exclude, and in the modernity it led to totalitarianisms. The dissonance between the political and spiritual sphere made the partnership between political and religious communities difficult, and brought about absolutist tendencies. There was the hierarchical-authoritative modus of the Church which supported the authoritative trainings of citizens. A Jewish woman who survived holocaust is convinced that the holocaust would not have been possible in England. On the other hand, the English were involved in many victimisations of the modern World. The lack of independence, autonomy, the will to implement dialogue, cooperation, and to include the weakest in the society everywhere led to non-living and authoritarian societies. Political power overruled or removed moral aspects of life. Nationalisms and class mentality demanded clean and closed nations in a single state, and caused also totalitarian exclusions. The fascination over capital and its exclusive rule over people did not respect the struggle for survival of the new societal class of workers and the peasants, which were being ruined.

This development introduced particular moralities, like the class morality of communism, the national morality of the Young Turkish Movement, the racial morality of Nazism and Fascism, the Japanese ethnocentrism. Their problems are non-acceptance of moral universalism and the exclusion of some living parts of the (whole moral) human community; every categorical morality should include all people. According to the Charter of Human Rights, all people should be granted basic human rights. Every morality which excludes any person or group is according to this Charter amoral.

The changes in 1989 also did not give satisfaction to the victims and their relatives. The new democracies are burdened by residues of past totalitarian exclusions; there are still only a few accepted democratic procedures in the society.

The same holds true for individual lives. Man is already burdened by his parents and other members of the society who are not ready to develop in him human potential, allowing others to take part in their own life. Lack of work on oneself and burdening others with one's own problems on the other hand brings about attacks on others, who thus become victims of someone else's unsolved problems.

Because the ethics is a practical science - art, the problems of the man and the society could be solved only by practical work. The ethical attempt should work in the human context which means that the ethical conditions for the relations among man should be worked out. This is the claim for the "horizontal ethics" Or. the "humanisation of morality" (Pieper 2000, 135). From our perspective it means to exchange the humanity and to involve all people in the process of the humanisation. This is much more needed after all humiliation of humans from the totalitarianisms (Jaspers 1962, Jonas 1987) and all modern globalised procedures of world human communion. The humanisation means to take part in the problems of humans. Everybody should be involved in the procedures of searching the ways to take up the burdens of all humans. All humans should be taken as integer human and not just as a means for different purposes.

The new morality

Adhering to bad habits, taking easiest ways, and fixating on austerities impede the development of man's central and vital abilities, thus the development of the society. The consequences are the social crisis of the today's world. The real causes of the financial crisis, the Fukushima disaster and climate changes are moral ones. Safranski quoted Nietzsche, who said that "man is not ready to know radically and 'coolly', and he (Nietzsche) criticised in this sense as early as Socrates (and Plato)" (Safranski 2010: 121). The finding of truth (true knowledge) presupposes the ability to discern between good and bad, to be moral and to develop the "sense of humility". We need "more spiritual people": "The love of truth has a salary in heaven and already on earth" (Nietzsche 1988, 53;III/45). To make changes implies searching after truth of oneself and one's societal companions, and to acknowledge one's humility and anthropological limitedness.

The Nietzschean philosophy struggles for this moral self-picture of man. He saw the solution in criticising the Christian (and modern man of technics) view of man. The humbled modest Christian man should be replaced by a strong, more high and self-resolute man: the Superman. Because the Christian God has died, a new strong and powerful man should be born. The Christian morality should be replaced by the morality of this Superman – Zarathustra. He is an ideal man, a personification of morality and an incorporation of the new morality, the morality of power.

According to Zimmermann (2008, 156ff.), Nietzsche influenced most of the modern political movements: Mussolini's Fascism, Hitler's Nazism, and also the Russian bolshevism (Lew Nikolayevich Trocky) and Zionism. Behind most of these influences is the Nietzschean idea of the self-redemption, which is a pillar of his philosophy. This philosophy advocates a modern, powerful, strong and exclusivist man. All these movements were built on Nietzsche's social philosophy, which promoted and cultivated special kinds of people: a concrete type of racial, national and class people. But it is impossible to accept all this Nietzsche's views of morality, like his badly grounded critic of the Christian morality and his exclusive view of man, which prefers special kinds of people and discriminates the others. We can understand his struggle for a moral man and accept his endeavour for high standards of morals, but we cannot accept his views that some kinds or types of men are moral and other not, because this means to exclude some people from the human (moral) community. And this was the case with Fascist, Nazi and communist morality.

Nietzsche's and any other morality of this kind are to be criticized due to its exclusiveness and limitedness to a concrete group of people. In contrast to this, the true moral principles are applicable to everybody and have thus universal character and value. The morality should be applicable to everybody, it should be universalised (Zimmermann 2008, 157). After post-Nietzschean era of the powerful man we have to find out what the true picture of man is.

Truth of man and victimisation

Because man is a being of reason, as the Greeks said, the problem of his knowledge is the touchstone. According to the Old Testament man cognitive ambition is to "be like God" (Gen 3, 5). Because man is not God and his knowledge is limited, the limitedness of knowledge is a supposition for truth of man. It is not in the first place a logical question but a moral one, the question of acknowledging his moral responsibility to others. The unwillingness to acknowledge this fundamental openness for truth of human reality is the cause and impediment to the knowledge of authenticity of human beings and thus the real humanity (Sloterdijk 2010, 135 ff.). According to Sloterdijk, the Greek term epistéme testifies this openness for truths and confirms man's dialogical openness to the other and to the higher Good, God. But the modern economic and technological processes point out an "ideal man", man without deficits. Despite this, the modern man experiences imperfectness and disorders in him and in the society. This increases anger, dissatisfaction and unsolved tensions in individuals and in the whole society, and brings about a search for scapegoats, for the weak, who should help resolve 'the mimetic crisis'.

The scientific and technical acquisitions in the modern society not only culminated these tensions, but also introduced new standards of the man "of austerities". Besides this, the industrial development caused great disproportions in the society. Workers were the bearers of the 'modern development', but they get the least of its benefits. Peasants lost their base for survival. And this story has not been finished yet. We are still struggling for solutions, and several groups of people are still excluded from societal processes. All those people are potential victims, and they became real victims of the societal changes in the last centuries. The problem has nowadays global dimensions. The indolence of leaders and institutions of the society (governments, aristocracy, the new class of capitalists, churches) causes revolt of upper classes, peasants and workers, whose position is becoming more and more unbearable. Oedipus as a victim has become worldly – with global dimensions. According to Adienne Lezzi-Hafter (2000, 1131/2), "Oedipus is very important in modern literature and philosophy." Man remains a complex being, his challenge is a passion and permanent victimization. This complexity made many people strangers to the society: from modern slaves at the beginning of modern times to workers, women and children as excluded classes of the society. Today this processes culminated in the status of global workers. These are victims of luxuries of the modern consumer society: organised trade of modern slaves: women and children for prostitution, war and drugs (Cacho 2011). The modern Oedipus is entangled in the wealth of modern productive procedure, which produces masses of victims.

All these processes are against man. According to Paul Valery, "the essential is against life" (Valery 1993, 629; and Sloterdijk 2010, 125), or we can say the modern life is against the essence of man. The main processes go on without man's personal decisions and do not serve the true prosperity of man or the prosperity of most people. Man is a prisoner of these processes, and there are more and more victims in general: modern consumers, the majority of poor global masses, but especially starving people, children and (young) women exploited for prostitution, cheep work, wars and drugs.

The Greek and the Christian view of man exposes the meaning of a victim for the survival of the humanity. Most of the non-Christian cultures prepared systems of victimization to prevent order and stabilization in the society. According to René Girard's late work *I See Satan Fall Like Lightning*, people knew that victims are necessary and systematically designed frameworks to justify them. Despite this, we have today extensive (verbal) care for victims, yet we cannot be proud of such care. After the end and fall of totalitarian regimes appeared new methods to victimize several groups and nations. Their number is still increasing. We are witnessing masses of victims, and there are many mechanisms (politics, media) to conceal this. We can paraphrase Girard by saying that the old myths were replaced by new (modern) ones (Girard 2006, 183ff.). Rivalries take place and the victims of this crisis of the humanity are increasingly excluded. The consequence of this development is the exclusion of most people from the goods of this earth. Let us look at it from economic point of view (besides other points of view), in numbers: there are 10 million millionaires who possess over 39 billion dollars. In contrast with this, 2.6 milliard people have to share only 1.4 billion dollars.

The human searching for truth has to take care for this very important dimension of the truth of man today.

The imperfect man searching for truth

Man of modern times was understood as a settled and scientific man, who stimulated, guided and governed the world and himself by science and technique. He perceived himself as a big, strong man empowered by science and technique. These are the prolonged organs of man (Kiepas 2010: 13). Man has a powerful sense of himself, which stimulated the faith that he would master the whole world. Nietzsche struggled against this monstrous man by inventing the individual superman, full of life and power. But the historical and societal limitedness did not and does not allow all people to get or to gain this ideal picture of man. Hannah Arendt (2005, ch. Fall Dawn of National State and the End of the Human Rights, 345ff.) in her work *The origins of totalitarianism* analyzed the history of the totalitarianisms of the 20th century as an usurpation of human rights. Only men who were true according to these totalitarianisms were granted perfection in contrast to others, who were excluded, diabolised and considered bad. The ideas of racism, nationalism, chosen classes and the "better people" prevailed. (They were usual for ordinary people, who had to serve the 'best classes' and refer to them as 'better people'). A contribution of the mimetic theory of Girard stresses the "anthropological constancy" (Uhl 2010, 323) of the rivalry, which makes the "other", the weak, who are to be victimized, declared bad and guilty for bad conditions of man.

René Girard resumed the basic Judaeo-Christian topic of man: every man is a limited being, there is an "original sin", due to which there are not only bad or good, all are involved in victimisation and guilty. It is not possible to exclude and not to see the breaches of human existence. Man is an individual being, a divided being and thus imperfect being. To obtain this consciousness means to convert (metanoia) and be related to the other as a completeness of oneself. It means to be open for real relations to the other. Without this fundamental change, work on oneself, individual and societal reconciliation are not possible. Anybody could undertake to change his relations to others, but nobody can do it without acceptance of the other. Change begins in mind. If man is not ready to change his mind, he will persist in the habits and customs he already has.

Nietzsche also understood this hour of truth of man and wrote about extrapolation of modern man and tried the ways to change it. Like many modern thinkers he saw the problem in the Christian teaching of a humble man. He was aware that this is not also a man of technique, but a self-confident, powerful man inspired by the Greek agon. The liberal paradigm of modernity strengthened this agonal, struggling and excluding relations among people. The Christian endeavour for interpersonal relations was thus reversed to rivalry and exclusion. Perhaps Nietzsche was beside of his psychological problems influenced by those modern tendencies and he saw the solution in a strong, powerful man who could change the modern strong systems which overruled the man. But according to Zimmermann (2008, 159), the Nietzschean ideal of man could and should be universalized in sense that all people are invited to realise the moral ideal of man. But this is not a man of technique, science, political (totalitarian) or consumer system, but only a "human man". Because of it the solution could not be reached in this world. There is no 'hyper-policy' (Zimmermann 2008, 157), the instrument of regulating this is no totalitarian system, no classless society, no world policy.

Such a man should implement universal moral power (Zimmermann 2008, 159). This calls for universal rules or ways of dialogue. The ways of reparation of humanity are the ways of dialogical man, of enlargement and deepening of his morality. Human dialogue is a struggle for acknowledging imperfections of everybody and implementation of inter-human relations. Nobody should be excluded from these processes (Dumouchel/Dupuy1999, 170, 232). The insatiable rivalry and unlimited enlargement of envy lead to more and more exclusions and do not allow the processes of reconciliation in the society. Dialogue among men should for this reason be completed by dialogue with God. Julia Annas (1994, 238) says: "The consciousness of the existence of ideas comes more from the conversion of the heart as from enlargement of intellectual sharpness". Paul Ricoeur thus terms the search for truth faithfulness. He speaks about "faithfulness of memories, of memories being true to ..., in order to express this search, this demand, this claim, which constitutes the veridical-epistemic dimension of the orthos logos of memory" (Ricoeur 2004, 55). Peter Sloterdijk (2010, 132–147) demands the "objective and epistemic view respectively ", which means holistic, (enough) deep view or the belief, which is directed to truth. One should be peritus skilled (Greek *episteme* means skilled, scientific, firmly). He warns that the humanity of today, together with intellectuals, is more concerned about killing truth than about discovering (finding) it.

This means that the metanoia, the conversion to full dialogue, which frees man from his entanglement in the myths of mimetic desire, averts him from victimisation of others and makes him ready to participate in processes of memory, which certificate his belief and faithfulness. Ocvirk (cf. Ocvirk 2011) is convinced that the metanoia as a Christian universalistic term is not applicable in the present secular society, which thinks in racial categories. The conversion to dialogue and to partnership can take place only (using Plato's diction) by memory of the eidetic world. So the supposition of Zimmerman to respect the Charter of Human

Rights or to practice the universal morality is possible only by supposition of orthos logos. This is the way to reconciliation and suspense of victimization. It is possible, because man has predispositions to good, but this should be always cultivated by dialogue (Ricoeur 2004, 491) and the will for truth. Ricouer mentions that in the "ultimate act of trust there is no recourse but to assume an ultimate paradox proposed by the Religions of Book" and which (I) Ricoeur (2004, 490) finds "inscribed in the Abrahamic memory". This dialogue is very difficult in the global society and in the Slovenian post-communist circumstances. The world crisis is caused by unwillingness to engage in dialogue, the Slovenian society is still permeated with the old Marxist manners.

Therefore, there are many sophisticated exclusions taking place in the modern world. Many people are made for victims, and are excluded from all societal processes. The violence has taken new and differentiating, subtle ways (trade with humans, terrorism, 'religious wars') which are consequences of these separation's processes of modern world. There are no possible ways for many people to avoid such circumstances of modern world.

Slovenian case

The Slovenian revolutionary case was a touchstone for creating a strong, revolutionary modern man without any compromises. This caused the fratricidal war which marked the Slovenian nation, and whose consequences are still felt. After the changes in 1989, we are still in the revolutionary euphoria, which takes mimetic dimensions at several decisive times, like in election campaigns etc. The dialogue among the divided parties has not taken place yet, because the post-communists believe that exclusions and rivalry is politically profitable. There are still many people affected by fear of the oppression from the former regime. The post-communists fear that the atrocious deeds of communist oppressors will be brought to light. The revolutionary values still prevail in the society. The mental, administrative and economic revolutionary revenge still takes place and hinders the reconciliation in the society.

The class enemy is predominant societal formula for exclusion of others and for maintaining the division of the society. The victims of the revolution are nameless, without graves, without compensations for their suffering. In this sense the post-communists are not ready to accept the principles of democracy. There is an ambivalent role of the Christians and the Catholic Church. The Church was in opposition to the regime. The Christians were prosecuted, exiled, more than 20,000 were killed during the war and revolution, the majority of them in the aftermath of war. Many Catholics were subjected to oppression and persecution by the secret police, there has been no lustration processes, be it political or in the Church. Many members of the Catholic Church still repeat the slogan of prosecution of Catholics. In general: the mentality of fear, isolation, powerlessness and rivalry as a sediments of the past system prevail instead of the trends of world's societal, economical and political processes. Slovenia will seriously begin with the reconciliation processes when the victims of the revolution are decently buried and the national declaration of reconciliation will not be only signed but politically and administratively accepted and implemented. They had to be declared as victims, so that other people could survive.

There was the moment in 2009, the 3rd of March, when the victims at Huda jama near Celje were discovered. After the long and tiring search and the removal of 100 meters of barriers, the excavating group found 427 fairly preserved corpses. Yet the search was stopped despite the fact that there are still more than 2000 corpses in the cave. The media showed the pictures of victims which moved the nation, and the compassion and empathy prevailed for some days. Under political pressure this lasted just about a week, afterwards political pragmatism prevailed over humane sentiments.

The disarrayed state makes, besides the old victims of the past regime (convicts, wronged parties, socially excluded), some new victims, newly socially excluded: workers, young generations with nothing to look forward to.

People in Slovenia are involved in the some processes of exclusions and with the same reasons as people from modern world, comparable to the world's processes but the revolutionary case gives the processes a special accent. From one point, it is the pragmatic reason which dictates the new transitorily class of the post-communist to survive by the manner of exclusion like it was in the communistic system. From the other side, the agonizing, rival mechanisms of consumer society leave more and more people aside of the societal processes. Because of the manner of communistic rivalry doctrine many people could turn to the dialogical ways of communication.

Empathy, dialogue and reconciliation

Jeremy Rifkin pointed out that dialogue and empathy are increasing in the global society. He is aware that it is "the climb to a global peak empathy" (Rifkin 2009, 423), which means that it is a very difficult task. On the other hand he is convinced that it will be reached. There is no doubt that it is a necessary task to reach freedom, reconciliation among different, mostly quarrelling human groups. There is an enormous need for empathy, but the ways to it are very difficult, combined with metanoia, with the change from rivalry to cooperation, compassion, and thus to the real essence of man. The agon, the logic of competition and revolution, still prevails, and not only politicians but also intellectuals, like Slavoj Žižek, promote and support theoretically and practically the revolutionary logic.

Rifkin speaks of the "births of humanism" (Rifkin 2009, 270), but could it be promoted by mimetic rivalry and 'scapegoat mechanisms', "the ones of really satanic relations-frameworks among men" (Uhl 2010, 318). This competition's mechanism among men should be converted to cooperation, dialogue and "solidarity with a suffering human being". Because so many people are speaking language of oppression and exclusion, the conversion is much more needed, but also much more difficult. We need prudence and ethical binding and responsibility.

According to Rolf Zimmerman, there are some criteria for historical moral responsibility. Generally observed, human rights are the criterion for meeting of people. We should not accept any particular moral criteria, the Kantian general law is to be observed. It is a frame worked out in the Charter of Human Rights from December the 10th , 1948, and it was worked out in detail at the conference in Vienna in 1993. The universal value of the Rights should be obtained. The human language has to take care for the intersubjective exchange of moral responsibility. States have moral responsibility for this communication. They have to deal with application of human rights in the historical and political area. The moral criteria of human rights should be globalized. There could be some particular cultural differences, but these should not go in different cultural blocs or different political powerful ideologumena, they should be discussed at the universal human level to suspend ideological particularities (Zimmermann 2008, 160–170).

The human rights should be cultivated and protected for "lower people", who are all humiliated, too. They have to take in account that their humanity should not be given up. It is very important to make the pedagogical and medial campaign to persuade all people to take such care for themselves. Political and other rulers have to open and to explicate frameworks of the genocide of Armenians, the holocaust of Jews, other nations and groups, and removal of "class enemies". In Slovenia and everywhere else the process of reconciliation exists, a long and difficult process which presupposes a conversion of mind and readiness to cooperate. The logic of revolution, which means lying, oppressing and exclusion, should be replaced by search for truth, freedom, cooperation … The latter are anthropological values, but to implement them we need steady willingness for dialogue at all levels of the society and in individuals.

There is a need for spiritual metanoia, which is a religious category, we need to combine the mystic and politics. Mystic is according to Leonardo Boff (2011:68 ff.) the awareness that we all are children of God, who is our common father. He enables us to take all people as our brothers and sisters, not merely rivals. We need also the politics to work out the "kingdom of God" on earth. This utopia can work if we are always sincerely praying "Our father in haven", and we thus have the will to build his Kingdom on earth. This endeavour is very exciting without faith. Because all things of a human life could be reached only through suffering (Cf. 1. Gen 3, 16–19), it is important and in the same sense very difficult – like all human affairs – to confer among ourselves the 'gravity (weight) of a day'. The victimization should be shared out also among human beings. The back side of the coin of human rights is the division of endeavour for humanity. If the victims are unavoidable, it is important that we are all ready to share the suffering among ourselves (whole human community). It is impossible that only some people are bearers of the world's salvation. There is only one Salvatore, Jesus Christ. If we are all going his way, we are bringing reconciliation in this world.

Perhaps the situation of the world is like that of the theatre of Soeren Kierkegaard. The theatre was on fire and its director urged a clown, who was just about to perform, to warn the audience. He tried, but the people thought he was pulling their leg, so they all died in the fire. The clown was trying hard to persuade them, but they took it as a good joke. The decisive people of today: politicians, financial and other rulers of the world, are staging plays and hiring clowns to put out the fire in the theatre. The clowns of this world are trying to persuade people that the situation is serious, yet nobody believes it (Boff 2011: 125 f.). Are we ready to acknowledge the truth of the world and humanity and to change our minds? This is the way to acknowledge victimizations and to reconcile people.

References

Annas, J. 1994. *Introduction à la République de Platon*. Pariz: P. U. F.

Anders, G. 1992. *Die Antiquiertheit des Menschen* I,II. München: Beck.

Anders, G. 1996. *Ketzereien*. München: Beck.

Arendt, H. 2005. *Izvori totalitarizma (The Origins of Totalitarianism),* Ljubljana: Študentska založba.

Bauman, Z. 1996. *Dialektik der Ordnung. Die Moderne und Holocaust*. Hamburg: Europäische Verlagsanstalt/Sabine Groenewold Verlage.

Boff, L. 2011. *Sehnsucht nach dem Unendlichen. Spirituell Leben*. Kevelaer: Butzon&Bercker.

Dumouchel, P./Dupuy, J.-P. 1999. *Die Hölle der Dinge. René Girard und die Logik der Ökonomie*. Thaur: Druck und Vergashaus MbH, Münster: LIT, 9–24.

Cacho, L. 2011. *Sklaverei. Im Inneren des Milliardengeschäfts. Menschenhandel.* Frankfurt: S. Fischer.

Girard, R.1989. *The Scapegoat.* Baltimore: John Hopkins UP.

Girard, R. 2006. *Gledam satana, ki kakor blisk pada z neba*. Ljubljana: KUD Logos (*Je vois Satan tomber comme l'éclair*. Paris: Grasset, 1999; *I See Satan Fall Like Lightning*. Maryknoll: Orbis Books, 2001).

Jaspers, K. 1962. *Der philosophische Glaube angesichts der christlichen Offenbarung*. München: Piper.

Jonas, H. 1987. *Der Gottesbegriff nach Auschwitz: eine jüdische Stimme*. Frankfurt: Suhrkamp.

Kertész, I. 2003. *Liquidation*, Frankfurt/M.: Suhrkamp.

Kiepas, A. 2010. *Der Mensch. Das vergessene Paradigma der Technikphilosophie*? Berlin: LIT.

Lezzi-Hafter, A. 2000. Oidipus. In: Cancik, Hubert/Schneider, Helmuth (Eds.). *Der Neue Pauly. Enzyklopädie der Antike*. Stuttgart: J.B.Metzler, pp. 1130–1133.

Nietzsche, F. 1988. *Onstran dobrega in zlega. H genealogiji morale (Beyond Good and Evil, On the Genealogy Of Morality*), Ljubljana: SM.

Ocvirk, D. K. 2011. Evangelijski metanoeite za spravo v sekularni družbi. In: J. Juhant, B. Žalec in V. Strahovnik (eds.), *Izvor odpuščanja in sprave: Človek ali Bog? Spravni procesi in Slovenci*. Ljubljana: Teološka fakulteta, pp. 43–53.

Ricoeur, P. 2004. *Memory, History, Forgetting.* Chicago/London: The University of Chicago Press.

Piper, A. 2000. *Einführung in die Ethik.* Tübingen/Basel: Francke.

Rifkin, J. 2009. *The Empathic Society. The Race to the Global Consciousness in a World in Crisis.* New York: Penguin Books.

Safranski, R. 2010. *Nietzsche. Biografija njegovega mišljenja*. Ljubljana: Literarno umetniško društvo.

Sloterdijk, P. 2010. *Scheintod im Denken. Von Pihilosophie und Wissenschaft als Übung*. Frankfurt: Suhrkamp (Edition Unseld 28).

Uhl, F. 2010. Religion, Gewalt und Relativismus. In: Wandinger, Nikolaus/ Steinmair-Pösel, Petra (eds.). *Im Drama des Lebens Gott begegnen. Einblicke in die Theologie Józef Niewiadomskis*. Wien: LIT, pp. 316–331.

Valery, P. 1993. *Cahiers/Hefte* 6. Frankfurt am Main: Suhrkamp.

Zimmermann, R. 2008. *Moral als Macht*. Reinbeck b. Hamburg: Rowohlt Verlag.

WHY THE CONCERN FOR VICTIMS REQUIRES FORGIVENESS: GIRARDIAN REFLECTIONS ON MONOTHEISM, VIOLENCE AND RECONCILIATION

Wolfgang Palaver, Innsbruck

René Girard's mimetic theory is today one of the most widely discussed theories that help us to understand the complex relationship between religion and violence. It is also an important anthropological approach to understand the importance of forgiveness as a precondition of reconciliation. In the following I will first introduce the three basic pillars of Girard's mimetic theory turning afterwards to its emphasis on forgiveness that has to prevent possible distortions of the biblical concern for victims.

1. Competition or Mimetic Rivalry as the Source of Violence

Not aggression but competition is according to Girard the main source of human violence (Girard, 2004: 9–10). By referring to competition Girard declares mimetic desire as a main cause of rivalries and violence. Whenever human beings imitate others and desire therefore the same objects they cannot share or enjoy together they easily turn against each other. This explanation of human violence brings Girard close to the English philosopher Thomas Hobbes who also emphasized this cause of violence at the beginning of the modern era: "If any two men desire the same thing, which nevertheless they cannot both enjoy, they become enemies; and in the way to their End, ... endeavour to destroy, or subdue one an other." (Hobbes, 1991: 87) But this affinity between Girard and Hobbes should not lead us to the assumption that they share a pessimistic anthropology or an ontology of violence. Whereas Hobbes assumes that human beings are necessarily prone to violence and war Girard's starting point is positive because he emphasizes in the very same book in which he accuses many social scientist to neglect the fragility of human relations that "mimetic desire is intrinsically good" (Girard, 2001: 15).

2. Archaic Religion: Peace Built on Violence

According to Girard, mimetic rivalries can lead whole communities into a deep crisis often close to a Hobbesian war of all against all. In his eyes, exactly such crises triggered the emergence of archaic religion at the dawn of human cultures. It was religion that helped archaic communities to overcome the crisis coming along with the spread of mimetic rivalries inside human communities. To understand this claim one has to focus on the importance of rites and prohibitions that play an essential role in early religions and must go beyond modern understandings of religions reducing it to merely cognitive concepts. This insight leads to the second pillar – mimetic desire is its first pillar – of mimetic theory: Girard's hypothesis that human culture roots in the scapegoat mechanism. According to Girard, early human communities had no cultural or social institutions to keep mimetic rivalries in check. The natural outcome was a general crisis because all were drawn into rivalries and violence. Without a solution to this war of all against all, human communities would have disappeared entirely. But according to Girard, mimesis - the source of the crisis - also helps to overcome a violent chaos. At the height of the crisis when all are drawn into violent rivalries and all objects have disappeared, mimesis can unify a group of people because all objects that created disunity have been replaced by hatred and violence between antagonists. Unlike exclusive objects, violence against a rival can be shared. The arbitrary blow of one of the rivals against another can fascinate others to such a degree that they imitate this deed and join in striking the momentarily weaker individual. The war of all against all suddenly becomes a war of all against one. The single victim is expelled or killed. Girard calls this unconscious, collective deed the scapegoat mechanism.

The expelled or killed scapegoat is seen by the lynchers in two ways. He is made fully responsible for the crisis; therefore, he is an absolute evil that must be expelled. But the sudden peace and the reconciliation that results among the lynchers is also attributed to the scapegoat. He or she is seen as both absolute evil and absolute good at the same time. This strange experience of badness and goodness at the same time is the archaic religious experience. The Latin root of the word sacred *sacer*, for instance, originally meant something that is both cursed and blessed at the same time. The victim is sacralized and deified. He or she becomes a god. Archaic religion is not an invention of priests to deceive their people but the result of an unconscious social mechanism to overcome a dangerous internal crisis. It is for this reason that Girard claims that "the peoples of the world do not invent their gods. They deify their victims" (Girard, 2001: 70). According to Girard, the scapegoat mechanism is the origin of religion and culture making all the central elements of religion (myths, rites, prohibitions) intelligible.

3. The Biblical Difference

Girard's analysis of archaic religion, however, does not explain religion in general or especially the religions of the Bible. He maintains a "biblical 'difference'" where he compares these two types of religion more closely (Girard, 2004: 14). This is the third pillar of mimetic theory. Girard was able to demonstrate that many myths and rituals of different cultures and epochs can easily be explained with his theory. When he turned to biblical texts, however, he discovered that the main passages are not like archaic myths telling the story of a collective murder from the perspective of the lynchers but side with the victim and expose the violence of the persecutors. Already in very old texts - like in the book of Genesis - we can find passages expressing a movement away from a world practicing human sacrifices. The most important text in this regard is the story of Abraham (Gen 22) who was going to sacrifice his son Isaac until God asked him to offer a ram instead. Other texts challenge the mythic pattern of archaic religions even deeper by directly siding with victims of collective persecution. Penitential psalms, the dialogues in the Book of Job, passages in the writing prophets -especially the Suffering Servant of Yahweh (Isa 52–53) - tell us about the collective violence against an innocent victim. The most important passages in the Bible in this regard are the passion narratives in the New Testament. Like mythical texts these narratives talk about collective violence against a single individual. Unlike myths, however they do not side with the persecutors but reveal the innocence of the scapegoat Jesus. In John's gospel a quote from the Psalms underlines clearly the innocence of Jesus: "They hated me without a cause" (Jn 15:25; cf. Ps 35:19). From a Girardian point of view, Judaism and even more so Christianity stand in opposition to archaic religion. This is also true of Islam. We can therefore justly speak of an Abrahamic revolution that overcame the stage of archaic religions (Palaver, 2009). The monotheistic traditions can be characterized by their concern for the victims.

4. The Ambiguous Cachet of Victimhood

There is, however, also a monotheistic legacy of violence. The Abrahamic exposure of the scapegoat mechanism does not automatically lead to a more peaceful world but has often terribly increased the amount of violence by distorted applications of it. To a certain degree such fragmented and distorted influences of the Abrahamic revelation help us to explain some of the temptations towards violence in our contemporary world. Girard has clearly been aware of this problem when he early on referred to such misuses of the biblical perspective: "As long as it remains intact it will be a force for peace, and only if it is fragmented can it be used in service of war. Broken into pieces it provides the opposing doubles with weapons that are vastly superior to what would be available in its absence." (Girard, 1986: 116) The most intriguing example of such a distortion of the Abrahamic tradition is connected to its siding with the victims. The Abrahamic concern for victims has led to the best and worst in our world. On the one hand it is one of the strongest sources that led to the still ongoing increase of the value of human beings resulting in our strong emphasis on human rights. On the other hand, however, we also recognize an increase of violence that follows a concern for victims that does not go together with forgiveness and reconciliation. The Abrahamic solidarity with the victims easily turns into an aggressive weapon if taking the side of the victim is not connected with forgiveness.

We can find many examples of this temptation throughout the history of the Abrahamic religions. From a Christian perspective, the most striking examples are the Crusades where Christians fought against Jews and Muslims legitimating their violence by emphasizing their solidarity with the crucified Jesus. The temptation of a vengeful religious lament has become a common dimension of contemporary religiously - and also secular -motivated violence, especially of terrorism. Muslim, Jewish and Christian terrorists legitimate their violent acts as deeds in defence of persecuted victims. Louise Richardson, one of the leading experts on terrorism, summarized the way terrorist all over the world see themselves today as representing the perspective of the victim: "Sociologist Mark Juergensmeyer asked Dr Abdul Aziz Rantisi, one of the founders of Hamas /…/, in what way he thought Hamas was misunderstood. He said, 'You think we are aggressors. That is the number-one misunderstanding. We are not: we are victims.' Bin Laden, characteristically, phrased it more dramatically: 'The truth is the whole Muslim world is the victim of international terrorism, engineered by America and the United Nations.' A member of the IRA explained to Kevin Toolis why he joined the terrorist movement: 'I knew that the IRA were our defenders, looking after our interests, fighting for our rights." (Richardson, 2006: 65)

We can discover a general tendency towards a "cult of the victim" in our world that easily leads to violence (Lasch, 1991: 67–68). Terrorism is closely connected to a vengeful instrumentalization of victimhood. It is part of what the psychiatrist Vamik Volkan called the "egoism of victimization" (Volkan, 1988: 176). Volkan explains plausibly, how a certain view of one's victimization, the inability to mourn properly and acknowledge one's own weaknesses may lead quickly towards terrorism: "The individual who perceives his group as victimized and whose own sense of self is threatened by that perception may be drawn to terrorist activities in the same way that a nation that perceives itself to be victimized may go to war." (Volkan, 1988: 176–177)

The temptation of vengeful religious lamenting has accompanied Abrahamic monotheism from its very beginning. It has remained, of course, a permanent temptation throughout Jewish, Christian and Muslim history. Many secularized versions of it are also contributing to our contemporary culture of a radical victimology often turning the concern for victims into an even more dangerous weapon. The Canadian philosopher Charles Taylor has taken up basic insights of Girard's mimetic theory explaining with its help also the dangers coming along with our modern cult of the victim that he calls the "powerful cachet of victimhood" (Taylor, 2004: 36). With Girard, Taylor maintains that the Gospel shows the innocence of the victim referring, however at the same time also to its abuses. The Gospel "points toward the raising up of victims, of the despised and rejected. … This becomes on one hand, a great force for battling against injustices. But it also becomes a way of drawing lines, denouncing enemies, the evil ones. … Because my being the victim means that you are the victimizer. I am pure. Claiming victimhood is an assertion of our purity; we are all right. Moreover, our cause is good, so we can fight, inflict a violence that is righteous: a holy violence. Hence we have a right to do terrible things, which others have not. Here is the logic of modern terrorism." Also Girard himself has addressed again and again this dangerous cult of the victim. According to him, we often "practice a hunt for scapegoats to the second degree, a hunt for hunters of scapegoats" (Girard, 2001: 158).

5. The Abrahamic Tradition of Forgiveness

The Abrahamic religions, however, are not automatically leading to violent abuses of victimhood. As we have already mentioned before it is only a fragmented use of the biblical revelation that turns it into a weapon in the mimetic struggles of today. A quick look at the New Testament shows how the concern for victims is accompanied by forgiveness. Contrary to all temptations of a vengeful lament the New Testament's solidarity with the victims does not at all legitimate retribution. Jesus' heavenly father personifies the love for enemies and the rejection of revenge: "Love your enemies and pray for those who persecute you, so that you may be children of your Father in heaven; for he makes his sun rise on the evil and on the good, and sends rain on the righteous and on the unrighteous." (Mt 5:44–45). In accordance with his father Jesus forgave his enemies when he was murdered on the Cross: "Father, forgive them; for they do not know what they are doing." (Lk 23:34) And when he met his disciples again after his resurrection he offered them his peace without blaming them for their weakness and cowardliness (Schwager, 1999: 146, 152, 207): "Peace be with you." (Jn 20:19) The true Christian spirit contradicts vengeful lamenting and is beyond all resentment.

Of course also in the other two Abrahamic religions, Judaism and Islam, we can find important ways overcoming resentment and preventing the vengeful exploitation of victimhood. Jacques Derrida refers to an Abrahamic tradition of forgiveness (Derrida, 2001: 28, 42). We are today so much in need of forgiveness that we should encourage all religions and world views to develop it as strongly as possible.

Charles Taylor has focused seriously on ways to overcome the deadlock of the cult of the victim in his recent writings. He recognizes a special danger in all attempts seeking a stance of purity that easily results in scapegoating. Drawing on the work of Dostoyevsky he contrasts the slogan "no one to blame" with its dangerous consequences to an attitude that characterizes all the redemptive characters in work of the Russian novelist who know that "we are all to blame". According to Taylor, only those who do not exempt themselves from all evil are able to forgive others and find "a new footing of co-responsibility to the erstwhile enemy" (Taylor, 2004: 39). Forgiveness is based on a "recognition of common, flawed humanity" (Taylor, 2007: 709). By this, Taylor indirectly refers to the concept of original sin that despite its many abuses and distortions throughout history helps us to overcome attempts to blame all evil on the other by adopting a violent moralism typical of crusaders (Taylor, 2007: 651–653, 698, 709).

For a modern example of the cult of the victim we can turn to Austria which for a long time did not properly deal with its own involvement in the Nazi crimes. Austria understood itself as the first victim of Hitler's aggression and felt therefore relieved from any obligation to take a critical stance towards its own past. It lasted until the 80s of the last century until more and more Austrians changed their attitude and started a serious reflection on our past. This challenging task has not yet been finished. In Germany, on the other hand, many people started to reflect on their own guilt after the Second World War. For the Germans, of course, there was not such an easy way to evade the question of their own responsibility. There were also important thinkers like the philosopher Karl Jaspers who emphasized early on in 1946 that Germans should not seek refuge in the role of the victim but should rather reflect on their own guilt and change their ways: "Therefore we, as individuals, should not be so quick to feel innocent, should not pity ourselves as victims of an evil fate, should not expect to be praised for suffering. We should question ourselves, should pitilessly analyze ourselves: where did I feel wrongly, think wrongly, act wrongly—we should, as far as possible, look for guilt within ourselves, not in things, nor in the others; we should not dodge into distress. This follows from the decision to turn about, to improve daily." (Jaspers, 2000: 108–109) We can ask us today if the different attitudes of Austria and Germany have contributed to the fact that Germany is today much less confronted by an extreme right in its parliaments.

To focus on our own shortcomings enables us to forgive those who have trespassed against us. From a theological perspective we know, of course, that it is God's grace that enables us to face our own guilt, forgive our opponents and seek reconciliation. Let me conclude with a political outlook that we can get from the work of Charles Taylor. He refers to current examples of ways to side with the victims without giving in to revenge and counter-violence. He mentions as important examples for our world of today the Dalai Lama, people like Adam Michnik in Poland and especially Nelson Mandela in South Africa: "Following the only too understandable path of revenge would have made it impossible to build a new, democratic society. It is this reflection which has pushed many leaders after periods in history to offer amnesties. But there was more than that here. Amnesties have the flaw that they usually involve suppressing the truth or at least consciousness of the terrible wrongs that have been done, which therefore fester in the body politic. Mandela's answer was the Truth and Reconciliation Commission, one which is meant to bring terrible deeds to light, but not necessarily in a context of retribution. Moreover, the deeds to be brought to light were not only those of the former ruling side. Here is the new ground of co-responsibility which this Commission offered." (Taylor, 2007: 710)

References

Derrida, J. 2001. *On Cosmopolitanism and Forgiveness*, translated by M. Dooley and M. Hughes, London: Routledge.

Girard, R. 1986. *The Scapegoat*, translated by Y. Freccero, Baltimore: The Johns Hopkins University Press.

———. 2001. *I See Satan Fall Like Lightning*, translated by J. G. Williams, Maryknoll, NY: Orbis Books.

———. 2004. Violence and Religion: Cause or Effect? In: *The Hedgehog Review* 6 (1), pp. 8–20.

Hobbes, T. 1991. *Leviathan*, Cambridge: Cambridge University Press.

Jaspers, K. 2000. The Question of German Guilt. In: *Perspectives in continental philosophy*, New York: Fordham University Press.

Lasch, C. 1991. Liberalism and Civic Virtue. In: *Telos* (88), pp. 57–68.

Palaver, W. 2009. Abrahamitische Revolution, politische Gewalt und positive Mimesis. Der Islam aus der Sicht der mimetischen Theorie. In *Im Wettstreit um das Gute. Annäherungen an den Islam aus der Sicht der mimetischen Theorie*, edited by W. Guggenberger and W. Palaver, Wien: LIT, pp. 29–73.

Richardson, L. 2006. *What Terrorists Want: Understanding the Terrorist Threat*, London: John Murray.

Schwager, R. 1999. *Jesus in the Drama of Salvation: Toward a Biblical Doctrine of Redemption*, translated by J. G. Williams and P. Haddon, New York: The Crossroad Publishing Company.

Taylor, C. 2004. Notes on the Sources of Violence: Perennial and Modern. In *Beyond Violence: Religious Sources for Social Transformation in Judaism, Christianity and Islam*, edited by J. L. Heft, Ashland: Fordham University Press, pp. 15–42.

———. 2007. *A Secular Age*, Cambridge, Ma.: The Belknap Press.

Volkan, V. D. 1988. *The Need to have Enemies and Allies: From Clinical Practice to International Relationships*, Northvale, NJ: Jason Aronson Inc.

IS IT POSSIBLE TO ESTABLISH A NEW TYPE OF NATIONAL RECONCILIATION ON THE BASIS OF THE OLD "SYMBOLIC" VICTIMS?

Tadej Strehovec, Ljubljana

Introduction

The national reconciliation is one of the most discussed topics in Slovenia public. Many politicians, thinkers, historians and opinion makers are trying to find new ways how to reflect on Slovenian modern history especially during and after the Second World War. Same thinkers and historians are looking for the new ways how to discover historical facts, trying to rewrite history and to put on trial still living responsible representatives of totalitarian communist regime. Other thinkers and politicians are much more in favor of the so called "soft approach", that means to discover historical facts in slow manner and to avoid decisions and interpretations which could be understood as one form of violence especially like revenge.

The aim of this article is to present and discuss one possible way of thinking about national reconciliation on the basis of the demythologizations of recent history and to find mythical elements in Slovenian modern society. On the basis of Girard's theory of mimetic violence and the "Scapegoat theory" the reflection could lead to another interpretation of violence during and after the Second World War in Slovenian newly (recent) history. Three fundamental questions will be discussed:

a. How the mimetic conflict was expressing itself in the time during and after the 2nd World War in Slovenia?
b. Why people of Slovenia got an independent country only after committing (so called) 'fundamental murder'?
c. Which could be the preconditions for national reconciliation from the perspective of Rene Girard?

At the end of this discussion a short description of indirect symbolical reconciliation will be presented, with the example of (so called) *Slovenian Yad Washem.*

1. Does mimetic violence exist in a Slovenian manner?

Girard's theory of mimetic violence consists of the thesis that religion is not a phenomenon of society, but rather that society is a religious phenomenon in which society restrains mimetic rivalry and violence. In his works, Girard analyses different kinds of biblical texts such as the story of Cain, the narrative of the scapegoat, the story of Job, and of the suffering servant (Girard 1985, 102). At the same time, he exposes the relation between rituals (victims) and myths. Therefore, his thesis is not only that an innocent victim links together the rival sides in society, but also that it establishes a kind of peace. The friendship between Herod and Pilate at the time of Jesus' trial is evident (Luke 23.12). In pagan mythological religion there seems always to be present the logic of looking for an innocent victim, one that is collectively condemned and killed. After the murder, it is usually divinized. But according to Girard, such logic is present not only at the temporal foundation of civilization. It is a hidden logic of everyday life in society. Society, full of tensions always generates new innocent victims. It is always a temptation for the majority in society to select and kill a weak victim from among the sick, suffering, strange, or guilty. The elimination of such "evil" makes it possible to live in peace. According to Girard, the main cause for such a process is mimesis or a mimetic mechanism. This process is related to the human desire to imitate. With this kind of desire, comes an envy that produces violence and hatred.

In the New Testament, we find four descriptions of Christ's passion. According to Rene Girard, these descriptions are part of a mimetic mechanism leading to the founding murder. On one side is the Jewish nation, a nation that is full of suffering under Roman occupation. On the other side there is the aggressive and corrupt Jewish leadership (priesthood), which would like to keep its power and its peaceful relations with the Romans at any price. On the third side, there are the Romans, who do not have sympathies from this nation. This world of tensions is the society in which Jesus of Nazareth lives. The Jewish people (apostles, women), representatives of the Romans and sometimes even the Jewish leadership (Nicodem), show respect and thankfulness to Jesus. But at a certain moment, when the danger of social conflict is high, the same people seek to resolve this tension through the selection of an innocent victim. The high priest, Caiaphas, was aware of such a possibility. He said, 'You know nothing at all. Nor do you understand that it is better for you that one man should die for the people, not that the whole nation should perish. He did not say this of his own accord, but being high priest that year he prophesied that Jesus would die for the nation, and not for the nation only, but also to gather into one the children of God who are scattered abroad.' (John 11.49–53)

The high priest is fully aware of the danger that is coming for the nation and for the Jewish leadership. He recognizes that only the murder of an innocent victim (the prophet from Nazareth) will save the nation from destruction and unite it into one body. This, as we have seen, is the main goal of the scapegoat mechanism.

Jesus Christ is aware of this decision of the Jewish leadership. After this decision, he did not go among the Jewish people, but rather he went with his disciples into the desert: 'Jesus therefore no longer walked openly among the Jews, but went from there to the region near the wilderness, to a town called Ephraim, and there he stayed with the disciples.' (John 11.54) The days near the feast of Easter were for Jesus of Nazareth the days of his mission. Before he entered into Jerusalem, he said, "O Jerusalem, Jerusalem, the city that kills the prophets and stones those who are sent to it! How often would I have gathered your children together as a hen gathers her brood under her wings, and you would not!" (Matthew 23:37) The magnificent reception organized by the citizens of Jerusalem for Jesus, in only a few hours changes into a collective condemnation of this innocent man. Even a substitute victim (Barabbas) offered by Pontius Pilate is not innocent enough and therefore is found unacceptable. Pilate's statement that the blood for this death should go on the heads of the people and his washing of hands reveals that Jesus Christ was innocent and unjustly condemned. Crucifixion, as the killing of an innocent victim, was the consummation of the scapegoat mechanism and one form of founding murder.

Rene Girard's theory of mimetic violence speaks about the view that the source of human violence is founded in human's desire for imitating the desire of fellow human being (Girard 1985, 61). The problem of this mimesis is in that, that such imitation could invoke violent reality at the one who is imitating and one who is imitated. On the inner personal and national level such rivalry could be soon changed into violence (Girard 1972, 65). The starting point for Girard's theory is "acquisitive mimesis". Girard proposes that much of human behavior is based on "mimesis", an all-encompassing expression of imitation, but focuses on acquisition and appropriation as the object of mimesis, contrary to most of the extant literature on imitative behavior (Jeremy Townsley 2003, 1). Girard describes a situation where two individuals desire the same object; as they both attempt to obtain this object; their behavior becomes conflictual, since there is only one object, but two people (Mathijs and Mosselmans 2000, 63). "Violence is generated by this process; or rather, violence is the process itself when two or more partners try to prevent one another from appropriating the object they all desire through physical or other means" (René Girard 1979, 9). This process could be recognized in every society where the exploitation and one form of colonization are present.

A look into the Slovenian recent history shows that the time before the Second World War was a time of many mimetic conflicts inside Slovenian society, especially in the so called catholic camp as well as in the relation towards liberal camp. Power as a common goal of all sides was invoking mimetic desires, which generated such a forms of unconscious tension, which came to be expressed in the time of the Second World War, when both sides armed themselves and performed violence in the logic "one against all others".

According to Rene Girard's theory of mimetic violence, tensions can develop so long until they do not threat the existence of a society or nation (Fleming 2004, 47). In the case that society is approaching that kind of situation, on the social level it starts with unconscious mechanism of searching a so called 'scapegoat' (Ushedo 1997, 131). It has to do with the unconscious searching of an innocent victim, which will by its death release tensions and return peace to society. According to Rene Girard, the best candidates in every mythical society for taking the role of innocent victim are children, old people, those with physical abnormalities, women, members of ethnic or racial minorities, the poor, and those whose natural endowments (beauty, intelligence, charm) or status (wealth, position) mark them as exceptional. In Slovenian historical context after Second World War, for the role of victim were selected those, which belonged to the most innocent, peaceful, and nonviolent group. These were the people, which (in majority) were Christian, probably deeply religious and in reality not capable of violent resistance.

With the extra juridical mass killings of between 12 and 19 thousand Slovenian citizens in months of May and June 1945, Slovenian society reached one form of social "peace". Two main protagonists found peace and relief – one in the power, the second one in the "status of victim" and in the so called "Slovenian apartheid system" of discrimination and stigmatization of Slovenian Catholics.

2. Was the committing of the "founding murder" a condition for the establishment of the Slovenian state?

Girard's theory of mimetic violence speaks also about the issue that every civilization begins with so called fundamental murder (Girard 1999). It has to do with the murder of the innocent human being or people, which society later divinizes and the perpetrators are demystified and put to justice. The stories like about Romulus and Rem, Cain and Abel, points toward the issue how the innocent victim reveals itself as a new divinity or as a positive character and a pounding point to establish new civilization. In the case of Abel's murder his brother Cain went to build cities that means new culture or civilization (Girard 1999, 114–115; Marr 1998, 590).

Something similar we could find in Slovenian resent history. For someone can be interesting, that Slovenians were almost 1000 years under the foreign, Hapsburgs power. Even more interesting is that we received our cultural and political independence only after we turned from the peaceful nation into the violent nation, which means into the nation well aware of its "founding murder". It seems that the blood of innocent victims' - on the spiritual and unconscious level - brought interior equality and energy, which was resisting to the external pressures and which established conditions for our national independence.

Slovenian society, from the Girard's point of view, has not come (yet) to the process of divinizing the innocent victims and to the demystification of perpetrators. It seems, that in the last 20 years we remained in some sort of 'status quo situation', where the ones who are in fact guilty, still enjoy immunity and the status of heroes and on the other side we still have innocent victims which are still demonized and stigmatized in our public space. The perpetrators basically remain heroes and victims still remain cursed.

3. The problem of Slovenian reconciliation from the Girarad's perspective

Rene Girard emphasizes that Christianity, with its gospels, is a religion which uncovers this mysterious and unconscious system of 'searching of a scapegoat' (Girard 1999, 163). That is why the murder of the innocent (for example Jesus Christ), the authors of the gospels didn't interpret from the point of the perpetrators, but from the position of justice and respect of human dignity. In such frame 'guilty and demonized victim' become divinized, and heroes revels themselves as murderers.

In Slovenia, reconciliation, in the light of Girard's theory, is very demanding. From this perspective for the reconciliation it is crucial to realize some fundamental postulates. Firstly it is important to reveal and establish the truth about historical facts into the collective memory of Slovenians. Secondly the identification of innocent victims and liberating them from the guilt (finding them innocent) is important task. The demystification and putting away symbols of the perpetrators and their totalitarian political system from the society is the third point. Finally, the non-government or religious organizations could create and establish different kinds of symbolic points in Slovenian society. These points would reveal the historical truth about violence, divinized the innocent victims and could "heal" national collective memory and collective subconscious. All these postulates will transform Slovenian mythical society into the society where violence will be unmasked and the reconciliation would be possible.

4. The Garden of peace or Slovenian version of Yad Vashem

In Slovenian historical context the Rene Girard`s perspective could become the source of different kinds of solutions, how to avoid the tensions on the field of the interpretation of Slovenian recent history. At the same time the Girard`s perspective could be the inspiration for creation of new type of symbols which could reunite and heal Slovenian society.

The excellent example of such inspiration could be the establishment of so called "Garden of peace" or Slovenian version of Israeli museum Yad Vashem. In 1953 the Israeli government has decided to build special memorial center for all the victims of the holocaust. This place became the place of memory and prayer for all Jewish people killed during the Second World War. It is interesting that the architects upgraded the idea of memory of innocent victims with the idea of celebrating the virtue of righteousness. They decided that in Yad Vashem should be place not only for victims but also for people of different nations which helped to Jewish refugees and saved their lives. With this purpose they established "The Garden of the Righteous Among the Nations" where all the names of righteous people are presented together with the planted tree for every righteous (wo)men. This is still an ongoing project that will continue for as long as there are valid requests, substantiated by testimonies or documentation. 449 individuals were recognized during 2010, and as of 2010, more than 23,700 individuals have been recognized as "Righteous Among the Nations". With the integration of this symbolic idea into memorial place, the architects transform the place of horrific memories into the place of the celebration of righteousness, courage, human dignity and love. And this is very important purpose not only from the point of history but also from the point of the healing of Israeli collective unconsciousness.

The experience of Israeli Yad Washem museum could help Slovenian society to establish for example a special memorial center called "The Garden of peace" which could be located somewhere between Brezje and Begunje villages in Gorenjska region. The construction of such memorial service would be the place of memory for all innocent victims irrespective of their political convictions. At the same time the Garden of peace could become place for every Slovenian or foreigner, which during the 2nd World War or after has showed human dignity, helped the persecuted, and has sacrificed his/her life for the others. Linden (Slovenian 'Lipa') planted with the name of every "just man" or "just woman" in the environment of all the innocent victims, could create such spiritual point, which will not make a division but help to restore national unity. With the establishment of such kind of memorial center, innocent victims will be physically changed into positive symbolic victims, which could reconnect society, and on practical and spiritual level establish such unity and peace, which will in long run, give basis for national forgiveness and reconciliation.

Conclusion

The theory of mimetic violence of Rene Girard could be one of many possible interpretations of Slovenian recent history and violence. The reconnection of the mimetic violence and the founding murder with the Slovenian history, mass killings, independence, and present initiatives for national reconciliation could be the starting point to overcome the historical divisions and to build the culture of dialogue, peace and unity. The divinization of innocent victims, the identification of justice and righteousness in Slovenian past are important preconditions for establishing symbolic places where the name of every innocent victim will be remembered and the righteousness as a virtue will be celebrated. Every civilized society should reveal the historical truth from the perspective of justice, overcome the frameworks of past violence and to embrace the truth and symbols which reunite, heal and finally give it hope and prosperity.

References

Fleming, C. 2004. *Rene Girard; Violence and Mimesis*. Cambridge: Polity Press.

Girard, R. 1972. *La violence et le sacré*. Paris: Grasset.

———.1979. Mimesis and Violence: Perspectives in Cultural Criticism. In: *Berkshire Review* 14, pp. 9–19.

———. 1985. *La route antique des hommes pervers*. Paris: Grasset.

———. 1999 The First Stone. In: *Renascence: Essays on Values in Literature*, Volume 52, Issue 1, 47, pp. 5–17.

———. 1999. *Je vois Satan tomber comme l'éclair*. Paris: Grasset.

Marr, A. 1998. Violence and the Kingdom of God: Introducing the anthropology of Rene Girard. In: *Anglican Theological Review* 80 (4), pp. 590–603.

Mathijs, E., and B. Mosselmans. 2000. Mimesis and the Representation of Reality: A Historical World View. In: *Foundations of Science* 5 (1), pp. 61–102.

Townsley, J. 2003. Rene Girard's Theory of Violence, Religion and the Scapegoat. www.jeramyt.org/papers/girard.html (10.10.2011).

Ushedo, B. O. 1997. Unloading guilt: The innocent victim as illustrated by James Baldwin and Rene Girard. In: *Journal of Religious Thought* 53/54 (2/1), pp. 131–149.

PHILOSOPHY AND ART

RECONCILIATION: A CONCEPTUAL ANALYSIS

Bojan Žalec, Ljubljana

1. Two aspects of reconciliation

We can consider reconciliation from two aspects: 1. regarding reparation and 2. as a way to handle conflicts.

2. Threefold system of justice[1]

We can better understand the reparative justice if we discern it from two other forms of justice: firstly, from the positive justice and secondly, from the retributive justice.

The positive justice consists of rights or entitlements and duties or obligations of persons that they have according to contracts, treaties or other historical acts.

The retributive justice has to do with the punishment for those who violate the positive justice. The reparative justice is usually understood as considered with restitution or compensation for such violations.

3. Punishment, reconciliation and inner motivation

Of course it is nothing wrong with punishment as such. However, our measure or guide by punishment shouldn't be revenge even if it brought some benefits to the victims. We should avoid any instrumentalization of any human person even if he/ she committed serious crimes. The suffering of other persons just for the sake of the relief of victims is not a morally acceptable compensation.

1 Cf. Thompson 2002, 38.

True reconciliation demands moral transformation. That means that it is rather internally and not merely externally motivated. If the need for reconciliation is not internalized then the conflict will not be permanently resolved. It may easily appear again if the circumstances change (cf. Assefa, The Meaning of Reconciliation). For inner or moral transformation auto-reflexion and a critical attitude toward oneself is needed.

4. Punishment, forgiveness, reconciliation and breaking off of violence[2]

Reconciliation of course doesn't mean that we merely forgive to a perpetrator. What is needed is rather a process and environment in which perpetrators accept the responsibility, confess, regret and remorse what they have done and become motivated to permanently improve the situation and the relationship instead of denying their guilt.

On the other hand even if the guilt is legally proved on the court this is not sufficient for reconciliation. This is especially true in the case of the group conflicts. A sole punishment will not hinder the perpetrators or their companions, followers or descendants from continuing to cultivate hatred or from wishing to revenge to those who have punished their models or (grand) fathers. Reconciliation has a much better chance to prevent a continuation of hatred and violence -which may transgress generations - as any other mechanism for handling conflicts. The effects of works and procedures of several truth and reconciliation commissions and also other experiences represent the evidence for this thesis. The mentioned commissions have been often successful in achieving that numerous perpetrators have publicly confessed their guilt. Yet they have not been so efficacious in respect of perpetrators` sincere regret and remorse or in their making active steps in direction of compensation and reparation of the relationship to their victims.

5. Foundations of reconciliation and healing[3]

Reconciliation is based on the following foundations:

1. A fair confession or estimation of perpetrators and victims of the harm or injury which has been done;

2 Cf. Assefa, The Meaning of Reconciliation.
3 Cf. Assefa, The Meaning of Reconciliation.

2. Sincere regret and remorse of the harm;
3. Preparedness to apologize;
4. Preparedness of the parties in conflict to get rid of anger and bitterness caused by the conflict and harm;
5. Commitment of the perpetrator to not repeat the crime;
6. A sincere effort of the perpetrator to repair - in possible measure - the wrong done or to compensate the harm.

Those six steps are surely positive factors of reconciliation. It is harder to say whether they are necessary and sufficient conditions of it. However I can't imagine a factual reconciliation to happen without presence of all of them.

Healing is a process of healing of deep emotional wounds (caused by the conflict) which follows the process of reconciliation.

6. The possible ways of reparation of relationship

What are the possible ways of reparation of relationship?

The first candidate is restoration. The problem with restoration is that it is often beyond human capacities to restore the wrong. For instance in a case of murder we can't undo the wrong. Restoration can provide the persons affected with the murder merely with money, property, psychological support, empathy, compassion etc. (Cf. Thompson 2002, 48)

The second candidate is reconciliation or reconciliatory reparation. Before we consider it let me notice that reconciliation is neither a necessary nor a sufficient condition of the restorative justice. It is not a necessary condition because a just restoration can take place even in case when no reconciliation has happened. For instance the perpetrator can do everything what is needed for restoration but the victim can be so adamant that no act will be sufficient for her reconciliation. Nor is restoration a sufficient condition. The sole fact that victims and perpetrators live in peace with each other (and that victims have even forgiven the perpetrator) doesn't mean that the restorative justice has been done. (Cf. Thompson, 49–50)

7. Reconciliation: a definition

Reconciliation is achieved when the harm done by injustice to positive relationship between individuals or groups is repaired or compensated in such a way that it no more hinders the establishing of a positive relationship.[4]

What can we observe regarding this definition of reconciliation?

Firstly: The sole (possibility of) reestablishment of a positive relationship - based on forgetting - without reparation of wrong is not reconciliation, not even a kind of reconciliation. It is not true that every (possibility of) reestablishment of a positive relationship is reconciliation. Only the (possibility of) reestablishment of positive relationship which is based on a reparation or adequate compensation of the harm done by injustice is reconciliation.

Secondly: Actual reestablishment of positive relationship is not a condition of reconciliation. It is enough that the conditions are fulfilled which make possible the actual reestablishment of relationship. Why is this last splitting of hairs important? One reason is that we can reconcile also with dead people. There are many positive relationships with dead people that can't be reestablished. However if we are reconciled with them the harm done by injustice is repaired or compensated in such a way that this positive relationships would be possible in the case that the dead people were alive.

8. Relativity of reconciliation and respect

Reconciliation is defined by the concept of a *positive relationship*. Our conception of a positive relationship obviously depends on morality we accept. It follows that our conception of reconciliation is relative to our moral view. To a degree that moral views vary also the conceptions of reconciliation vary.

Reconciliation is relative in another way. Reconciliation is a matter of reestablishing of certain positive relationships. So in a sense we can speak of different kinds of reconciliation depending on the kind of a positive relation in case: political reconciliation, erotic reconciliation, business reconciliation ... Yet the emotional attitude or relationship that is a necessary condition in all these possible

4 Cf. Thompson 2002, 50 for similar definition. However Thompson`s definition includes that harm is repaired or compensated *by perpetrators*. I don't think that the words in italics belong to the definition of reconciliation.

different kinds of reconciliation is some kind of personal emotion i.e. emotion that is directed to persons. There are basically two pairs of such emotions. The first pair is related to persons, the second to the Person i.e. God. The first pair consists of love and respect. The second pair - prayer and cult - is analogous to the personal feelings directed to humans. Prayer corresponds to love and cult corresponds to respect. (Cf. Veber 1930) So whatever positive relationship is reestablished in the case of reconciliation in every case some kind of personal emotion must be present. Without personal emotion we can't properly speak about any kind of reconciliation. In short: without some kind of personal emotion reconciliation is impossible.

Further we might say that reconciliation can be obtained only among persons and only among persons who mutually recognize each other as persons. This recognition must be mutual because reconciliation is possible only as a bilateral relationship. To the contrary, forgiveness is in principle a unilateral act: I can in principle forgive John (because of some act x) without any relevant action exercised by John.

Of course the following thought immediately crosses the mind: Reconciliation is relative in the third sense: we have different understanding of what a person is so we have different conceptions of reconciliation. In a certain sense I agree with this observation. Yet I think that no matter the differences among us regarding our concepts of a person, every one of us in his emotion of respect uses some concept of a person and hence distinguishes between persons and non-persons. And this is what is important for my point.

There is another argument for the thesis that personal attitude is necessary for reconciliation. The first premise of the argument is that we take ourselves as persons. Second premise: Process of reconciliation is essentially a dialogical process (cf. Juhant 2011, 13). Conclusion: Reconciliation is possible only when the mutual personal emotions among parties involved in reconciliation obtain. The implicit premise of the argument is that at least some basic equality of the participants in a dialogue is its necessary condition. If I don't treat somebody as a person I don't treat him as sufficiently equal to cultivate a dialogue among us.

9. Reconciliation and justice

Let me add also a short finding about the relation between reconciliation and justice: Reconciliatory approach consists of adopting restorative, compensational and (other) demands of justice (cf. Thompson 2002) including the future justice. So justice is an essential part of the process of reconciliation. On the other hand reconciliation is a positive factor, background or even a condition of (future) justice (cf. also Wildfeuer 2011).

10. Forgiveness and reconciliation

What is the relationship between those two concepts? Especially interesting is the question whether forgiveness is a necessary condition for reconciliation.

In order to answer those two questions we must take into account the characteristics of the concepts *reconciliation* and *forgiveness*: both concepts are transitional and both concepts are manifold, differentiate.

Both concepts are transitional, like the concept of tolerance. Strictly speaking we must always know - when we say that A is tolerant - what is the object of his/her tolerance. Similarly is true when we talk about reconciliation and forgiveness. When we say that A has forgiven B we must always know what was it that A has forgiven B, which his/her act or attitude was the object of forgiveness. Similarly it is true when we say that A and B reconciled. If we are precise and explicit we must say in regard of which relation have A and B reconciled or which relationship they established again.

Is it true that in all cases or kinds of reconciliation forgiveness is a necessary condition for reconciliation? I do not think so. We can refer to the fact that there is a repeated establishment of several relationships that does not demand any forgiveness. Motifs and causes for this repeated establishment may be different however we may speak about reconciliation although there is no forgiveness involved. Thus person A can reestablish erotic relationships with person B (A erotically reconciles with B) - because B immensely attracts A - although A did not forgive B that she/he has swindled her/him. This is maybe not a good example because one could object that A is addicted with B and hence she/he cannot act freely. However freedom is a necessary condition to talk about personal action. Reconcile can only persons and only as far as their actions are free. Reconciliation is founded on a free action of persons. We may answer that it is not necessary that A acts unfreely when she/he reestablishes erotic relationship with B. This could be in agreement with her reason and conscious and she may consider such a relationship as something rational and morally positive. However let us allege another clearer and less disputable example in favor of the thesis that forgiveness is not a necessary condition for reconciliation.

Thus we can allege an example of possible reconciliation between two states or collectives, social groups, nations etc. Two countries can reconcile after one country inflicted damage on another. The reconciliation can take place after the representatives of the country A (perpetrator) accept responsibility for some actions of their state and they make certain steps that satisfy the citizens of the country B (victim). No forgiveness takes place in this since the action has happened many years ago, the perpetrators are already dead and the citizens of B do not consider the ancestors of the perpetrators from A as guilty. But all this does not mean that the two countries did not reconcile because they (re)established a whole set of positive relationships. The unjust damage from the past is repaired or compensated in the way that it does not prevent any more a cultivation of positive relationships between two countries. Here another difference between the two concepts reveals. Forgiveness is conceptually connected with guilt. We can forgive only to someone who is guilty. Guilty can be only an individual, not a group or a collective. There is a collective responsibility, but not a collective guilt. Ancestors may be responsible for the crimes of their predecessors but they cannot be guilty of them. For this reason strictly speaking we cannot forgive collectives but only individuals. Yet we can reconcile (or not) with the predecessors of the perpetuators which cannot be blamed (and we do not blame them) for anything. That may depend on their attitude and actions. If those are right we may reconcile with them without any our forgiveness directed to them. In any case the essence is the following: we can forgive only to someone who is guilty (or, more precisely, whom we consider as guilty) but we can reconcile with someone with whom we have broken off the relationships (because she/he is in some connection with crimes) although we think that she/he is without any guilt (regarding those crimes). Those crimes can prevent a cultivation of positive relations between me and this person although I do not consider her/him as guilty. When the damage of the crime is repaired or compensated so that it does not prevent any more the establishment and cultivation of positive relations between me and this person, the reconciliation between us has taken the place although no my forgiveness directed to this person happened.

In the light of the above considerations the opinion that forgiveness is a necessary condition for any reconciliation turns out as dangerous because as a matter of fact it demands not only our acceptance of collective responsibility but also of collective guilt and hence of punishment of people for the crimes that they did not commit and above which they had no control or influence (for instance they were not born in the time when they happened).

If we consider reconciliation on the social level – reconciliation between social groups – we notice that in reality there is actually no side totally pure or faultless (nobody is without sin) but rather that also the victim side itself contributed to ramification of force that (at the end) (criminally) affected the victim side. In order to reconciliation happen it is needed also that the victim side comes to awareness of its negative contribution and that it shows or expresses that. In any case an expression of empathy with the side that committed crimes (even of compassion), of understanding of the situation of that side, understanding of the (historical) genesis, function, logic etc. of the relevant (historical) subjects (even criminal) is a positive factor of a transformation of the "criminal" side and at the same time also an indicator of the corresponding state or transformation of the victim side. For reconciliation (expressed) life in truth is needed: not only of the victim side but also of the "criminal" side. Only the truth will set us free (cf. Jn 8:32). We all have needs to be understood, for empathy and compassion, even criminals and members of their social group. The feeling of the absence of empathy, compassion and understanding is a negative factor of reconciliation. For that reason the statements like "I don't understand how they could commit such crimes ..." etc. are - in regard of reconciliation - counterproductive. Besides we should be aware of the fact that the part of the misfortune of violence and crimes lies in the possibility that it can in a sense corrupt also the victim itself. That is why reconciliation demands not only a transformation of the perpetrator but also of the victim. A totally satisfactory transformation is hard to achieve and often practically impossible. Consequentially reconciliation is often - at least to a certain degree - a utopian project and only a regulative idea.

Yet from the above it does not follow at all that the endeavor for the realization of reconciliation does not make sense. Actually it belongs to the essence of the Christian doctrine. Genuine Christianity is actually an effort for an adequate moral and spiritual transformation and for reconciliation (as in the relationship between man and man as in the relationship between God and man). Moral and spiritual transformation or conversion has an inestimable value, in any case higher than non-reflected, effortless or even ossified acceptance of Christianity. Let us only recollect the Biblical parable of the lost (or prodigal) son (cf. Lk 15: 11–32). That is why the reaching of reconciliation in the environments where ossified (or collectivistic) mentality and morality are dominant is very difficult, including environments with the "Christian" ossification or closed minds.

References

Assefa, H. The Meaning of Reconciliation. Available at http://www.gppac.net/documents/pbp/part1/2_reconc.htm (2. 11. 2011).

Juhant, J. 2011. Sprava kot projekt slovenskega postkomunističnega dialoga. In: J. Juhant, V. Strahovnik in B. Žalec, *Izvor odpuščanja in sprave: človek ali Bog? Spravni procesi in Slovenci.* Ljubljana: Teološka fakulteta, pp. 13–41.

Thompson, J. 2002. *Taking Responsibility for the Past: Reparation and Historical Justice*. Cambridge: Polity Press.

Veber, F. 1930. *Filozofija: načelni nauk o človeku in njegovem mestu v stvarstvu*. Ljubljana: Jugoslovanska knjigarna.

Wildfeuer, A. G. 2011. Justice and Reconciliation. In: S. Adwan & A. G. Wildfeuer (eds.), *Participation and reconciliation: preconditions of justice*, Opladen & Farmington Hills, MI: Barbara Budrich, pp. 119–132.

HISTORY AND (IN)JUSTICE. LEVINAS' ADVOCACY OF HUMAN SINGULARITY

Branko Klun, Ljubljana

If, according to Hegel, philosophy is "its own time apprehended in thoughts" (Hegel 1967, 13), then we could regard the philosophy of Levinas as an attempt to face the "incomprehensible" events of the last Century, in particular the Holocaust, which is for Levinas the "paradigm of gratuitous human suffering, where evil appears in all its horror" (Levinas 1991, 107). Levinas dedicated his second major work, *Otherwise than Being*, to "the memory of those who were closest among the six million assassinated by the National Socialists, and of the millions on millions of all confessions and all nations, victims of the same hatred of the other man, the same anti-Semitism" (Levinas 1998, v). The impossibility in "apprehending" the meaning of violence and suffering in history, however, does not attest to the defeat and renouncement of philosophical questioning, but rather intensifies the question about the signification of meaning (*la signification du sens*). Perhaps the traditional interpretation of meaning as a "conceptual apprehension" should be overcome by a new reflection on sense, where passivity – as in the very essence of suffering (Latin: *passio*) – may uncover its own way of signifying (meaning) beyond the active role of intellection.

Hegel, with his triumphalism of rationality and its inherent meaning, which embraces the totality of being and history, in many ways represents the antipode of Levinas' philosophy. In the face of the events of the 20th century, not only is there doubt in the rational progress of human history, as Hegel interprets it, born, but this doubt is now transferred to the moral capabilities of man, which is bound to his faculty of reason. Levinas begins his first major work, *Totality and Infinity*, with the astonishing question that "it is of highest importance to know whether we are not duped by morality". Does not the "permanent possibility of war", asks Levinas, render morality "derisory" (Levinas 1969, 21)? He is all too aware of the merciless realism of history and the injustice it often brings about, and for that reason morality cannot represent a false consolation for man, in the sense of a utopian eschatology, which either expects or is waiting for a happy ending to history. Levinas stands before the demanding task of defending morality and the meaning of man, which in a specific way goes beyond rationality and history. In contrast to Hegel's universality and totality of history, he speaks in favour of the individual, whose singularity and uniqueness is drawn from his moral calling. Levinas counters Hegel's judgement of history with the judgement of the Other, which calls me to responsibility for him. With that, he then opens up a new understanding of messianism which is not bound to the expectations of the end of history, but rather becomes a motive for ethical action, here and now.

1. The Judgement of History and the Singularity of the Will

Hegel's philosophy represents a grandiose attempt to include time and history within rationality itself. Traditional metaphysics, in the context of its Greek origins, considered true being (which corresponds to the true logos or the true rationality) to be immutable and non-temporal, since time represents change and mutation. In contrast, the biblical tradition is "historical" in an essential way, as history is the place where God reveals Himself, enabling us to consequentially regard history as God's (rational) plan of salvation. Hegel combined the two traditions in a unique way by enlarging the notion of rationality with the dialectics of becoming, introducing the notion of time into the very "happening" of rationality. God's plan of salvation is thus replaced by the rational course and the actualisation of the "logos" (dialectical logic) itself, and the belief in a transcendent eschatology becomes an immanent logical necessity of historical development. The biblical separation between the secular course of events and the history of salvation is cancelled out; it is "sublated" (*aufgehoben*), and for Hegel the history of the world is also the Last Judgement (adopting Schiller's epigram: "Die Weltgeschichte ist das Weltgericht"). The inherent rationality of history delivers judgement on every historical event and also on every individual. In fact, every particularity or individuality is only a moment of in the dialectical movement toward a concrete universality (or totality) which, in the dialectic meaning of sublation (*Aufhebung*) simultaneously leaves behind and preserves individuality.

From the Hegelian perspective, the "meaning of individuals (invisible outside of this totality) is derived from the totality. The unicity of each present is incessantly sacrificed to a future appealed to to bring forth its objective meaning" (Levinas 1969, 22). Levinas was inspired by Franz Rosenzweig who, in the opening sentences of his *Star of Redemption*, reflected on the absolute uniqueness of one's own death and its impossibility to be integrated into a superior universality (Rosenzweig 1988, 3–5). Here, in contrary to Hegel's view, history is not only unable to express the absolute singularity of an individual, but it can also never do him justice. Levinas distrusts the judgment of history and writes: "The verdict of history is pronounced by the survivor, who no longer speaks to the being he judges, and to whom the will appears and offers itself as a result and as a work"

(Levinas 1969, 240). In this sentence Levinas stresses two interrelated aspects of what could be called the objectification of the person who is judged. Firstly, the survivor speaks *about* the one he judges in the third person – he does not speak *to* him or her. There is no face-to-face relationship, in which the judged person could appeal the pronounced judgement, and there is no possibility for an apology either. Secondly, the person is judged according to his or her results and work, representing an objectification of the person's subjectivity. But, a judgement based solely on the works (or actions) of a person can never do justice to that person.

How can we save the meaning of a human individual from being absorbed into the anonymous totality of history? The only possible way of transcending history seems to be the advocacy of "an irreducible singularity, exterior to the totality into which he enters" (Levinas 1969, 242). Is not the human will – in contrast to reason and its universality – the expression of this irreducible individuality and singularity? The will stands for the freedom of a subject, which, in its interiority, appears to be intangible by exterior powers. Cannot this invisible interior freedom of the will be regarded as a transcendence of the visible world and history? Levinas does not believe that the will alone can be the foundation for this singularity of subjectivity, because of the essential ambiguity within the will itself, and in this point he agrees with Hegel, who demands objective institutions so that freedom (or the will) can be truly realised. In other words, the individual will, or freedom, cannot remain purely in the interior, but must objectify itself in the exterior world. It has to form these objective, rational institutions in order to come to its genuine realisation. But, it is precisely in subordinating himself to the objective order of universal rationality that man finds himself within a new totality, under the neutral judgement of "pure reason". For Levinas, "the virile judgement of 'pure reason' is cruel" (243), and he speaks of "a tyranny of the universal and the impersonal, an order that is inhuman though distinct from the brutish" (242). The impersonal universality of reason is unjust, and there is an "offence" to human singularity "inevitably produced in the very judgement issued from universal principles" (247).

But one could argue along with Kierkegaard that the genuine transcendence of the will and of human singularity lies precisely in its impossibility to be subjected to the universality of reason. Kierkegaard defends the single individual against Hegel's dialectics "as the single individual is higher than the universal" (Kierkegaard 1983, 56). However, Levinas fears that the mere advocacy of individuality may lead to the morally questionable self-affirmation of subjectivity. It is for that reason that he refuses "the egoist cry of the subjectivity, still concerned for happiness or salvation, as in Kierkegaard" (Levinas 1969, 305). According to Levinas, "[t]ruth cannot *be* in tyranny, as it cannot *be* in the subjective" (245), which means that the tyranny of universality (totality) cannot be overcome from the confines of one's own subjectivity. But where then can the singularity and meaning of a human being, which would be able to transcend the impersonal universality of reason and the totality of history, be found?

2. Ethical Singularity and the Judgement of the Other

In contrast to the verdict of history and the impersonal judgement of reason, Levinas introduces a new kind of judgement which he calls the "judgement of God". But, for Levinas "[t]he Dimension of the divine opens forth from the human face" (Levinas 1969, 78); the judgement of God is inseparably connected with another person, with the Other. God only comes to me through another person; He speaks to me through the face of my neighbour. The face is a specific phenomenon, which, beyond physical visibility, uncovers an unseen ethical dimension. It is precisely this ethical excess regarding the phenomenal appearance of the Other that ensures his transcendence. The Other does not allow himself to be integrated into the totality of the world and rational cognition. According to Levinas, the face is first and foremost an ethical expression, in the sense of an imperative and command; the face calls me and commands me. In contrast to its *physical* fragility and weakness the face reveals an *ethical* sovereignty and power which commands me in an unconditional way: thou shalt not commit murder. The ethical call of the Other demands an answer from me, it places me in the position of "the one who must respond", and this is a position I cannot avoid. Levinas' responsibility is first and foremost an expression of this passive state of "the one who must respond", a state in which the subject finds himself in front of the face of the Other. Responsibility is therefore not a rationally assumed accountability, which would be a consequence of my free choice. It is not a capability of a rational being to "give an account" (Greek: "logon didonai") of one's own behaviour, but rather it is a responsibility that comes before freedom. Since this is not about an actively assumed responsibility which would be limited, just as a subject is limited and finite, but concerns instead the passivity of the one who must answer, one who is called unceasingly and without limit, this "passive" responsibility of the subject is infinite. It is here, in this infinite vocation of responsibility, that Levinas sees the ethical transcendence of the otherwise ontologically finite subject.

I am under the judgement of God when I find myself in front of the face of the Other. The ethical response to this face can be both a command and a judgement over me. However, Levinas emphasises that this judgement is not "a verdict set forth impersonally and implacably out of universal principles" (Levinas 1969,

244). This is not a verdict of reason which, in its universal pretension, alienates my subjectivity; rather, the judgement of the Other confirms it. Even more so, the call (and the judgement) of the Other establishes my singularity, or my uniqueness (Levinas 1998, 56), in the first place. For Levinas, the uniqueness or "unicity" (*unicité*) of the self does not consist in the egoistic individuality of my being, or in the freedom of my will. Subjectivity lies in the ethical vocation, in the uniqueness of my responsibility for the Other. Beyond the order of ontology there is a transcendent order of ethics. In the same sense as a fellow human being ethically transcends the phenomenal appearance of his/her visible face, my ethical subjectivity surpasses my ontological identity. As an ontological subject with a will, I still belong to the totality of being and history, but through this ethical responsibility my subjectivity receives a new meaning beyond ontological and historical determinations. According to Levinas, "principium individuationis", which individuates human subjectivity, is that unique and irreplaceable responsibility which is prior to both my consciousness and the constitution of my self-understanding. But the "source" of my subjectivity lies beyond me – it is the Other who calls me and who assigns me with this unique responsibility.

For Levinas, subjectivity can be described in terms of the response which we see in the biblical tradition, when a person is called by God. "Here I am" (sometimes followed by "send me"), does not mean that the one who is called merely *gives* a response, but rather that in his entirety he *becomes* the response. His subjectivity becomes the actual happening of the response, which derives its identity from its vocation, to which his identity is called. "Here I am," is not an ontological statement confirming my own being, but a giving up of one's own being for the vocation to which one is called. Paradoxically, this "being-for-the-Other" represents an ethical singularity beyond ontological identity (or what Levinas also refers to as "uniqueness without identity" – Levinas 1998, 57). In a similar way to the biblical call of God, with the call of the Other I am charged with a unique ethical mission or responsibility for the Other. And, since the subject is in a state of passivity, and is called without any limit, he is subjected to an infinite responsibility. The more we become aware of our vocation and responsibility, the more obvious it is that we are not responsible enough. That is why Levinas writes, "the infinity of responsibility denotes not its actual immensity, but a responsibility increasing in the measure it is assumed" (Levinas 1969, 244). This infinite vocation gives a finite human being an infinite meaning.

This infinite responsibility for the Other goes beyond any norms of reason and requirements of the law. Justice is not associated with equality, reciprocity and reasonableness, but it requires exception, uniqueness, singularity, and infinite responsibility. Only infinite responsibility can do justice to the Other. Levinas writes: "I am therefore necessary for justice, as responsible beyond every limit fixed by an objective law. The I is a privilege and an election" (245). That is why justice, to which the judgement of the Other refers, demands more than a reasonable ordering of society, or the objective judgement of history. The traditional understanding of justice as a universal law, equality and reciprocity cannot protect the absolute singularity of human beings. However, this singularity does not consist in a narcissistic confirmation of the subject against universal structures, but in its ethical "exception" and uniqueness concerning his responsibility for others, for all of society, and for the whole of creation. "At this point", Levinas writes, "the real universality [...] can affirm itself. It consists in serving the universe. It is called messianism." (Levinas 1997, 95)

3. Ethics and Messianism

Overcoming history is not equated with the idea that a history of salvation exists beyond the history of the world, which would translate to meaning a realisation of God's plan of salvation. Levinas fears that in this case we would be dealing with a new totality, which would equally fail to recognise subjectivity and singularity (Levinas 1969, 246). We cannot overcome history with another, or a new history. So, Levinas simply states that he has "no philosophy of history" (Levinas 1989, 15), and especially emphasises that he does not have an "optimist philosophy for the end of history" (Levinas 1991, 133). However, despite this fact, it is possible to overcome this entrapment in history. "When man truly approaches the Other he is uprooted from history" (Levinas 1969, 52). The ethical call of the Other transcends history and judges it. For that reason, with Levinas we are dealing with a special kind of overcoming of history, one which does not search for a solution in the end of history, or in the last judgement, but demands instead that we uncover transcendence in history ourselves, here and now. According to him, it "is not the last judgement that is decisive, but the judgement of all the instants of time, when the living are judged" (Levinas 1969, 23). So, we should not wait for justice to be done by God in the future; it is we who are called to realise the justice of God in this very moment.

From this point of departure Levinas develops a special understanding of messianism, which is not equated with the belief that God will send a saviour who will stop history. Messianism begins to be realised in the moment when I recognise my universal responsibility, "my power to bear the suffering of all" (Levinas 1997, 90). The messiah cannot come if I myself do not take over his task. This paradox of transcendence in immanence permeates all of Levinas' philosophy and also affects the question of God. God only enters into the world through ethical actions, and if I do not bear witness to him in my infinite ethical calling, there is no God. Levinas intentionally exchanges the usual order: it is only in my responsibility that I become aware of the fact that I have been called by God; only in my obedience that I discover his command (Levinas 1998, 148). That is why Levinas believes that obedience and faithfulness to the Law are more important than the wait for the fulfilment of God's (messianic) promise. And what's more, perhaps it is only service without any thought given to the promise which deserves the promise at all, or which has already realised it (Levinas 1991, 184).

Such an understanding of messianism is closely tied to Levinas' conception of time. History represents time of the Same, a time of totality. It is synchrony, which, according to Levinas, is not real time at all. In order for real time to be established, what is necessary is an irruption on the part of the absolute otherness, or transcendence, which cannot be synchronised into the present-time of totality. That is why the ethical transcendence of the Other means the introduction of time as diachrony, in which the Other is not a part of my (present) time. For Levinas, the Other remains both, the absolute past and the absolute future. The absolute past of the Other, whom I cannot bring into the present by means of re-presentation, implies the absolute priority of his call which forms the foundation for my subjectivity (qua responsibility). On the other hand, the diachrony of the transcendent Other also opens the absolute future (Levinas 1991, 179), as the Other is the one who never enters into the presence (present time) and is always coming. In that way real time becomes time-in-relation-to-the-Other, a temporalization of my ethical subjectivity, mirroring the paradox of my being which becomes being-for-the-Other.

The temporalization of ethical subjectivity occurs as a passive endurance, as a time of patience and passivity, with the connotation of suffering ("passio"). Despite its passivity, this time nevertheless has a clear direction – namely "to the Other". Levinas also calls this ethical time "A-dieu" (181), "to-God" – since it is a paradoxical temporalization, where, in my responsibility for the Other, I take leave (adieu) of myself. Simultaneously, and in precisely that way, I make it possible for God to "occur". At that moment I am the messiah, God's witness. This kind of ethically understood time makes it possible for the messianic future to happen here and now. However, to be messiah does not mean bolstering one's ego, but an "eschatology without hope for self or liberation with regard to my time. [...] it is passage to the time of the Other" (Levinas 2003, 27).

Levinas' advocacy of human singularity, which began with an analysis of the ethical transcendence of the Other, finishes with the transcendent ethical vocation of my own subjectivity. If I do not bear witness to transcendence, if I do not subjugate myself to the judgement of God, history will remain unjust. If, however, my suffering for the Other testifies to the possibility of another signification, which goes beyond intellection and Reason (in the Hegelian sense), then I am permitted to believe that there also exists a meaning for the suffering and death of those innocents who are threatened by, or have already experienced, the unjust judgement of history.

References

Hegel, G. W. F. 1967. *Philosophy of Right*. Oxford: Oxford University Press.

Kierkegaard, S. 1983. *Fear and Trembling. Repetition*. Princeton: Princeton University Press

Levinas, E. 1969. *Totality and Infinity: An Essay on Exteriority*. Pittsburgh: Duquesne University.

Levinas, E. 1989. Entretien. In: Jean-Christophe Aeschlimann (ed.). *Repondre d'autrui: Emmanuel Levinas*. Neuchâtel: Éditions de la Baconnière.

Levinas, E. 1991. *Entre nous: Essais sur le penser-à-l'autre*. Paris: Bernard Grasset.

Levinas, E. 1997. *Difficult Freedom. Essays on Judaism*. Baltimore: The John Hopkins University Press.

Levinas, E. 1998. *Otherwise Than Being or Beyond Essence*. Pittsburgh: Duquesne University Press.

Levinas, E. 2003. *Humanism of the Other*. Urbana and Chicago: University of Illinois Press.

Rosenzweig, F. 1988. *Der Stern der Erlösung*. Frankfurt/M: Suhrkamp.

RECONCILIATION, AN ACT OF COURAGE AND INNER FREEDOM

Anton Jamnik, Ljubljana

The Bull of Indiction of the Great Jubilee of the Year 2000, *Incarnationis mysterium* (November 29, 1998), includes the purification of memory among the signs "which may help people to live the exceptional grace of the Jubilee with greater fervor." This purification aims at liberating personal and communal conscience from all forms of resentment and violence that are the legacy of past faults, through a renewed historical and theological evaluation of such events. This should lead - if done correctly - to a corresponding recognition of guilt and contribute to the path of reconciliation. Such a process can have a significant effect on the present... and is thus an act of courage and humility (Communio 2000, 5), as it is written in the introduction of the document 'Memory and Reconciliation: the Church and the Faults of the Past', published by a special International Theological Commission and proposed by its President, Joseph Cardinal Ratzinger.

In the above-mentioned bull, John Paul II adds: "As the successor of Peter, I ask that in this year of mercy the Church, strong in the holiness which she receives from her Lord, should kneel before God and implore forgiveness for the past and present sins of her sons and daughters." The purpose of this document is not to search for particular cases in history but to explain the assumptions which justify the regret of past faults. "Christians are invited to acknowledge, before God and before those offended by their actions, the faults which they have committed," (Communio 2000, 7–8) the Pope concludes, "Let them do so without seeking anything in return, but strengthened only by 'the love of God which has been poured into our hearts' (*Rom* 5:5)."

Beside stressing the importance of assuming responsibility for the past faults and thus recognition of guilt, the document exposes the readiness for forgiveness of all injustice sufferred by Christians. The Jubilee Year offers an opportunity for the purification of memory and thus reconciliation, which is a sign of a new start. Our purpose here is not the analysis of the document of the Theological Commission in detail, as its contents are rich and compact, and thus difficult to summarize. It is right to understand it as an encouragement and an excellent starting point to think about reconciliation in our place and time, and at various levels.

The Jubilee Year has opened the door of hope: the door of believing in salvation, in the power of reconciliation and forgiveness. This door was opened by

God, who 'loved us first', who was the first to offer his hand in reconciliation through Christ. He proclaimed Good News of Peace and reconciled the world with God the Father. He came to show us the way out from the vicious circle, or better: the devil's circle of an eye for an eye. Jesus did not eliminate justice, he completed it with the commandment of love, charity, and forgiveness, the corner stones of the new civilisation. Since then man has been able to cut the growing spiral of revenge.

Whoever claims that reconciliation is impossible has given up hope upon mankind. The point of the Jubilee Year was to stress the possibility of reconciliation, because first and foremost, reconciliation is the work of God, and only then it is the fruit of man's efforts. Forgiveness has roots in salvation: there is only one true and sincere forgiveness, God's forgiveness. It is essential for Christians to include God in reconciliation, to ponder upon Christ's death and resurrection. This does not mean, of course, that those who have different convictions cannot join the process of reconciliation. The dignity of each individual, his conscience, open to truth and effort to do right in life, are the most common anthropological (philosophical) starting points which are common to everyone who is genuinely ready for reconciliation. In Christianity, these starting points are based on the Revelation, and given new dimensions through the Gift of Faith.

Reconciliation means a new conversion and a new quality of being on both personal and communal level: 'The Slovenian nation will never rise and gain moral healing until it confronts all evil which has accumulated between us, until it wipes away the tears from the suffering faces and rights the wrongs we have inflicted upon each other. The nation's reconciliation is one of the most urgent tasks we are facing… it is the price for the future of Slovenia. Without reconciliation, we are a nation with no future'. (Rode 1995, 133)

This reflection has no intention to analyse any actual events. My intention is to offer some general starting points which should form the basis of any reconciliation, from the theological and philosophial point of view. We shall focus on the personal level, the inner cosmos of human mind and heart, 'the most secret *core and sanctuary* of a *man,* where he is *alone* with *God*', according to the Second Vatican Council, face to face with his Creator, as well as on the communal level, as this personal activity leads to a new quality of interpersonal relationships in striving for a nobler life.

1. What reconciliation is not

The word reconciliation is used in many different contexts, which is why it is often misunderstood and misinterpreted. This is particularly the case when reconciliation is applied to the social context, in order to right the wrongs suffered by a particular group of people. In this case the word reconciliation is often simplified, only partly close to its true meaning, and at the same time grossly misunderstood. So what, then, is not reconciliation? (Schreiter 1992, 18–27)

a) Reconciliation is not 'instant' peace of mind

The first and most common misunderstanding of reconciliation is the attempt of eliminating the violence that has been inflicted upon someone out of one's memory, or talking about reconciliation without recognising the facts. Not confronting or rather ignoring the facts is justified by the excuse that the past should be forgotten, that one should make a new start, without any traumatic memories. This sort of 'reconciliation' is favoured by those who have either inflicted violence and caused injustice or participated in it. They would like the victims to forget the violence, forget and forgive what has happened. Such reconciliation, a form of 'instant' peace of mind, reluctant to confront the facts and the truth, is far from the true purification of memory.

Thus the suffering of the victims is presented as unimportant, or even ignored; the victim who has suffered injustice is humiliated and the perpetrator is neither able to face the truth nor start a new life. The victims should not be asked to forget about or ignore their suffering, as this would imply that the violence inflicted upon them continues, and those who express such demands are indirectly saying that their suffering is not important, that the victims are irrelevant in the process of reconciliation. By devaluating and ignoring the memory, we devaluate and ignore human identity, and by devaluating and ignoring human identity, we humiliate and ignore human dignity. That is why reconciliation as 'instant' peace of mind is the exact opposite of true reconciliation. Forgetting about the suffering means forgetting about the victim, and thus the causes for the suffering remain hidden and unsolved.

Reconciliation as 'instant' peace of mind tries to avoid the analysis of the causes of suffering. If these causes are not defined then the suffering continues in a certain form; the vicious circle of violence continues and more and more people are hurt in the process. Reconciliation cannot be something that happens quickly and declaratively, it takes its time and contextual basis.

This sort of reconciliation, which ignores the facts and refuses to face the truth, exclaiming the need for overcoming the past and forgetting what has happened, is far from the proper reconciliation and true peace. Shutting one's eyes from the past, ignoring and supressing one's memory do not indicate the end of violence, they only prolong its destructive effects. Reconciliation is about reclaiming people's dignity, of those who have suffered injustice as well as those who have inflicted it, and have the courage and the power to confess the bad deed. It is a demanding and gradual process, which requires personal readiness and determination to regain one's basic quality of life.

b) Reconciliation should not be a negotiating process

True reconciliation is sometimes considered to be replaceable, as a sort of negotiating process the purpose of which is to eliminate the conflicting situation or at least to alleviate it. In this case, reconciliation is reduced to a particular process in which skilled negotiators try to mediate between the conflicting parties by evaluating their interests and trying to reach the most agreeable solution by means of negotiation. Thus reconciliation is reduced to the process of trading and negotiating, in which each party is trying to protect its interests.

Reconciliation as a negotiating process, based on interest, has very little to do with Christian views on reconciliation. Everything is reduced to a kind of trade which is very often far away from the truth and true values. The problem here is that reconciliation is only considered to be something human, leaving aside the aspect which is essential for the Christian understanding of reconciliation: the initiator of reconciliation is God, and man only tries to follow him with his endeavours and actions. The other problem is the fact that reconciliation in this case is reduced to the level of technical-pragmatic reasoning; reconciliation becomes a certain skill, a form of negotiation, unable to solve the initial conflict which calls for reconciliation.

We have only discussed two points of view so far of what reconciliation is not. Perhaps the following reflection will clarify certain aspects which are important in terms of reconciliation.

2. Reconciliation as an act of forgiveness

a) Forgiveness as a new quality of being and interpersonal relationships

The God of Christianity is the God of unlimited forgiveness. The God of Jesus Christ is first and foremost the God who through his own Son proclaimed to people forgiveness of their sins. His words and actions prove the firmness of this truth in the Bible. The gospels describe forgiveness as a break from a certain logic of human relations, which follow the principle of just payment. In his sermon on the mount, Jesus says: "You have heard that it was said, 'Eye for eye, and tooth for tooth.' But I tell you, do not resist an evil person. If anyone slaps you on the right cheek, turn to them the other cheek also. And if anyone wants to sue you and take your shirt, hand over your coat as well. If anyone forces you to go one mile, go with them two miles." (Mt 5: 38–41).

The above words may lead to believe that Jesus was naïve. But he is trying to tell us something completely different. He requires neither passivity nor renouncing the fight against evil and basic endeavours for truth and justice. He shows us that by returning evil with evil, even if in the name of justice, does not change human society. A new attitude is required, which does not search for measure in the past actions, but instead it searches for an action which creates something new and breaks the vicious circle of hatred. Otherwise we are closed into the logic of continuous repetition of one and the same thing. This logic is destructive in its core, and in the end it leads to exclusion or even death of at least one of the opponents.

This novelty, the break of the vicious circle, presents itself in forgiveness. Forgiveness does not mean forgetting about what has happened, it is a brave decision for a new kind of future, different from the past actions locked in our memory. Man is liberated by the act of forgiveness, and granted new strength to enter an adventure of encountering something new. Forgiveness opens the door to new hope and new future, and thus to new quality of being on personal as well as communal level. We can well imagine the future of the paralysed man, had Jesus not forgiven and healed him; or the future of the sinful woman and the Pharisees. As soon as the law of eternal repetition or retribution is interrupted, the future is unpredictable and open. This way a believer copies his Creator in the act of forgiveness. He develops a new relationship with the person he is forgiving. Forgiveness in its core changes interpersonal relationships and thus reveals the face of God. (Duquoc 1986, 104)

We can only hope that forgiveness will have a healing effect upon the perpetrator, but we can never be sure. Forgiveness without proper moral grounds is based on 'hope against hope'. The hope a person has for the perpetrator includes risk, either great or small.

Jože Krašovec writes in his book *Reward, Punishment and Forgiveness*: 'The perpetrator can either refuse or even abuse forgiveness, and such risk can turn into a threat. That is why risk is a part of consideration about the propriety or impropriety of forgiveness. We must not overlook the fact that basically every fogiveness or reconciliation presents a risk, even if the perpetrator recognizes and acknowledges the injustice he has inflicted upon an individual. There is always the danger that a person who has committed an evil act will do something similar again. The question of God's forgiveness without adequate basis with the perpetrator needs to be dealt with the fact that no person is just enough in God's presence, and that people keep insulting each other and God, despite our later regrets; which means that God keeps forgiving each and every person. God's mercy would therefore stop only in the case of complete impenitence. Until then, we believe that God is merciful despite man's unworthiness, as the sincerity of the repentance can often be doubted.' (Krašovec 1999, 841–842)

The reasons for forgiveness and mercy are much more significant if the perpetrator can prove with positive actions that he is worthy of indulgence. Forgiveness is about expecting the perpetrator to admit his guilt and distance himself from it. Once he does that he may be forgiven in accordance with three basic facts: self-respect, respect towards the perpetrator, and moral rules. This is an act of courage and sincere humility, when an individual faces his wrongdoing and starts a relationship or dialogue with the person who has been hurt by his injustice, and it is the beginning of mutual respect. Repentance is the most basic thing after an unjust deed. It is also the most natural demand and expectation of the people who have been hurt. True repentance means a sincere internal change. The perpetrator who faces his guilt, admits and repents it, refuses his unjust deed, wants to reconcile with the victim and start a new relationship. (Krašovec 1999, 843)

The suffering inflicted upon a man with an unjust deed has various effects upon him. Some people harden after the blow they have received and continue their unjust deeds. Others are softened by suffering, they recognize their own limitations, bond with other people, and wish to make a new start. (Krašovec 1999, 834) Admission of guilt is thus an act of courage, inner strength and sincere humility, and at the same time an expression of man's willingness to start a new, more authentic and harmonious life. One of the most important things here is facing the truth, which is enabled by starting a dialogue and by admission and mutual respect, despite the deeds that have been committed.

b) Forgiveness as an act of remembering

If we observe the history of humankind we can quickly establish that it was full of violence and injustice. Liberation theologies in Latin America have clearly shown, despite their many disadvantages, that the history of the world (including Slovenian history) was written from the point of view of the winners. Hence the tendency to write a new history, based on what is called 'the back side' or the other side of history, which is the history of the oppressed, and those whose names have been forgotten and hidden forever.

Jesus does not forgive by calling the perpetrator and his deeds irrelevant. Quite the opposite, he connects a murder with the deepest power of evil, Satan. John the Evangelist writes that 'the devil had already put it into the heart of Judas Iscariot, Simon's son, to betray him' (John 13:2) and that right after the first morsel given to him by Jesus 'Satan entered into him' (John 13:27). This clearly shows the whole tragedy of the event. 'Forgiveness does not mean trivialising and belittlement of the crime and the guilt. It proves that the perpetrator or the oppressor only has a future if he admits his guilt, changes his attitude towards the victim and thus acknowledges the victim's rights.' (Dolenc 1997, 11)

God's forgiveness is neither forgetting nor yielding of the weak. It penetrates into human relationships and transforms them. It neither creates any debts nor asks for favours in return. It is revealed through Him, who was the victim of a crime, and it stands for God's solidarity with all victims of the history. This solidarity does not mean God's encouragement for revolution and resistance, but it enables new relationships between people and thus renovates the world. God's forgiveness means proclaiming the Kingdom of God, which is nearing through conversion and through the change of government. (Duquoc 1986, 109–110)

We often hear that only he who forgets truly forgives. It happens, however, that in our strong desire to forget, the memory of an old insult or wound is kept alive. The lack of power to forget is accompanied by strong feelings of guilt: man feels guilty for not forgiving, for not being able to forgive. In Paris, a monument was erected for the French who had been deported to German concentration camps. The sign reads: 'We forgive, but we never forget!' This inscription might be considered rather shocking, but we must realise that the basic message of Jesus' words and deeds was mutual forgiveness, whereas he never asked us to forget. A true virtue of forgiveness is shown when man remembers things at the same time. If he were able to forget, there would be no need for him to forgive, as there would be no reason for forgiveness. Only because the evil inflicted upon him is still locked in his memory, is he able to forgive with all his heart. And that is the key point of forgivenes: it is absolutely not about forgetting, it is the liberation from inner anger, resentment and the desire for revenge, which is gnawing at every fibre of man's being. (Elizondo 1986, 127)

Forgiveness in this sense means reliving the past in one's memory, 'working through' it and making it a part of one's own history. By remembering a past injustice, man can radically change his position when he releases and liberates his negative emotions and thus dismisses them. Anger at the perpetrator of the injustice, which has been burdening his memory, suddenly vanishes, and man can accomplish inner freedom and start living a fuller life. This can be done because man no longer perceives the other person solely as a perpetrator, as someone who has inflicted violence and injustice upon him; he views him from other aspects as well. When I forgive, I distinguish between the person who has inflicted injustice upon me, and the injustice itself. I judge the other person by his value as a human being, who, as well as I, lives in an imperfect world, marked by various conflicts.

In the creative part of remembering I try to view the person who has inflicted injustice upon me with my spiritual eyes, and at the same time I try to go over that. I no longer see him as a perpetrator, I try to understand him at a deeper level, where he is human, as irreplaceable and precious as I, despite his human weakness and limitations. This sort of remembering, which is deeply permeated by forgiveness, enables me to perceive myself in a completely new way: not only as a victim or an insulted person, but as someone who is capable of rising above the injustice. Forgiveness is, in the end, the act of faith in the basic goodness and good of man. (Dolenc 1997, 12)

Therefore forgiveness is readiness to let past events remain in the past, not letting them take control over other people and myself. It is an act of receiving and uniforming: I accept a painful experience into my own history as a past event which no longer determines my future. When speaking of forgiveness, we always encounter a problem that injustice or insult is impossible to forgive and forget. From man's point of view it would be extremely difficult to find an answer to this difficult question. But forgiveness reaches much further than forgetting. It is levelled with grace. The experience of forgiveness provides man with a revelation that he is not the source of his own life; his life has been gifted to him. It is rather typical that the verb 'forgive' is close to 'give' in many languages. The experience of forgiveness is the experience of being given a life at the same time. (Peters 1986, 87)

3. Reconciliation as an act of man's greatness and dignity

On the one hand, man is a being of immense dignity and ontological goodness, but on the other hand he is a being of limitations and sin, which also have an extremely powerful effect on his life. If man is neither untouchable nor is he the greatest value in his individualism and personal dignity, the most natural response to insult and injustice is hatred, which tries to destroy the perpetrator. Moral hatred is inevitable, and it is not only directed at the insult or injustice alone, it is also, or even solely, directed at the perpetrator.

'Forgiveness and mercy are moral values in those views which acknowledge the transcendental source, transcendental core and transcendental purpose of man. The faith that man and universe derive from one and the highest Being provides the ontological-existential basis of equality and irreplaceable value of each person.' (Krašovec 1999, 837) This fact is one of the basic characteristics of the Judeo-Christian tradition. The peak of the Biblical revelation is the fact that the entire God's work is good, and man was created in God's own image. From the point of view of creation we can say that God's love towards man is unconditional. 'The evil caused by man cannot completely eliminate his basic dignity. This leads us to believe that we must always distinguish between the deed and the perpetrator, and despite our dislike for evil, we need to acknowledge the 'inner' dignity of the perpetrator. This principle is masterfully shown by St Augustine, who says that God loves and hates man at the same time. He hates human deeds, including sin, and he loves him, who is created in his own image.' (Krašovec 1999, 838)

God does not judge man, who is a relative being, by his absolute standards. When he judges man's unjustness and unfaithfulness, he considers man's basic imperfection as his general extenuating circumstances. When a man judges an unjust deed, a question arises as to what extent he will be able to judge the circumstances of a particular deed. It is of vital importance that he is conscious of his own imperfection. Man's right to hatred and vengeance is disabled by a truly existential starting point. The Book of Sirach provides a very convincing argument for forgiveness:

> 'Anger and a hot temper are horrible things,
> but sinners have both.
> The Lord is taking note of your sins,
> and if you take vengeance on someone,
> the Lord will take vengeance on you.
> But if you forgive someone who has wronged you,
> your sins will be forgiven when you pray.
> You cannot expect the Lord to pardon you
> while you are holding a grudge against someone else.
> You yourself are a sinner, and if you won't forgive another person,
> you have no right to pray that the Lord will forgive your sins.
> If you cannot get rid of your anger, you have no hope of forgiveness
> —you are only a human being. Think about it!
> Some day you will die, and your body will decay.
> So give up hate and live by the Lord's commands,

> the commands in the covenant of the Most High.
> Instead of getting upset over your neighbor's faults, overlook them.
> (Sir 27:30 – 28:7).

Imperfection on both sides, which is clearly grounded in the Bible, is the most evident proof in the eyes of Mr. Krašovec that moral hatred towards perpetrators is not justified. A person who would want to judge others under the assumption that he himself is just, assumes a position of an undisputed arbiter and thus places himself next to God. This sort of behaviour is strongly advised against by the silent voice of the suffering servant in the Book of Isaiah (Isaiah 52,13–53,12) or by the Apostle Paul: 'Do not take revenge, my dear friends, but leave room for God's wrath, for it is written: "It is mine to avenge; I will repay," says the Lord.' (Romans 12:19). Even more evident is Jesus' encounter with the teachers of the law and the pharisees, who challenge him with the role of the judge for the woman caught in adultery: 'Let any one of you who is without sin be the first to throw a stone at her.' (John 8:7). The readiness to forgive best corresponds with the basic human dignity and it can easily be considered a distinguished sign of man's greatness. (Krašovec 1999, 840)

4. Reconciliation as the internal liberation

A sense of justice and our desire for reconciliation naturally lead us towards force, which we would like to use in order to right the injustice, pay back and get satisfaction for the inflicted insult. A crime must be punished. Offended honour demands satisfaction, which is obtained if the perpetrator is forced down on his knees. It appears that only violent punishment can satisfy a violent crime. If I am insulted, my anger is not soothed before the perpetrator receives what I believe he has deserved. But the fact is that I cannot find peace even after the perpetrator has been punished. The memory of evil remains a constant source of anger and unrest. Bitterness and disappointment prevail. (Dolenc 1997, 13)

Experience shows that by persistence of hatred and by refusing forgiveness man is disfigured and can eventually become completely depersonified. Natural sense tells us that a man who continuously refuses forgiveness cannot be respected. At the same time, life teaches us a valuable lesson that forgiveness has a healing effect on both the perpetrator and the victim.

The greatest damage done by an insult can be limitation of my personal freedom, so that I can no longer be who I am. Very often this damage is much greater than the insult. Man's personality continues to be controlled by anger and resentment, which is like spiritual poison, permeating man's entire being and subconsciously determining his life. I am getting irritated, offensive, I helplessly yield to my inner impulses. When I hate the perpetrators who have inflicted evil upon me, I enable them with my hatred to be masters and controllers of my life. Their life becomes a dominant force which controls my entire life. A person who hates is his enemy's slave, he is dependent on him, and completely defined by his actions, decisions, creations, responses etc. The perpetrator is thus the commander of my life.

We need to live with past events. Who has the right to ask the Jews to forget about the holocaust? Will prisoners ever be able to forget concentration camps? Who has the right to ask us to forget about Kočevski Rog, or Teharje, or many other mass graves?

The deeper the wound or the insult, the more powerful the controlling influence of the consequences which takes away man's freedom, self-respect and inner peace. The real tragedy of sin and crime is in the transformation of the victim, who may not be able to let go of the hatred. The wounds inflicted upon one's heart, memory and soul are in themselves a kind of spiritual cancer, which eats away the victim's life and transforms him into a person he does not wish to be. The Apostle Paul writes about such a state when he says: 'I do not understand what I do. For what I want to do I do not do, but what I hate I do... What a wretched man I am! Who will rescue me from this body that is subject to death?' (Romans 7:15.24). (Dolenc 1997, 13)

If man was left all to himself he would probably destroy himself as well one day by paying an eye for an eye. Even after the perpetrator has been punished, we are cursed with remembering the evil deed, which evokes a number of negative emotions. Spiritual cancer does not heal in a wounded heart. So what happens with a person who has suffered great injustice and become a victim, does he have to spend the rest of his life in misery, in a way a slave to his perpetrator?

General, natural human request for vengeance and retribution makes God's loving mercy seem unnatural, even unjust and unreasonable. Considering all this, God's incarnation – in human standards – was the only way to protect humankind from self-destruction. The basic principle of his life was love. Jesus' love goes all the way to the end, and this, in its own way, means the healing of the humankind. Because of sin, Jesus died on the cross, but his love for man never died. Jesus did not conceal the presence of evil, as he was tempted himself, but he took away its power to rule and control the lives of people. Mercy and forgiveness are the only way to end the cancerous spreading of sin and violence. The vicious circle, ready to spread, is broken. A new start is made possible. (Elizondo 1986, 129–131)

When we talk about reconciliation as inner liberation in our relationships towards other people, it is vital to realise the importance of forgiveness or self-forgiveness. 'Many people cannot forgive others because they are unable to forgive themselves to have let, one way or another, the injustice being inflicted upon them. They keep pondering upon how the whole thing should not have happened at all. Self-directed anger is very common, people are certain that they should have prevented the injustice. Injustice means insult of a narcissistic image the victim projects upon himself.' (Dolenc 1997, 17–18)

For this reason, the forgiving self faces a task to accept its own self first, with all its limits and vulnerability. Forgiveness can help him achieve a more realistic self-image. It is a possibility to face the truth about himself and face his aggressive emotions, his often exaggerated expectations and his past. Forgiveness is the sort of love which tries to accept the other just the way he is. I try to approach my perpetrator with some sort of understanding and compassion, which derive from destructive impulses in my own consciousness. Mutual acceptance is based on the ability to accept oneself first, with all his inner hurt, responsibility, and readiness to face the reality of being. They both need to realise how seriously they have been estranged by the injustice.

If I am capable of receiving the undeserved love of another human being upon whom I have inflicted injustice, I am clearly aware of my own imperfection and limits, and my dependence on the love of the forgiving person. Mutual confession and acceptance can transform the inflicted injustice and make it a firm basis of the newly started relationship. Forgiveness is a very hard mental work, which requires an enormous amount of time and energy. It also contains hidden risks and thus requires a lot of courage.

5. Reconciliation as a call for conversion

Believing in Jesus means conversion from the way we consider natural and normal, towards his way, which is the way of forgiveness. As stated before, forgiveness is not a matter of forgetting or closing one's eyes to the injustice. On the one hand, forgetting can mean ignoring the unimaginable pain and suffering that people are able to inflict upon one another. On the other hand, remembering can help us grow and develop compassion. A wound or an insult, transformed by love, can turn into a source of mercy and a basis for reconciliation. One's decision to follow Jesus, a true conversion, is a beginning of a new way, and not running away from the truth or forced forgetting of facts.

When I forgive another person, I accept into my life God's generous offer of universal forgiveness. When man forgives, he is similar to God in a very special way, he experiences divine qualities in the act of forgiveness. To err is human and to forgive, divine, close to God. Observed with human eyes alone, the life of Jesus may seem absurd and unreasonable, even unjust, but it is the only way to break the destructive, vicious circle which transforms the victim into a new perpetrator. We shall only be able to truly forgive if we convert to Jesus and embark on his journey. Our forgiveness to another person is not a condition to earn God's mercy, it is more of an accompanying act.

Our God-given chance to convert is an excellent opportunity for us. Renowned psychiatrist, V. Frankl, once stressed in a television interview that a worthless favour is done to perpetrators, convicts and criminals by those psychiatrists who try to convince them that they are not responsible for their own actions, that they are ill, and not sinful or wicked. This deprives them from a possibility and logicality of conversion. They are forever locked in their crime and left there, instead of being pushed into taking the guilt. They are not being given a chance to act as free and responsible people, to convert from their crime and become new, different people. God's call to conversion reflects his trust in man, and not God's bitterness.

A true Christian does not behold his broken wings. Judas went away and hanged himself, and Peter went out and wept bitterly (ex. Matthew 27:5, Luke 22:62). There is an enormous difference between the two. The first one was damned by his sin, whereas the other one was blessed. There is a similar comparison between the hero of Greek tragedies, Oedipus the King, and Mary Magdalene from the Gospel. In the Greek tragedy, Oedipus the King plunges long gold pins into his own eyes in despair, and Mary Magdalene keeps her eyes in the Gospel. She needs them too much, so that she can cry and scoop the water out of them, which Simon the Pharisee did not pour on Jesus' feet. This is Christianity. Just man Simon considered himself to holy to get close to Jesus, whereas Mary Magdalene got close to Jesus through her sins, which helped her recognise the true God. A question comes up in the end whether I am ready to accept an apology in the form of forgiveness, or do I want to give it to myself, so that I can hold my head up high above everyone else, even God? It is a question whether my sinfulness opens me towards other people or closes me into self-sufficiency, arrogance or even despair, if there are no reasons for me to be happy with myself.

A Christian is aware of not having any moral right to judge others. He has no right to think himself better than Judas Iscariot, or Pontius Pilate, or your average Jerusalem dweller who shouted along with the crowd: 'Crucify him!' Whoever takes a close look into his heart, he has to admit that he considers nothing that is human alien to him, neither Judas' betrayal, the fear of the apostles, Peter's denial, gregariousness of Jerusalem dwellers, Pilate's cynicism and ambitiousness, nor the flattery of the Jewish magnates. I can personally take the blame for many hardships in this world, I am responsible for the injustice and violence, even though I do not directly participate in them. I am part of general human sinfulness, and I am responsible for it. K. Gibran made this perfectly clear in his 'Prophet': 'Oftentimes have I heard you speak of one who commits a wrong as though he were not one of you, but a stranger unto you and an intruder upon your world. But I say that even as the holy and the righteous cannot rise beyond the highest which is in each of you, so the wicked and the weak cannot fall lower than the lowest which is in you also. And as a single leaf turns not yellow but with the silent knowledge of the whole tree, so the wrongdoer cannot do wrong without the hidden will of you all. Like a procession you walk together towards your god-self… And when one of you falls down he falls for those behind him, a caution against the stumbling stone. Ay, and he falls for those ahead of him, who, though faster and surer of foot, yet removed not the stumbling stone… You cannot separate the just from the unjust and the good from the wicked; for they stand together before the face of the sun even as the black thread and the white are woven together. And when the black thread breaks, the weaver shall look into the whole cloth, and he shall examine the loom also. (Gibran, holybooks.com/the-prophet-by-khalil-gibran 23–25)

The entire humankind, different communities, each society, we are all cloths woven from more or less white and sometimes black threads, and we are thus responsible for each other in the very core of our beings, as well as for the crimes committed by some.

Final thoughts

Man's existence has always been burdened by experiencing guilt. We constantly face the task of forgiveness and asking to be forgiven. Forgiveness as a form of behaviour and as a proper deed belongs to the basic coordinates in one's personal structure. Therein lies the special mission of the Church and of various forms of civil society, as stressed by bl. John Paul II: 'The light and the power of the Gospel, from which the Church lives, have the ability to enlighten and support choices and deeds of a civil society, as if from swelling abundance, in full respect of their autonomy… On the treshold of the third millenium we may hope that the politicians and nations in charge, especially those who are involved in dramatic conflicts, fed by hatred and often memory of very old wounds, will let themselves be led by the spirit of forgiveness and reconciliation, as testified for by the Church, and they will try to resolve the differences with the help of sincere and open dialogue... A truth acknowledged is the source of reconciliation and peace, because, as stressed by the same Pope, 'the love of truth, sought by humility, is one of the great values, capable of re-uniting the people of today...' (Communio 2000, 53).

References

Aurelius Augustinus, 1975, Sermo XLII caput IV. V Minge: P.L. XXXVIII, 45.

Dolenc, B. 1997. Sprava kot krščanska obveza in možnost. In: *Na poti k resnici* (ed. J. Juhant). Ljubljana: Teološka fakulteta Univerze v Ljubljani.

Duquoc, C. 1986. Die Vergebung Gottes. In: *Concilium* 22. Ostfildern : M. Grünewald, pp. 55–67.

2. vatikanski cerkveni zbor. 1980. Cerkev v sedanjem svetu (CS) V: *Koncilski odloki*. Ljubljana: Nadškofijski ordinariat, pp. 570–667.

Elizondo, V. 1986. Ich vergebe, vergesse aber nicht. In: *Concilium* 22. Ostfildern : M. Grünewald, pp. 22–36.

Floristan, C.; Duquoc, C. 1986. Vergebung in einer unversohten Welt. In: *Concilium* 22. Ostfildern : M. Grünewald, pp. 15–23.

Gibran, K. 1981. *Prerok*. Ljubljana: Mladinska knjiga.

Janez Pavel II. Spomin in sprava: Cerkev in napake preteklosti. In: *Communio* 10. 2000. Ljubljana: Svet Mednarodne katoliške revije Communio pri Slovenski škofovski konferenci, pp. 33–42.

Janez Pavel II. 1998. *Incarnationis mysterium*. Vatikan: Libreria editrice Vaticana

Krašovec, J. 1999. *Nagrada, kazen in odpuščanje*. Ljubljana: Svetopisemska družba Slovenije.

Peters, J. 1986. Die Funktion der Vergebung in sozialen Beziehungen. In: *Concilium* 22. Ostfildern : M. Grünewald, pp. 5–22.

Rode, F. 1995. *Spomin, zavest, načrt Cerkve na Slovenskem*. Ljubljana.

Schreiter, R. J. 1992. *Reconciliation -Mission and Ministry in a Changing Social Order.* New York: Orbis Books-Boston Theological Institute.

FORGIVENESS AND RECONCILIATION: FROM JOSEPH OF EGYPT TO SHAKESPEARE'S PROSPERO AND PHILOSOPHICAL INTERPRETATIONS

Irena Avsenik Nabergoj, Ljubljana

Forgiveness, mercy and reconciliation are central in the Bible both of the Old and of the New Testament. The Bible is based on the belief that forgiveness is a sign of love, tantamount to love, or better the supreme, the most sublime sign and the most saving sign of divine and human love. The Bible of the Old and the New Testament is replete with moving narratives and statements about the greatness of divine and human forgiveness, mercy and reconciliation. (see Krašovec 1999). In the Old Testament, the most well-known and popular is the narrative of Joseph in Egypt (Gen 37–50); in the New Testament the parable of the prodigal son (Lk 15:11–32). In recent decades some philosophers discovered the centrality of forgiveness and reconciliation in the Bible and contributed good interpretations of this topic.

1. Forgiveness and Reconciliation in Shakespeare's *The Tempest*: Comparison between Joseph of Egypt and Prospero

Critical presentation of approaches to the topic of forgiveness and implications for understanding of conditions and reasons for granting forgiveness is an appropriate ground for presentation of some literary works dealing with this topic. In this limited framework, a presentation of the play *The Tempest*, the last play that William Shakespeare (1564–1616) wrote alone, presumably in 1610–1611, seems a most suitable example. The play is based on the story of Prospero, the rightful Duke of Milan, who came to a remote island, after his brother Antonio removed him with the help of King Alonso of Naples and put him to sea to die with his three-year-old daughter Miranda. Prospero and Miranda appear on a remote island and they have inhabited it twelve years. After a lapse of some time, Prospero recounted to Miranda the dreadful crime of his brother who abandoned them to the sea. On Miranda's question: "How came we ashore?" (1.2.159) Prospero professes: "By providence divine." (1.2.160).

It is the underlying call for justice that dictates that Prospero with the power of wizard conjure up a storm when his brother Antonio accompanied by his counsellor Gonzalo, the king of Naples Alonso, his son Ferdinand, and his brother Sebastian are sailing home from Africa to Italy. The tempest brings them to his same island. Alonso's son Ferdinand wanders around the island and meets Prospero and his daughter Miranda. At this point the play reaches the first happy climax. When Miranda sees Ferdinand, they fall in love.

After many dramatic events Prospero feels that the time of confronting with his enemies, especially with his brother Antonio, is near, and expresses his satisfaction to his loyal servant Ariel, who is airy spirit. He says:

> At this hour
> Lies at my mercy all mine enemies.
> Shortly shall all my labours end ...

Prospero reveals his view on both the nature of the three men's guilt and on his decision to forgive them under the condition that his dukedom be restored to him. In conversation with the airy spirit Ariel Prospero declares that he is prepared to forgive even the impenitent Antonio and Sebastian, in order to help them to regain their personal moral identity so that "they shall be themselves". He says:

> Go, release them, Ariel.
> My charms I'll break, their senses I'll restore,
> And they shall be themselves.

At this point, the ghost Ariel, under the direction of Prospero, brings Antonio and his friends to Prospero. When they stand before him "charmed", Prospero reveals his identity. He forgives them their guilt. Alonso in turn restores Prospero's dukedom, and Prospero promises to return all home safely to Italy. At this point, the main themes of the play become fully transparent: guilt, punishment, friendship, love, repentance, forgiveness and reconciliation based on restoration.

Commentators do not generally recognize that Prospero's destiny of being thrown into the sea and later "presenting" himself before the lords recalls the story of Joseph of Egypt (Gen 37–50), who was thrown into the cave and later presents himself before his guilty brothers in the position of his power in the Egyptian court (45:1–15). In fact, there are many similarities between the story of Joseph and of Prospero: both were stripped of their original position by "brother(s)"; both were guided by God's Providence through many vicissitudes; both organize a solemn moment when they present themselves to their "brothers" who are so "charmed" that they are not capable of recognizing them; and, most chiefly, both forgive their "brother(s)" when they are in the hands of Joseph/Prospero in order to restore their families.

Joseph believes that selling himself to the Ishmaelites had been an unwitting carrying-out of God's will. In Shakespeare's play, on the other hand, Prospero similarly as Joseph explains to Miranda what happened twelve years ago. When she asked the "How came we ashore?" he answered: "By providence divine" (1.2.158–159). In both stories, sinners are driven to confession of their guilt by the extreme distress. In such a situation Joseph's brothers confess: "Alas, we are paying the penalty for what we did to our brother; we saw his anguish when he pleaded with us, but we would not listen. That is why this anguish has come upon us" (42:21). Similarly, Alonso confesses his guilt once he finds himself, after the shipwreck on the remote island, totally helpless (3.3.95–102).

Prospero, however, treats the "traitors" Antonio and Sebastian more harshly. His brother Antonio does not manifest any sign of repentance. Nevertheless, he forgives his "rankest fault", as we read:

> For you, most wicked sir, whom to call brother
> Would even infect my mouth, I do forgive
> Thy rankest fault – all of them – and require
> My dukedom of thee, which perforce I now
> Thou must restore.

In the Introduction of the Shakespeare's play *The Tempest* David Lindley explains Prospero's difficulty to forgive his unrepentant brother Antonio by referring to the priestly words of the absolution in the Morning and Evening Prayer and comments: "But the forgiveness there offered to a congregation 'being penitent' is not in the priest's power to command or bestow, but only for God to afford. Prospero finally accepts that he, likewise, cannot set conditions on forgiveness, recognising instead that he is bound by another biblical imperative – to forgive a brother, not seven times, but seventy times seven (Mt 18:21–22). With gritted teeth and in grudging words Prospero acknowledges that his human 'virtue' is to be found in forgiveness which is unconditional" (Shakespeare 2007: 52).

The twenty-line Prologue brings the theme of forgiveness and reconciliation to a fitting conclusion. Happy because he has regained his dukedom "and pardoned the deceiver," Prospero affirms the fullness of restoration (lines 14–20):

> And my ending is despair,
> Unless I be relieved by prayer

Which pierces so, that it assaults
Mercy itself, and frees all faults.
As you from crimes would pardoned be,
Let your indulgence set me free.

The solitary life of on the remote isle transformed Prospero so far that he discovered weakness of power and the strength of generosity.

Prospero's will to forgive and his concern with restoration is reminiscent of the divine declaration in the context of the "utopian" promise of the "new covenant" from Jeremiah 31:34, quoted in the Epistle to the Hebrews (8:12): "I will be merciful toward their iniquities, and I will remember their sins no more." David Lindley is certainly right when he comments the role of "the language of religion" in the play *The Tempest*: "The language of religion, necessarily implicated in the representation of magic, cannot be neglected in any comprehensive account of the play. This is not, emphatically not, to claim that *The Tempest* is a religious allegory; but rather to observe that its engagement with religious paradigms of repentance and forgiveness, power and its limitations, animates yet another 'discursive field' that must be taken as seriously as all the other contexts we have so far discussed." (Shakespeare 2007: 53)

2. Contemporary Philosophical views on Forgiveness and Reconciliation

Jean Hampton is one of very rare modern philosophers capable to penetrate to the last resorts of biblical implications for the greatness of forgiveness, mercy and reconciliation. In the Introduction to the book she published in cooperation with Jeffrie G. Murphy she explains the point: "Jeffrie Murphy is a philosopher of law and I am a political philosopher. Hence, as his portion of this Introduction indicates, the discussions that follow are primarily informed by the theories and methodology of modern moral, political and legal philosophy. However, my interest in these topics also has a religious source, and this source provides another focus for the present book." She was faced with the contrast between the logics of mind and the heart: "Why, I wondered, do people accept with their heads, but not believe in their hearts, the Christian message of forgiveness?" This kind of disappointment leads her to the decision to find out whether she can "follow – or at least try to follow – the commandment to forgive them if, *but only if*, the commandment was right"; moreover, "to come to grips with the Christian teachings and texts from outside the tradition of theological reflections on these subjects." (Hampton 1988: 10–13)

Jean Hampton searches the answer to the issue of forgiveness on the ground of the question of human worth: "The forgiver does not wait for the wrongdoer to prove himself to be morally reborn in order to reassociate with him. Instead, the forgiver *trusts* that, although he has undergone no rebirth, he is still 'good enough' despite what he has done. Forgiveness is thus the decision to see a wrongdoer in a new, more favorable light." (Hampton 1988: 84)

Such a trust might seem psychologically an impossible attempt, but exactly this is the essence of the biblical belief in human being as the crown of Creation: "God created humankind in his image, in the image of God he created them." (Gen 1:27) This principle is behind such statements as those in the book of Ezekiel declaring that God did/will not act according human evils: "Then I thought I would pour out my wrath upon them and spend my anger against them in the midst of the land of Egypt. But I acted for the sake of my name." (Ezek 20:8–9; also vv. 13–14, 21–22, 44) The literal meaning of the phrase "for my name's sake" (see also 36:22; 1 Sam 12:22; 1 Kings 8:41; Jer 14:7, 21; Ps 106:8; etc.) implies the doctrine that God who is all-righteous and against whose righteousness men have sinned, yet acts toward them in mercy. In human terms, there is no explanation for this logic; we can only recognize that God is so. The reason God forbears and forgives is to be found in him, in his transcendent greatness and the universal purpose with his Creation. He is a God whose property it is to have mercy and to lead the world to completion. In spite of all abominations of Israel, God always finds a core of dignity in sinners and declares his faithfulness to them in order to save them.

The exclusively positive purpose of Creation offers proper foundation for understanding of punishment and forgiveness. Forgiveness is possible only when the offended party is able to see the wrongdoer in a favourable light in terms of the belief that human beings are "treasures beyond price." This implies change of heart in the offended person, i.e., warmer feelings and compassion towards the wrongdoer that open up the way to forgiveness and reconciliation. Once the offended party is capable to recognize an intrinsic worth in wrongdoer, she/he must be able also to understand the role of punishment in right sense. Punishment or retribution should not be reaction of hatred to wrongdoer but asserting moral truth about intrinsic value and equality of all human beings. When the essence of wrongdoing is a wrong claim to elevation over the victim, punishment must be in essence a declaration of infliction of a defeat that annuls the wrongdoer's incorrect claim to superiority, with the purpose to restore the equality of rank and value. (Hampton 1988: 11–161)

Nearly twenty years later Charles L. Griswold published his study *Forgiveness: A Philosophical Exploration*. How can an expressly philosophical account of the issue of forgiveness cope with literary presentations of love, forgiveness, mercy and reconciliation, characteristic of biblical poetry, narratives and parables and of literature in general? An in-depth analysis of extant texts and the common sense make it clear that purely rational philosophical arguments are not sufficient when it comes to most important points to observe. But in contrast to Jean Hampton, Griswold limits the scope by declaring in the Prologue: "In the present book I offer an analysis of forgiveness as a secular virtue (that is, as not dependent on any notion of the divine), although I will also make reference to theological discussion as appropriate, both by way of contrast and because the touchstone of modern philosophical discussion of the topic is to be found in Bishop Butler" (xv, cf. also p. xvii) Griswold explains that his proper meaning of forgiveness is limited to the secular understanding of "interpersonal forgiveness," but for the sake of clarity he distinguishes five other meanings related to the term of forgiveness: political apology, economic forgiveness, political pardon, judicial pardon, metaphysical forgiveness. For the term *metaphysical forgiveness* he has the explication.

Griswold's view that forgiveness is "governed by norms" precludes his admission that forgiveness could be in the final analysis unconditional. The assumption that forgiveness is governed by norms causes conceptual confusion especially when one tries to explain the relationship between personal versus non-personal and normative versus non-normative, and especially how forgiveness relates to love. Interpersonal relationships are based first of all on trust, therefore they cannot be reduced to norms. Forgiveness has to do with love, but true love is of true self, so it is clear that true forgiveness comes from the true self. Unconditional love means love without condition. By its nature it stretches beyond reciprocal love to love of everyone and everything. In relation to humans true love separates individuals from their behaviours and is capable to treat all people as equals and in their inner core worthy of redemption in spite of questionable things they commit. Experience of unconditional love has little to do with personal views, societies and religions that tend to become a system of norms. Martin Luther King Jr. declared in his Acceptance Speech on the occasion of the award of the Nobel Peace Prize in Oslo, December 10, 1964:

> Sooner or later all the people of the world will have to discover a way to live together in peace, and thereby transform this pending cosmic elegy into a creative psalm of brotherhood. If this is to be achieved, man must evolve for all human conflict a method which rejects revenge, aggression

> and retaliation. The foundation of such a method is love. /.../ I believe that unarmed truth and unconditional love will have the final word in reality. That is why right, temporarily defeated, is stronger than evil triumphant. /.../ I believe that what self-centered men have torn down men other-centered can build up. /.../ I still believe that We *Shall* overcome!

The recent monograph of David Konstan *Before Forgiveness* follows Griswold's interest to point to the development of "the modern concept of forgiveness" on interpersonal human level. He argues that the modern notion of interpersonal forgiveness is absent from the Greco-Roman world and not fully developed in the Bible, ancient Judaism, Patristic and mediaeval authors. Konstan argues that this modern notion developed in the framework of Kant's moral philosophy, namely of his notion of "a change of the self" in the process of repentance. The tendency of the book is pointing to "missing" notions and definitions of interpersonal forgiveness instead of understanding the reasons for lack of interest in such notions and definitions.

Conclusion

This paper indicates that the entire direction of such biblical texts, as the story of Joseph of Egypt, is shown in the future, that is, in the time of interpretation. The broad representation of similar motifs invites an uncovering of similarities and differences in terms of content and form. Here the question arises of the degree of the formative influence of the Bible on European and world literature. Any comparative study determines whether a text originally or in terms of sense adapts the Bible or literature, and it is especially interested in the effects of the narrative on readers who are faced with a similar crisis, albeit in another time and in other external circumstances.

References

Griswold, Ch. L. 2007. *Forgiveness: A Philosophical Exploration*. Cambridge: Cambridge University Press.

Hall, G. R. W. 1999. *The Tempest as Mystery Play: Uncovering Religious Sources of Shakespeare's Most Spiritual Work*. Jefferson, NC / London: McFarland & Company.

Hampton, J., and Murphy, J. G. 1988. *Forgiveness and Mercy*. Cambridge: Cambridge University Press.

Konstan, D. 2010. *Before Forgiveness: The Origin of a Moral Idea*. Cambridge: Cambridge University Press.

Krašovec, J. 1999. *Reward, Punishment and Forgiveness: The Thinking and Beliefs of Ancient Israel in the Light of Greek and Modern Views*. Supplements to Vetus Testamentum 78. Leiden / Boston / Köln: E. J. Bill.

Shakespeare, W. 2000. *The Tempest*. Edited by Christine Dymkowski. Cambridge: Cambridge University Press.

-----. 2007. *The Tempest*. Edited by David Lindley. The New Cambridge Shakespeare. Cambridge: Cambridge University Press.

-----. 2007. *The Tempest*. Edited by Rex Gibson. Cambridge School Shakespeare. Cambridge: Cambridge University Press.

-----. 2008. *The Tempest*. Edited by Stephen Orgel. Osford Wolrd's Classics. Oxford: Oxford University Press.

GUILT, SHAME AND RECONCILIATION WITHIN THE CONTEXT OF HUMANITY

Vojko Strahovnik, Ljubljana

"Now Zeus, fearing that our race might perish altogether, sent Hermes to bring shame (aidos) and justice (dike) to human beings in order that there might be principles of order in cities and unifying bonds of friendship."
(Plato, *Protagoras*, 322c; transl. Robert C. Bartlett (*Protagoras and Meno*, Cornell University Press, 2004))

1. Introduction

In this paper I want to address some of the key characteristics of guilt and shame as moral attitudes – especially regarding their interconnectedness with the concept of humanity – and to present their importance in the processes of reconciliation. I base my argument on the postulate of the ethics of humanity or personalism, which can be defined as a view that *"every person is a supreme value in itself"* (Žalec 2010: 29; cf. also Žalec 2011) and on the *"recognition and acceptance of a human being as a being that given his innermost foundation has dignity."* (Juhant 2009: 348) The greatest threat to such a stance is to use the other as a mere instrument in attaining some other end (Žalec 2010: 31–32; cf. also Žalec 2011) or even to not recognize the other as a (complete) human being and thus fully human. Such a horizon further implies that "*human dignity in its concern with status and stature has to do with the proper recognition of the identity of every human being and identity of the human species"* (Kateb 2011: 12–13) and although we often associate morality with suffering *"being made to suffer, bodily and materially, is not conceptually the same wrong as being treated as if one is not a human being."* (Kateb 2011: 13) This will prove crucial for the proposed understanding of reconciliation. Within such a personalistic perspective good and evil are not only the extreme limits of our moral approval or criticism, but distinctively fundamental moral concepts (Gaita 2002: xix), which together with the concept of humanity are basic for attaining a full understanding of morality, including the concepts of guilt, shame, and reconciliation.

2. Shame and Guilt as Moral Emotions and Moral Attitudes

Both guilt and shame are essentially related to our moral lives and play an important part in it. They can be characterized as moral emotions or moral attitudes that arise in relation to our past or present actions. In what follows I centre my attention to the felling of shame and the feeling of guilt (as opposed to some objective state, e.g. that somebody committed a wrongful act and is therefore guilty of it). Both can be understood at the individual level as well as on the level of groups.

Shame is closely related to our sense of excessive exposure, of not being covered and being powerless in relation to other(s) and further to the sense of the loss of status. (Williams 1993: 220) Moral shame can be understood as such uncoveredness, a sense of weakness and powerlessness that we feel when we are truly aware of our moral wrongdoing(disclosed either by others or by ourselves), weakness or defects of our characters. Williams has pointed out that within the horizon of modernity (highly marked with a notion of guilt) we often feel that there is no real place in morality for the notion of shame, and further, that from our modern perspective ancient Greek ethics and culture could be legitimately described as being marked with *"culture of shame"* (Williams 1993: 94–95). Furthermore, some view this development as a sign of moral progress and label the Greek culture of shame as underdeveloped and more primitive. (cf. Haggerty 2009: 307) The origins of such a conviction lay in the modern picture of a moral agent or a moral subject – formed e.g. in the name of the Kantian idea of autonomy – that is not determined by character, since reasons or revelation enables her or him to know the moral law that binds all moral agents and which she or he must obey or follow in action. A proper response to the breach of this moral law is first and foremost a feeling of guilt that one has done something contrary to it than that of shame. Shame usually presupposes *"the other"* that watches us from the outside and *"before whom we feel ashamed"*, but such a figure would imply the heteronomy of a moral standard that is excluded from the described autonomous nature of modern moral agency and morality.

Guilt or the feeling of guilt is our response to the realization that our action was morally wrong and that we are responsible for the consequences of this action. Guilt arises when we violate certain moral norms or inflict pain or damage to the other. Typical reactive responses to guilt (or the ways of overcoming it) include confession, correction of the wrongs done, apology, acceptance of punishment and alike. Guilt could be understood as a painful response to the moral wrongness of my action and its consequences. (Gaita 2002: 34) It seems that guilt (as opposed to shame) is closely connected with the possibility of deciding and acting differently and that therefore presupposes that we could have done otherwise.

Guilt and shame should not be considered as a two completely separated or mutually exclusive moral phenomena. We cannot draw a clear boundary between the two. In the space between them there is a gray area that could be characterized as a kind of a feeling of moral weight or burden. In addition to that an individual can feel both guilt and shame in relation to the same action, so both as moral stances do not preclude each other, neither as actual feelings nor given their adequacy.

Within the ethical debate on guilt and shame both moral emotions are nonetheless characterized by some important differences between them. The basis of most of the discussed differences is a recognition that guilt usually focuses on the moral wrongness of our acts (guilt is *act-centred*), while shame is closely related with vices and moral deficiencies of our character or ourselves (shame is *agent-centred*). Guilt is thus associated with wrongness of our action, while shame points to us as agents, to our person(ality); i.e. we are of feel ashamed of ourselves and not (only) of our actions or their consequences. (Haggerty 2009: 304; Doris 2002: 155.) Williams (1993: 89) argues that shame as opposed to guilt affects our whole personality; it implies a certain feeling that we need to protect and shelter ourselves in which our whole personality is revealed to ourselves as diminished, weakened, lessened or damaged; we feel, or better, wish not just to hide our face or ourselves but that we weren't here at all, we wish to sink through the floor. Guilt, on the other hand, is tied to a concrete and particular action that was morally wrong. In a sense we know that the guilt would follow us and we cannot escape it, because the wrongness of that action cannot be changed or corrected. Shame is primarily connected with vision, with a look or an image, while guilt is related to (inner) voice and listening. With guilt we therefore speak about the voice of conscience inside us or a voice of judgment above us, while with shame we speak about our image (as seen by others), we cannot bear to look others in the eyes, we find even our own perception of ourselves burdensome. This is most radically demonstrated by Oedipus that blinds himself and says that *"every look is painful for him"*, that he is *"dirty"* and *"unpleasant and disagreeable even to the goods"* and urges others: "*O, I adjure you, hide me anywhere, far from this land, or slay me straight, or cast me, down to the depths of ocean out of sight.*" (Sophocles, *Oedipus Rex*) Guilt is most often associated with a breach of a given command or prohibition, while shame concerns some ideal and us not achieving it. Shame in a sense presupposes the other, the observer, while guilt presupposes only our recognition that we have violated a certain moral command.

Further differences between guilt and shame are revealed when we look to other reactive attitudes that usually accompany them. Guilt emerges with our wrongful act to which others may respond to with anger, resentment, indignation and demand from us a compensation or an apology. A thing that arouses shame in us is usually accompanied with contempt, ridicule or avoidance by others. Guilt is directed to the other, it concerns the damage we have caused, and requires its correction and apology, reparation or retribution for it. Shame on the other hand focuses on ourselves; it calls for confrontation with ourselves, for improvement and for moral progress that must be achieved. Most of the mentioned differences between the two attitudes are also supported by empirical research (cf. Karlsson and Sjöberg 2009).

Shame is essentially *restitutive* (it requires a change in ourselves, to restore the ideal), while guilt is *retributive* (it requires punishment, retribution or apology). In this sense, forgiveness of a victim or a person who has been harmed by my action is closer to guilt than to shame, because forgiveness can relieve me of my guilt of my inner voice, but not necessarily restore my desired ideal, image or moral character. I myself must do this. (Williams 1993: 91) A still further difference is that although both guilt and shame in some way presuppose the other, this other occupies quite different roles. In the case of guilt the other is in the role of the victim or an executor as an independent authority, which represents the need for compensation or a threat of punishment. With shame, this other occupies a role of a spectator or a witness. *"The watcher or witness before whom we feel shame is not necessarily critical and punitive. Instead, the other may represent potentially affirming attitudes such as acceptance, admiration, respect, love and resolve, as well as more painful ones such as disappointment, rejection, avoidance, or contempt. Moreover, the watcher or witness is not experienced as an impersonal judge, an enforcer or a victim. The approval or disapproval of the watcher or witness is felt by the self directly. With shame, we experience this appraisal personally, as an evaluation of our character. Thus, when we feel shame we do not fear punishment at the hands of an impersonal other, but instead loss of love, honor, and respect in the eyes of our community. The threat is not punishment, but abandonment."* (Haggerty 2009: 306)

3. A Common Humanity as a Standard for Moral Shame

Shame is not linked only with the external expectations of the society and with our fear of being exposed and disclosed before the other; although it in a sense presupposes the other (we can remember Sartre's description from *Being and Nothing-*

ness of a man peeping through the keyhole and suddenly realizing that he himself is being observed and thus the subject of others' view) we may interpret that the other is not necessarily real or concrete, but it can also be an imaginary other. It can represent an ideal or a standard. Such other might be internalized, abstract, generalized and idealized, that is composed of my ethical concerns. I propose the following general understanding of shame. Shame is based on the standard of humanity, which is positioned within ourselves as a standard (Williams 1993) and this criterion should not be seen only pertaining to the damage suffered by the victims, but more deeply, as a violation of humanity, as an overlooking of humanity in the other. (Gaita 2002: xiv, 4, 43–50.) Shame also establishes a relationship between us and the other(s). (cf. Rawls 1999: 392–434)

Moral shame can thus be understood as a response to the violation of this internalized standard of humanity, against which other(s) must be recognized as a valuable human being(s) just like us that possesses a fully equivalent status. Within the context of ethics based on human dignity and humanity, it is particularly important that also in our moral attitudes such as guilt, shame and regret, the other is not overlooked as being fully human, as a victim in all her individuality. (Gaita 2002: 31–32)

If we overlook victims' humanity and reduce their human status, then those victims in this case are deprived of any meaningful depth, and thus we hinder their defence, for example, by reference to the injustice of such treatment. With the breach of this standard we have not only caused damage to others, but we have violated humanity in them and in ourselves, since we failed to achieve it as our own ideal. When such a violation against humanity arises, an adequate response to it cannot simply be guilt or regret, but it must be accompanied also by shame. Such felling of shame should not be seen merely as something negative, but as an opportunity to help us overcome defects and shortcomings of our character, which we feel ashamed of (this is a sense of restitution of humanity in ourselves and in others); shame in this case should not follow the logic of stigmatization but of reintegration.

4. Guilt, Shame and Reconciliation

Guilt, shame and regret can also be understood at the level of groups or communities, not only in the context where we are talking about a certain type of complicity and collective guilt. National and other social groups have their own histories, which to a large extent determine the present emotional experiences of members of these groups, including for example, that of pride, guilt, shame or a desire to correct things from the past. These emotional responses are not necessarily related to our taking part in events or practices of the past, but are established on the basis of group membership or social identity emerging out of the evolving dynamics of relations within and between groups and communities. Collective guilt can be seen as a response of the members of the community to the immoral acts that affected a selected group, when those actions become prominent and our community identity is strong enough. Guilt could thus lead to reparation and apology for the acts and events in the past. The above-mentioned understanding of shame as a restitutive/restorative moral stance on the other hand enables us not only to remedy the injustices done to victims, but also eliminate the attitude towards them, which is at the basis of acts committed. Shame can therefore be felt in the context of the community either as perpetrators, as persons associated with the perpetrators or as mere observers of fact that the ideal or standard of humanity has been respected and still is not satisfied (e.g. by the state, which waives certain actions) and is in this sense appropriate.

A significant difference between aspects of guilt and shame is that guilt directs us to the victims, to those who have been harmed or suffered injustice or wrongs, and requires reparation. In a much lesser extend does guilt help us understand our relationship to the actions and to the victims. This is an area of shame that could disclose these relationships and establish or re-build our personality or our moral identity, both at individual level and at the level of community. *"Shame can motivate us to try to reconnect, to work for forgiveness and reconciliation."* (Haggerty 2009: 304)

In some cases an attitude of (restorative) cultivation of shame rather than retributive guilt and retaliation is more productive for reconciliation. Within the horizon of the debate on reconciliation is also important that it is often shaped by (too) weak or (too) thin concept of responsibility, which overemphasises the dimensions of guilt and underemphasises shame. (Haggerty 2009: 304–305) A similar deficiency of focusing only on the exposed guilt is also discussed by Williams, who calls for a renewed reflection on the meaning of shame. Guilt *"can direct one towards those who have been wronged or damaged, and demand reparation in the name, simply, of what has happened to them. But it cannot by itself help one to understand one's relations to those happenings, or to rebuild the self that has done these things and the world in which that self has to live. Only shame can do that, because it embodies conceptions of what one is and how one is related to others."* (Williams 1993: 94)

Shame enables us to look beyond the inflicted damages and directs our attention to the standard of humanity. *"When our shame is a lucid expression of collective national responsibility for the wrongs done by our ancestors, we have risen in truthful response to the evil in our history – of the fact that it is our history. Because it is an acknowledgement of the fact that we must rise in truthful moral responsiveness to the meaning of what we have been caught up in, often through no fault of our own, it is rightly called an acceptance of responsibility."* (Gaita 2002: 102) This also requires the following: *"When people's souls have been lacerated by the wrongs done to them, individually or collectively, openness to their voices requires humbled attentiveness. When one's nation has committed those wrongs, shame is the form that humbled attentiveness takes. Without it, there can be no justice."* (Gaita 2002: 102)

Shame also allows us to establish a basis in a community to avoid such practices of political, judicial or other state institutions in the future that could encourage or set an example to members of the community to foster such indifference towards suffering of those who are victimized, excluded or marginalized. On the contrary, we should promote the full recognition of the humanity of others and our responsiveness to them as our equals. Without such a full attention to the victims there cannot be real justice. In this sense we can conclude that justice so understood is a basis for the establishment of peace and reconciliation between different groups, because only in this way they are regarded on the same level having the same status. A genuine correction of injustices is possible within such horizon.

5. Conclusion

In the paper I discussed the role of shame as a moral response to acts or practices from the past. I defended the understanding of moral shame as an emotional response or attitude, the appropriateness of which is based on the standard of humanity, which is harboured within us as a moral standard. This standard of humanity should be understood not only at the level of damage caused to others or at the level of suffering, but deeper, as a violation of humanity in the other. Only such recognition of humanity in the other(s) makes resolution and reconciliation possible. The formation and proper understanding of the moral emotions and attitudes (especially shame) are an important part of national reconciliation, which must necessarily be accompanied with sanctions and reparations for wrongs committed. In this process our commitment to the truth plays an important part, since *"[l]ies can destroy the integrity of the national life only because we value truthfulness in ways not reducible to the practical benefits it may bring. People find it terrible to live a national lie just as they do to live a lie in their personal lives. In neither case is truthfulness merely a means to something whose value we could understand without appreciating the need we have of truth, for its own sake, as we sometimes say.*" (Gaita 2002: 188–189) Otherwise we could easily be subverted into a *"shameless society"* on the outside, but full of traumas and pains on the inside that could lie at the heart of many negative phenomena in the community.[1]

References

Doris, J. 2002. *Lack of Character – Personality and Moral Behaviour*, Cambridge: Cambridge University Press.

Gaita, R. 2002. *A Common Humanity. Thinking about Love and Truth and Justice,* London and New York: Routledge.

Haggerty, D. 2009. White Shame: Responsibility and Moral Emotions. In: *Philosophy Today* 53 (3), pp. 304–316.

Juhant, J. 2009. *Etika I. Na poti k vzajemni človeškosti*, Ljubljana: Študentska založba.

Karlsson, G. in Sjöberg, L. G. 2009. The Experience of Guilt and Shame: A Phenomenological–Psychological Study. In: *Human Studies*, 32 (3), pp. 335–355.

Kateb, G. 2011. *Human Dignity,* Cambridge, MA/London: The Belknap Press of Harvard University Press.

Rawls, J. 1999. *A Theory of Justice (Revised Edition)*, Cambridge, MA.: Belknap Press.

Strahovnik, V. 2009. *Moralne sodbe, intuicija in moralna načela,* Velenje: IPAK.

Strahovnik, V. 2011a. Občutje krivde in sramu v kontekstu sprave. In: J. Juhant, V. Strahovnik and B. Žalec (eds.), *Izvor odpuščanja in sprave: človek ali Bog?*, Ljubljana: Teološka fakulteta, pp. 111–126.

Strahovnik, V. 2011b. Identity, Character and Ethics: Moral Identity and Reasons for Action. In: *Synthesis Philosophica*, 26: 1, pp. 67–77.

Williams, B. 1993. *Shame and Necessity*. Berkeley: University of California Press.

1 This paper was prepared as a part of the research project *Dialogue in the Global Multicultural Society* (J6—4139), financed by the Slovenian Research Agency (ARRS). I would like to thank to Janez Juhant, Bojan Žalec, Erika Prijatelj, Drago Ocvirk, Matjaž Potrč, Jernej Letnar Černič, Günter Prueller Jagenteufel, Bela Mester and Robert Petkovšek for a valuable discussion on its topics.

Žalec, B. 2010. *Človek, morala in umetnost. Uvod v filozofsko antropologijo in etiko,* Ljubljana: Teološka fakulteta.

Žalec, B. 2011. Personalism, truth and human rights. In: J. Juhant & B. Žalec (eds.), *Humanity after Selfish Prometheus: Chances of Dialogue and Ethics in a Technicized World*, Berlin: Lit, pp. 29–41.

CAN THE MEDIA AFFORD RECONCILIATION? RECONCILIATION AS A PRINCIPLE OF A MINIMALISTIC ETHICS

Claudia Paganini

1. Media Ethics in Today´s Scientific Debate

The intellectual's basic constitution as being critical of the media is as old as are the print media themselves. Media ethics, however, has been practised for a long time – and along with the increase of the technical possibilities and the rapid development of the media landscape, generally in simple response to individual cases or, most frequently, to scandals. As opposed to this approach, today's debate about media ethics is characterised by a very conscious endeavour to place the ethics of specific areas on the solid ground of theoretical reflection. Whoever practises media ethics today no longer needs to insist continuously on the fact that media praxis cannot do without basic (and regulative) codes of conduct; he finds himself surrounded and supported by a highly committed academic community and can lean on a number of informed networks favouring journalistic self control, news criticism, etc.

The strong presence of journalistic contributions in the field of media ethics as well as its interdisciplinary orientation have lead to a situation in which questions and answers are being presented from diverging perspectives, with diverse methodologies and, at times, not on homogeneous levels of discussion. Existing reflections on the challenges media ethics has to cope with, on its limitations, and on the ways in which these limitations can be overcome frequently diverge from each other. The attempt to agree on a common language in the face of the competing interests of the humanities, the social sciences and journalism often turns out to be futile. Besides, the new media have increasingly taken possession of the private sphere and are far from being in line with what had once been considered as the journalistic code of honour. All in all, journalism, public relations, advertising, visual media communication, and new media are faced with such very different challenges that it seems doubtful whether there is such a topic as the ethics of media.

At the same time, however, it is obvious that the individual domains of media overlap and cannot always be strictly separated from each other – as is the case with online games which integrate blocks of information, documentation or even blogs, with digital advertising worlds which camouflage themselves as games, with TV or broadcast programs based on interactive participation models. Therefore, at the same time that an ethics of media comprising the whole range of specific media ethics may prove to be too big a challenge (Rühl / Saxer, 1981: 475), it is clearly unsatisfactory to merely accept the disintegration of media ethics into its sub-domains.

If it turns out impossible to discuss, judge and 'shape' media reality as a whole and if in the place of one comprehensive media ethics small and smaller ethical sub-domains come to exist next to each other, media ethical discourse risks relegating itself to insignificance. In order to bring light into the question whether it is possible to develop a comprehensive media ethics and whether the idea of reconciliation could thereby play a significant role, it seems advisable to first present the sub-domains of journalism, public relations, advertising, visual media communication, and new media and to point out their claims, their challenges and their ways of posing problems.

2. Media Ethics and Its Fields of Application

Journalism is basically targeted at the emergence and functioning of publicness, it creates publicness by means of discourse and acts on the maxim of making things public by publishing (Pöttker, 2008: 299, Funiok, 2007: 129). Journalism reports and comments, provides the recipient with factual knowledge and strategic perspectives, meets the public's need for information and takes a critical stance in public discussions. The dual orientation of journalism – with its double goals of transmission of facts and opinions creating two different relational fields – aggravates the problem by producing competing norms which both claim validity. For insofar as journalism asserts its claim to represent facts, it is supposed to deliver objective knowledge and a maximum of information, and insofar as it is an opinion-former, this very objectivity ceases to be a criterion and the well-founded choice of information is being substituted for a maximum of information. The postulation of objectivity itself, however, includes both the likelihood of revision and correction and the respect for the human being as the object on which is being reported; it also requires the protection of the individual (protection of privacy, presumption of innocence, etc.) and – with regard to the sources – the thoroughness of research (versus speed), combined with the protection of the informant.

With regard to the audience, caution[1] and a sense of responsibility are considered indispensable, particularly in the case of opinion-marking reporting.

On the other hand, journalists themselves oppose censorship and insist on the freedom of the press, which has to be defended against political intervention and pressure, just as it has to be defended against imposed conformity by market mechanisms and audience opinion. The obligation to achieve the highest possible (and sold) print runs, and the highest possible TV and radio ratings, curtails the journalist's freedom and can be compared to the constraints exercised by any totalitarian political regime. It incites the journalist to go beyond factual and informative reports, to manufacture sensations and scandals and thus seemingly[2] renders more poignant the tension between the rights of the (human) object of the report and those of the receiving public. Compliance with the prohibition against accepting presents and benefits, compliance with the separation of PR content and information content – two rules of behaviour so justly proclaimed – can only be controlled and revealed on a superficial level, while in practice there are clearly more subtle and more permeable ways for paying clients to attract the media's attention.

In contrast with journalism, public relations activities can be defined as an interested communication,[3] destined to produce preliminary products for a subsequent treatment by the media (Westerbarkey, 1995: 160f.), thus attempting to gain influence on public discussion and opinion-making for the benefit of their clients. Quite similar to advertising, public relations aims at improving the competitive positions of its customers. Although its persuasive character is less prominent than that of advertising, it still is in conflict with such claims as truth and sustainability[4].

1 Thomaß – 2003: 159–168 – develops five ethical principles of journalism which have basically been touched upon in this paragraph.

2 "Seemingly" for the very reason that – on closer examination – an exaggerating and tendentious press does not give preference to the right to information (to the disadvantage of the object of the report), but by targeted disinformation becomes guilty both in the face of the object and the consumer.

3 As to the complex relationship between organisations and their stakeholders, see Karmasin, 2008: 268–280.

4 As to the concept of a "Corporate Social Responsibility", see Starck / Kruckeberg, 2003: 37. J. L'Etang (2003: 64) qualifies this position by referring to the agents "bad reputation" and "fear of disadvantage".

What seems particularly problematical in this respect and has hardly been dealt with in literature so far, is the fact that very frequently political PR contributions are being adopted by editorial staffs, who are compelled to produce and increase their output, without proper research and verification. And since public relations activities – at times almost independent of factual reality – constitute "reported reality", there is a clear danger that the fiction resulting from this procedure may later on be considered as past reality.

The problems mentioned above, however, do not call into question the legitimacy of public relations and advertising in general (Göbel, 1999: 648f). In their function as instruments of communication of economic relevance they represent the most important financial resources of the media. They help to finance and render possible the journalist's work and in their interaction with journalism they guarantee that all three sectors can comply with their respective tasks within the system. Besides, advertising is a component of "economic freedom of opinion", which is to be tolerated as long as it neither restricts other economic subjects in their rights nor attacks the persona of human beings. Advertising is legitimate when it announces its "products", when it reminds of them, when it informs us about them or when it makes the recipient experience them, but it becomes clearly problematical when – in promotional advertising or strategic publicity campaigns – its deliberately persuasive method turns into an obsessive pursuit of manipulation, as is the case for instance with subliminal, camouflaged or intentionally false publicity (Bohrmann, 1997: 37. 50ff; Hausmanninger, 1992: 231f; Schweiger / Schrattenecker, 1992: 23f). As to the form of advertising, ethically relevant questions impose themselves with regard to visual media communication. Ethical questions also impose themselves with regard to the quality of the products presented and to the way human beings are being treated, be it in their function as objects or as subjects, that is, as recipients of publicity. Are they being taken seriously as human beings in their respective situations or are they being exploited for economic purposes and thus abused?[5]

Visual media ethics is often dealt with in a comparatively superficial, albeit not insignificant, way when the representation of excessive violence, war, death, etc. – particularly in media that is at risk of falling into the hands of minors – is

5 This is the case, for instance, when publicity – word and image – deliberately wishes to shock or to break a taboo. See Bohrmann, 1997: 112ff; Könches, 2001: 18ff; Schulze 1999: 238ff.

being discussed. Apart from such scandalous images, however, images generally present themselves as a positive and accurate witness and seem to guarantee truth[6]. Images convey the illusion of authenticity (Barthes, 1985: 84ff; Bazin, 1981: 260; Wehner, 2000: 116.) and their immediateness induces the consumer to forget that as the recipient of images that are transmitted in visual communication they will always remain an observer of second order. Images are subject to human determinants and must therefore be apprehended less in their function as passive witnesses than in that of active agents in the process of journalistic communication. Given the low visual competence of the average consumer, a responsible handling of visual material in the media would at least require a contextualisation of the material, an identification of feigned images (functioning as symbols) and a concomitant verbal elucidation of the conditions of their production (Isermann / Knieper, 2010: 313.). In a second step, the postulations of an ethics of journalism should then be equally applied to the field of visual journalism (Gordon / Kittross, 1999: 72).

The so-called new[7] media and their "unlimited" access to "unlimited" information promise freedom to the consumer but are in fact characterised by the strong divide between rich and poor and a cultural imbalance to the benefit of – economically potent – western thought (Tapscott, 1998: 255–280; DiMaggio, 2004: 355–400). The existence of parallel streams of information which are difficult to evaluate produces over-information (Debatin, 2010: 324), which is then exposed to filtering mechanisms that restrict freedom and therefore hardly qualifies as promoting knowledge. Apart from these structural difficulties[8] and several problems of (basically) legal relevance[9] it is a fact that the area of digital media has become the playing ground for a multitude of individual actors who have not received

6 With regard to the pre-eminence of the image in mass communication, William J. Thomas Mitchell (1994: 11–34) suggests the term "pictorial turn".

7 The term 'new media' is a relational concept but nonetheless particularly suitable in this context since it refers simultaneously both to existing realities and to further developments that cannot yet be foreseen.

8 As to the positioning of internet ethics between media ethics and computer ethics, see Greis, 2001.

9 Such as the formation of ideologically motivated gangs that threaten inner security, the emergence of certain forms of organised crime or the increase of fiscal crime, made possible by the acceleration of transactions, etc.

any journalistic education, who are audience and authors in one and who erroneously believe in the anonymous character of the world wide web. Besides, they increasingly belong to the age group of minors. And if in publicity there is a shift from information to the simulation of lived experience, in the new media, too, games and entertainment become more and more important, bringing with them a double challenge. Actors in the new media not only have to be motivated to act responsibly (from the point of view of media ethics) in the face of the community but at the same time they also have to be protected against their own exhibitionist exposure of the private sphere.

3. Media Ethics and the History of its Investigation

The central position that the journalist occupies in classical print media presumably is one of the reasons why in its beginnings media ethics has presented itself as an ethics of the individual. While in the Christian context the opinion prevailed that the journalist's work should be guided by altruism and care (Wild, 1990: 44) for both the (human) object and the audience, Otto Groth described the good journalist as a man of conscientiousness, trustworthiness, determination, discretion and self-control (Groth, 1962: 387ff). Following Kant, he defined the guideline: "Act according to the maxim whereby your decision – while carefully preserving and cultivating your personality – will serve the greater good of the human community."[10]

Not unlike Emil Dovifat's (1890–1969) concept of the "publizistische Persönlichkeit" (journalistic personality), Otto Groth's (1875–1965) media ethical considerations largely ignore the fact that the interactions of the individual with society have an impact on the journalist's work. While taking up the reception and critique of these early positions marked by an ethics of the individual, Hermann Boventer (1928–2001) – in accordance with Gerhard Maletzke's approach – gives up the one-dimensional approach of mass communication. However, in his rejection of a situational ethics that puts values into perspective, Boventer still focuses on the moral responsibility of the individual journalist[11]. In contrast to these early

10 Groth (1962: 630): „Entscheide dich so, dass deine Entscheidung unter sorgsamer Erhaltung und Ausbildung deiner Gesamtpersönlichkeit dem Wohle der Gesamtheit dient."

11 The special attention Hermann Boventer pays to the journalist's moderation brings him close to virtue ethics – not unlike Hermann Lübbe who however places stronger emphasis on the role of

positions media ethics is presently discussed in its multidimensional relations. Rüdiger Funiok's approach with his concept of an ethics of responsibility should be mentioned here just as a number of different approaches from the perspectives of constructivism, of systems theory or of discourse ethics. However, to present these approaches in an adequate way would clearly go beyond the possibilities of this article, which is the reason why they – just like cultural studies (Fiske, 1987; Fiske, 1989; Fiske, 1993; Fiske, 1996) – cannot be dealt with here.

4. Reconciliation as a Principle of a Minimalistic Ethics?

Given the diversity of the philosophical approaches, it is surprising to see that so far the conceptual framework of Tom Beauchamp's and James Childress's principlism, an approach that can be considered as predominant in medical ethics, has hardly been applied to the field of media.[12] Principlism is a deliberative ethics based on a limited number of moral principles such as autonomy, beneficence, nonmaleficence, and justice. What speaks in favor of these four principles is the fact that from the beginnings of history most moral decision-makers in the field of medical ethics have used them in a descriptive or prescriptive way. By appealing to this common morality Beauchamp and Childress intend principlism to reach a high degree of consensus. The four mid-range principles – which are less general than fundamental principles and more general than casuistic rules – generate *prima facie* duties, but have to be put into perspective and weighed against one another in each individual case. They thus help find a well-reasoned response to problems of ethical relevance and give reason to believe that they remain valid as core elements of moral behaviour even in a pluralist society exposed to constant change.

If we ask whether reconciliation can be a principle of such a minimalistic ethics, the answer seems to be negative at first. A principle like reconciliation would be a positive demand, whereas we look for regulations for media ethics that signal clear limitations like for instance the principle of nonmaleficence. But is the principle of nonmaleficence itself suitable for media ethics? Well, there is probably

the recipient.

12 In *Medienethik als Prinzipienethik* (in print) W. Löffler makes a proposal of how to conceive and develop media ethics as an ethics of principles.

consensus that the goal of publishing must not be valid without any restrictions. And given the fact that media deal with human beings who become objects through the act of publishing or figure as informants or audience and consequently have to be protected against the loss of privacy and manipulation, the principle of nonmaleficence seems promising at first sight. It might even include cases of exhibitionist self-exposure provided the fact that doing damage is understood in its broadest sense, including all forms of psychic harm and injuries to the person's integrity.

Yet, almost simultaneously the limitations of the principle of nonmaleficence with regard to media ethics become apparent here: On the one hand, it has to be asked whether the principle of nonmaleficence, when applied to media self-representation, does not assume so broad a meaning that it comes to lack the specificity that would be necessary to constitute a principle. On the other hand, there are situations in media work where nonmaleficence is too limited as long as the focus remains on the protection of the human being. In publicity, for instance, human beings may be put on the media stage for economic reasons; it may be their own choice, they may be paid for it and the general framework may be appropriate. They do not suffer damage in the strict sense of the word, yet they are a means, not an end in themselves for what counts is the profit that can be made through them.

This problematics is far from characterising advertising alone. Journalists, too, sometimes write about people, not so much because they would feel concern for the person and his unique destiny, but – possibly – because they have to care about positive reactions to a gripping story. Last but not least, in visual media communication the principle of nonmaleficence does not seem to respond to the specific problematics of the field either. Not all situations where the visual representation of human beings does not do justice to their dignity and uniqueness are synonymous with damage. This is the reason why a principle of respect seems more appropriate in order to cover the whole range of possibilities and necessities to protect human beings in media communication. However, respect is a positive demand just as autonomy – to continue the series of principles.

Perhaps we should add that autonomy can basically be understood both in a negative and in a positive sense: in a negative sense with regard to the objects of media comments and their need for protection; in a positive sense as the freedom of the press, the right of organisations, business companies or politicians to present their respective positions with the aid of public relations, the right of economic agents to advertising, etc. It thus seems possible and reasonable to admit not only negative, but also positive principles like for instance reconciliation. In this context the fact that reconciliation represents a very special demand does not seem to be a grave problem either, for we do not want to develop a general morality, but suggest principles for applied ethics which have to enclose special obligations for the media and need not be general in the first place. However, does reconciliation really correspond to the proper character of the media?

Media work implies publishing, and this above all in the professional domain. For journalism, public relations, and advertising consist in the very task of making information, facts and opinions public and projecting them to the outside while leaving behind the small group of persons originally involved. In this respect publishing seems to be the *proprium* of professional media work and as a principle it would correlate with one of the traditional claims of journalism, the freedom of the press. Publishing is characterised by a strong dynamics of its own, which interestingly enough also appears to determine the sphere of private media work, and in particular visual media communication and the handling of new media. If one notices how private persons show an increasing interest in posting everyday details, private convictions, etc., one might object that publishing should rather not constitute such a principle because of its own strong dynamics. Therefore, instead of publishing, publicness could be considered as a convenient principle. Such a principle would not legitimise the compulsive publishing of insignificant or even private or intimate contents and would have to be clearly differentiated from negative forms of publicness – as outlined in Jürgen Habermas′ *Strukturwandel der Öffentlichkeit* (Habermas 1990).

Another principle that suits the ethical specificity of the field very well seems to be that of truth. Both everyday intuition and the lawmaker stress the principle of truth when they claim correction, etc. And yet, if truth becomes a principle in the sense of principlism, a number of difficulties arise. First of all, truth cannot easily be recognized or identified but has to be 'fathomed' and explored and it is doubtful whether something to be explored can at the same time constitute an authority or an ethical obligation. This problem however could be eluded if instead of truth one would speak of correctness in the sense of a correct presentation of facts.

But even the principle of correctness is too strong, in my opinion, for at closer examination it only covers the small area of informative journalism. As soon as we turn to opinion-making journalism, the claim for correctness does not work since the latter does not report on facts that could be right or wrong. The situation is similar in public relations and advertising, which both place facts into a perspective. Eventually, with regard to visual media communication and that part of the new media that does not deal with journalistic contents, it remains unclear how correctness can be stated at all. This is also true for a possible principle of objectivity, which is difficult to identify where it is required, while it is not intended at all in other – mostly more extensive – media sectors. What might be promising is to reflect on a principle like truthfulness – which means to be convinced of the contents one distributes –, or of a principle like transparency – which means declare facts as facts, opinions as opinions, entertainment as entertainment and so on.

With regard to the importance of possible principles like publicness, truthfulness or transparency reconciliation seems to be too narrow in sense and meaning as a principle for a minimalistic media ethics and at the same time not specific enough. Nevertheless, one might reflect on whether – beyond a limited number of core principles – there is space in media ethics for the idea of reconciliation. Reconciliation could give an orientation to media ethics, it could constitute the frame for understanding and discussing mid-range principles. Such a project would go beyond the approach of Beauchamp and Childress and would need a metaethical foundation which cannot be discussed here. Hence, I will limit myself to some concluding considerations as to how far the idea of reconciliation could enrich media ethics.

Reconciliation does not mean to forget or to continue as if nothing had happened. Reconciliation rather means the deliberate and intensive discussion of preceding actions or events, the articulation of criticism just as the consciousness of one's own mistakes. Since positive publicness does not allow to cover up information but implies to dealt with it seriously, a reasonable interaction is to be expected between journalism and the idea of reconciliation. What is important, however, is not to humiliate the opponent but to pacify conflicting parties instead.

Besides, it seems as if public relations and advertising in particular needed reconciliation since in a long-term perspective the very interests of their clientele can only be represented profitably in a well operating society. To uphold reconciliation means to opt for underrepresented voices and to counterbalance the one-sided representation of those groups that have the economic power to sell their own visions successfully on the market. At the same time we realize that new media make communication inevitable. The faster and more intensely people exchange their ideas, the greater the possibilities for misunderstanding and quarrel. If the new media do not wish to find themselves in a situation of blockade of communication, reconciliation must be considered as an important perspective in online interaction, no matter whether emails, facebook entries or online-games with interactive play modes are concerned.

I am well aware of the fact that in the context of this paper, a systematic processing of these potentials is not possible; there is not enough space to adequately argue the approach of a principle ethics nor to develop a metaethical foundation of a higher central theme. What seems evident, however, is that media should all the more afford reconciliation and that media ethics certainly could be enriched by it.

References

Barthes, R. 1985. *Am Nullpunkt der Literatur.* Frankfurt am Main: edition Suhrkamp.

Bazin, A. 1981. Ontologie des photographischen Bildes. In: Wiegand, W. (ed.): *Die Wahrheit der Photographie. Klassische Bekenntnisse zu einer neuen Kunst*, Frankfurt am Main: Fischer S.

Bohrmann, Th. 1997. *Ethik – Werbung – Mediengewalt. Werbung im Umfeld von Gewalt im Fernsehen. Eine sozialethische Programmatik.* München: Fischer.

Debatin, B. 2010. New Media Ethics. in: Schicha, Ch. / Brosda, C. (eds.): *Handbuch Medienethik*, Wiesbaden: VS Verlag.

DiMaggio, P. et al. 2004. Digital Inequality: From Unequal Access to Differentiated Use. in: Neckerman, K. (ed.): *Social Inequality*, New York: Russell Sage Foundation.

Fiske, J. 1987. *Television Culture.* London: Menthuen & Co. Ltd.

Fiske, J. 1989. *Reading the Popular.* Boston: Unwin Hyman.

Fiske, J. 1993. *Power Plays, Power Works.* London: Verso.

Fiske, J. 1996. *Media Matters. Race and Gender in U.S. Politics.* Revised Editions. Minneapolis: University of Minnesota Press.

Funiok, R. 2007. *Medienethik. Verantwortung in der Mediengesellschaft.* Stuttgart: Kohlhammer W.

Göbel, E. 1999. Werbung. in: Korff, W. et al. (eds.): *Handbuch der Wirtschaftsethik 4*, Gütersloh: Gütersloher Verlagshaus.

Gordon, D. / Kittross, J. M. 1999. *Controversies in media ethics.* Boston: Routledge.

Greis, A. 2001. *Identität, Authentizität und Verantwortung. Die ethischen Herausforderungen der Internetethik zwischen der Medien- und Computerethik.* München: Kopäd.

Groth, O. 1962. Die unerkannte Kulturmacht. Grundlegung der Zeitungswissenschaft. In: *Periodik* 4, pp. 387–390.

Hausmanninger, Th. 1992. *Kritik der medienethischen Vernunft. Die ethische Diskussion über den Film in Deutschland.* München: Fink Wilhelm.

Isermann, H. / Knieper, Th. 2010. Bildethik. In: Schicha, Ch. / Brosda, C. (eds.): *Handbuch Medienethik*, Wiesbaden: VS Verlag.

Karmasin, M. 2008. Stakeholder Management als Ansatz der PR. In: Bentele, G. / Fröhlich, R. / Szyszka P. (eds.): *Handbuch der Public Relations. Wissenschaftliche Grundlagen und berufliches Handeln,* Wiesbaden [2]: VS Verlag.
Könches, B. 2001. *Ethik und Ästhetik der Werbung. Phänomenologie eines Skandals.* Frankfurt am Main: Peter Lang.
L´Etang, J. 2003. The myth of the "ethical guardian": An examination of its origins, potency and illusions. In: *Journal of Communication Management* 8, pp. 53–67.
Mitchell, W. J. Th. 1994. *Picture Theory. Essays on Verbal and Visual Representation.* Chicago: University of Chicago Press.
Pöttker, H. 2008. Öffentlichkeit als Sisyphusarbeit. Über unlösbare Widersprüche im Journalismus. In: Pörksen, B. / Loosen, W. / Scholl, P. (eds.): *Paradoxien des Journalismus: Theorie – Empirie – Praxis*, Wiesbaden: VS Verlag.
Rühl, M. / Saxer, U. 1981. 25 Jahre Deutscher Presserat. In: *Publizistik* 26, pp. 471–507.
Schulze, A. 1999. *Werbung an der Grenze: Provokation in der Plakatwerbung der 50er bis 90er Jahre.* Wiesbaden: Deutscher Universitäts-Verlag.
Schweiger, G. / Schrattenecker, G. 1992. *Werbung. Eine Einführung.* Stuttgart [3]: UTB.
Starck, K. / Kruckeberg, D. 2003. Ethical obligations of public relations in an era of globalization. In: *Journal of Communication Management* 8, pp. 29–40.
Tapscott, D. 1998. *Growing Up Digital: The Rise of the New Generation.* New York: McGraw-Hill Professional.
Thomaß, B. 2003. Fünf ethische Prinzipien journalistischer Praxis. In: Debatin, D. / Funiok, R. (eds.): *Kommunikations- und Medienethik*, Konstanz: Uvk.
Wehner, J. 2000. Wie die Gesellschaft sich als Gesellschaft sieht – elektronische Medien in systemtheoretischer Perspektive. In: Neumann-Braun, K. / Müller-Doohm, St. (eds.): *Medien- und Kommunikationssoziologie. Eine Einführung in zentrale Begriffe und Theorien*, Weinheim: Juventa.
Westerbarkey, J. 1995. Journalismus und Öffentlichkeit. Aspekte publizistischer Interdependenz und Interpenetration. In: *Publizistik* 40, pp. 152–162.
Wild, C. 1990. *Ethik im Journalismus. Individualethische Überlegungen zu einer journalistischen Berufsethik.* Wien: Verband der wissenschaftlichen Gesellschaften Österreichs.

CHURCH, MINISTRY AND RELATIONAL THEOLOGY

RECONCILIATION IN A WORLD OF EXCLUSION: THE POSSIBILITY OF A RADICAL NOVELTY "IN CHRIST"

Corneliu Constantineanu, Bucharest

Introduction

The tragic realities on the global scene in a context of worldwide increasing violence as well as an amplification of various forms of intolerance and exclusion, are all pointing to an unambiguous *urgency* of reconciliation. In such circumstances faith based communities, in particular, need to consider more seriously and without delay their task and possibilities for a real contribution to a much needed ministry of reconciliation. Moreover, throughout the history of Christian thinking "reconciliation" has been regarded as fundamental for Christian faith and theology, a central theological category expressing the very heart of the gospel. This represents yet another reason to explore without delay the theme of reconciliation.

Even though the church has a special call to proclaim and embody reconciliation, it is with sadness and much pain that we note the failure of the various Christian communities, in many different circumstances, to enact reconciliation in their context. Gregory Baum is thus very perceptive when he remarks that even though "*the Christian gospel summons the church to exercise the ministry of reconciliation in situations defined by strife and hostility ...churches have rarely exercised the ministry of reconciliation;*" even where present, such ministry is still "*a pioneering activity*" (Baum, 1997, 184–192; italics in the original). This situation constrains us not simply to reflect seriously on the inability of Christian communities to incarnate the message of reconciliation but also to look for adequate resources that will enable them in such a crucial ministry. There is, therefore, a great need for serious enquiry into the biblical concept of God's reconciliation of the world in Christ in such a way as to be both exegetically sound and relevant to the social and political needs for reconciliation in today's world. I am convinced that a new understanding of the social and political meaning of reconciliation in the biblical and theological tradition will represent an important resource for churches in their social engagement (for a detailed, exegetical study of the social relevance of reconciliation in Pauline theology, see Constantineanu 2010). In this paper I would like to explore, briefly, Apostle Paul's understanding and presentation of reconciliation, especially the novelty he brings to the concept when compared with the classical paradigm of reconciliation in his days. I will argue that his concept of reconciliation was radically shaped by his own encounter with Christ and his personal experience of reconciliation. It was the new reality accomplished by God "in Christ" that made him re-evaluate and change the old paradigm of reconciliation.

Paul's Encounter with Christ and Reconciliation

It is commonly accepted by students of the NT that Paul's encounter with Christ on the road to Damascus Paul had changed fundamentally his theological convictions and his course of life (see particularly Kim, 1981; Donaldson, 1997; Gager, 1980). The experience on the Damascus road introduced a radically *new* element into Paul's symbolic universe: Jesus of Nazareth, crucified in Jerusalem, appears to him as alive, confronting Paul with a reality he could not deny – Jesus was raised by God and thus confirmed that he was the Messiah of Israel and the Saviour of the world. Paul was thus forced to re-examine his entire worldview in the light of this new and undeniable reality.

The Damascus road event meant for Paul, among other things, a profound experience of God's grace and reconciliation which significantly shaped his theology, life, and ministry as expressed well by Kraftchick: "a full appreciation of Paul's theological construction must consider his personal experience" because "Paul's theology is shaped not only by his heritage, his religious convictions and his struggles with his congregations, but also by his experience of the human condition" (Kraftchick, 2002, 145. See also Longenecker, 1997; Everts, 1997; Dunn, 1998). Other scholars too observed the close connection between his remarkable experience and his theology (Roetzel, 1998; Hodgson, 1998; Oakeshott, 1985). It is significant to understand that Paul met Christ while he was an enemy of God persecuting the church and that, contrary to his own expectations, he was not rejected and destroyed by God but found himself reconciled. He experienced personally the profound and radical nature of God's grace and forgiveness, a God who did not count Paul's sin against him but rather accepted and forgave him. One can agree with Wolff who stated that "this experience of reconciliation shaped Paul's apostolic existence" (Wolff, 1989, 93).

One important biblical passage that describes the significant implications of Paul's experience of reconciliation is 2 Corinthians 5:14 – 6:10. There are several important truths regarding reconciliation which are presented in this passage and I would like to briefly comment on them. First, Paul understood in that event that reconciliation is purely *God's gift of grace* offered to an estranged and rebellious humanity. Indeed, we have a window into the radical nature of God's grace, of a God who reached out to his enemies. *The victim takes initiative*. This is what Schwöbel refers to as "*the asymmetry of reconciliation*":

> The asymmetrical character of divine reconciliation and of divine love defines the reconciling act in Christ as of identification and exchange. Since reconciliation with those who cannot initiate reconciliation by themselves because they are captive in separation from God can only be achieved through the identification of God in Christ with his enemies, so divine love is directed to those who cannot love God (Schwöbel, 2003, 25).

Second, the reconciliation of the world by God is presented to Paul as an *objective reality*. Everything else that Paul says about reconciliation at personal, social and political levels can be properly understood only in that light (Gunton, 2003, 6). It was this truth for Paul that *gives the possibility for present reconciliation*. By referring to his experience of reconciliation, Paul does not limit the reconciliation of God simply to those who have such an experience. On the contrary, and more fundamentally, that very experience revealed to Paul the permanent nature, attitude and action of God towards an estranged and rebellious humanity. God has reconciled the world to himself once and for all! And God's gracious stance towards Paul is an illustration of his stand towards the whole hostile world. This is what Paul understood on the Damascus road. The appearance of the resurrected Christ to him as well as Paul's own experience simply confirmed the objective nature of reconciliation. Thus, a ministry of reconciliation in the world is not merely *analogous* to what God has done, but it *is* what God has done. Reconciliation on the horizontal plane is not doing the sort of thing God did with us but it is doing the very thing God did with us. It is an extending of that cosmic reconciliation. It is not an extending of our terms of reconciliation but extending God's reconciliation.

Third, it is through *Christ's death and resurrection* that the objective reconciliation is accomplished and so it is Christ the reconciler that Paul focuses his attention on; thus, it is around Christ that any thought of reconciliation should be based. One cannot separate the concept of reconciliation – especially in its political and social aspects – from Christ, in whom the reality of reconciliation is found and realized.

Fourth, by echoing his own conversion experience, Paul wants to direct the Corinthians towards their own radical experience of reconciliation by God's grace so that they will be able to relate differently to each other, and even to their enemies. This may be seen clearly in 2 Cor. 6:1–10, where Paul insists that the Corinthians should not make the grace of God in their lives to be *in vain*... Indeed, the whole point of 6:1–10 is to illustrate that "the gospel message, to be the gospel message, must be embodied, not just spoken" (Kraftchick, 2002, 151). There is thus an *intrinsic relationship* between *the message* of reconciliation and *the messenger's* own reconciliation and life.

Lastly, it is significant that for Paul *there is no reconciliation without a cost!* Reading through Paul's catalogues of afflictions and sufferings (2 Cor. 6:3–10) one gets a very strong sense of this aspect. Schwöbel again captures well this dimension of reconciliation:

> ...in view of the message that has been entrusted to them Christians know that the reality of reconciliation can spread – but at a price. Reconciliation understood from this theological perspective is not based on mutual agreement that has to be established first, but on a one-sided step to break up the pattern of the mutuality of enmity. Reconciliation is based on a one-sided offer of peace where there was conflict. As such, it is costly: it requires withdrawing from all attempts at retribution. The one who offers reconciliation is the one who must pay the price for the renewal of the relationship in the sense that there can be no retribution for the past misdeeds (Schwöbel, 2003, 35–6).

Christ Makes All Things New!

There are at least three additional important aspects, beyond his reconciliation, that were fundamentally shaped by Paul's encounter with Christ. He realizes that, somehow, a new world is beginning to take shape because of Christ, a new existence is available for those who are "in Christ." First, it was *a new way of understanding and constructing his identity*. In 2 Cor. 5:17 Paul states:

> *"if anyone is in Christ, there is a new creation: everything old has passed away; see, everything has become new!"*

Paul's encounter with the risen Christ on the Damascus road had a dramatic impact on his life. Not only was his new identity irreversibly shaped by Christ, but he was also "shaken" in his previous definitions and construction of identity. He discovers that Christ lives in him, that he is, in fact, embraced by Christ (and so, he realizes that Christ was open and made space for Paul, his initial enemy); that Christ's opening made it possible for Paul to open himself for Christ and, at the same time, for others; that he is now, paradoxically, both sure of who he is in Christ, and, at the same time not so sure: that his new identity is constantly in negotiation and interaction with "the other"; that there is a somewhat mysterious dimension of who he is and who others are which requires a good deal of faith (Gal. 2:20); and that his new sense of identity has enabled him to relate differently to those around him, to value and appreciate people from a completely different perspective (2 Cor. 5:16). Paul has now a different set of values through which to judge everything and everyone else and a new basis from which to perceive and relate to "the other."

Another significant novelty which Paul realized was possible now "in Christ" was *an intellectual reorientation, a new way of knowing, a new understanding of reality.* In the new age inaugurated by Christ, the true knowing surpasses the knowing of the old age (*kata sarka*). And this is true not only for Paul but also for all those belonging to this community of "new creation."

When Paul and his converts accepted the revelation of God in Christ they have experienced

> an *intellectual reorientation* in which they had to *change their understanding* of *human nature* and *the obligations* flowing from their new relationship to God, as well as *a new view of the cosmic scheme of things.* … In turning to God, they were required to change their understanding of the divine and service to him; they had to think anew of human nature, no longer in terms of human potentiality and virtue, but from a perspective of their relation to God and his will; they had to reconstruct their view of a cosmic order to one that is under God's judgment while they themselves had a hope of deliverance from that judgment. And running through all of this new understanding was the theme of their moral responsibility (Malherbe, 1998, 237–38, 240).

The new way of knowing is not simply a spiritual, ecstatic, or mystical way of knowing available to a few, nor a knowing in abstraction or isolation from the other. On the contrary, as Martyn remarks, "it is life in the midst of the new-creation community, in which to know by the power of the cross is precisely to know and to serve the neighbour who is in need." (Martyn, 1997, 109). Everything is now known, defined and lived out in the light of Christ – his love, cross and resurrection. Martyn continues:

> For, as the second half of 2 Cor 5:16 and the first half of v. 17 show, the epistemology characteristic of this community is thoroughly and without remainder christological. That is to say, together with the community that is being formed in him, *Christ* defines the difference between the two ways of knowing, doing that precisely in his cross. The cross of Christ means that the marks of the new age are at present hidden in the old age (2 Cor 6:3—10). Thus, at the juncture of the ages the marks of the resurrection are hidden and revealed in the cross of the disciple's daily death, and only there (Martyn, 1997, 110).

There is yet a third new reality that is made possible now "in Christ," namely a *new way of relating to others, including the enemy.* His own reconciliation with God has completely altered his perception of, and relation to, his enemies. Not only was he able to acquire a different understanding but he was reconciled with his former enemies! Those he once persecuted now embrace him and they are reconciled. "From now on, therefore, we regard no one from a human point of view" (2 Cor. 5:16). And this is all made possible by Christ who first embraced Paul while he was an enemy. And this is enough for Paul to understand that he can now follow Christ's example.

We can conclude this section by saying that beginning with Paul's own radical experience of reconciliation on the Damascus road, a new vision of reality started to emerge for Paul. A *new reality* was brought about by the death and resurrection of Christ: a world of new possibilities and radical innovations is opened up now "in Christ," with serious implications for all those living within this new reality.

The New Paradigm for Reconciliation

It was this new understanding of reality in the light of Christ and his reconciliation that determined Paul to re-examine and make a paradigm shift in the Hellenistic concept of reconciliation (Fitzgerald, 2001, 231–62). Following Fitzgerald, in a very schematic presentation, the standard Hellenistic paradigm of reconciliation contained the following elements: presupposing a wrongdoing of one or more parties which created the conflict, the basic principle in the standard paradigm was that *those responsible for the conflict* were to take initiative in restoring the relationships and seek reconciliation, while the offended party had to willingly accept the offer of reconciliation; the guilty party's initiative in reconciliation took the form of an *appeal*, often accompanied by some gesture showing affection and concern for the wronged person; *reparations* were necessary in order to pacify the estranged party and achieve reconciliation; there were both *benefits* and *responsibilities* involved in the fact of reconciliation: "one of the benefits was the knowledge that one could fulfil one's tasks in the full confidence of a restored relationship"; as for the responsibilities, "the reconciled were to live in light of their renewed concord with one another and henceforth to live irreproachably" (Fitzgerald, 2001, 231–32).

Due to his own experience of reconciliation and of his understanding of the new reality "in Christ," Paul makes several significant changes in the paradigm of reconciliation. The first thing to be noted is that Paul takes the term used in diplomacy and politics, applies it to the divine-human relationship (2 Cor. 5:18–20; Rom. 5:10–11), and shifts the paradigm so that *God, the offended party is taking the initiative* in reconciliation. That God intervenes prior to and apart from human repentance is most clearly expressed by Paul in Romans 5:8, 10 where Paul states that God has taken the initiative and reconciled human beings while still sinners and hostile to God. As Fitzgerald correctly remarks, this is "of momentous import, for it suggests a radically new and unprecedented understanding of God" (Fitzgerald, 2001, 233).

The death of Christ could be understood as the "reparations" payment necessary for effective reconciliation between God and humanity. The shift Paul makes here, however, is that it is not the offending humanity who makes the reparations but God, who "reconciled us through the death of his Son" (Rom. 5:10). One last important note we would like to make here refers to one of several features that remain intact from the traditional paradigm, namely *the responsibility* of those being reconciled, to live their lives in the light of their achieved reconciliation, i.e., to live irreproachably. Paul maintains this element as essential and shows that he has assumed that responsibility and lived appropriately to his reconciliation with God. He is thus "offering proof of the reality of his own reconciliation" by pointing to the blamelessness of his ministry (2 Cor. 6:3), to the virtues he exhibits (6:4–7) and to the way in which he gives himself for the benefit and spiritual enrichment of the other (6:10).

Such an analysis brings significant insights and advances substantially the discussion of reconciliation in Paul. It shows that within the traditional paradigm reconciliation dealt with interpersonal, societal, and political aspects of life. While Paul maintains these elements, he also brings God into the picture, thus enlarging the political concept of reconciliation with a vital, religious dimension and integrating these two elements into one reality. In addition, Paul regards as important the element of responsibility for those being reconciled to live in accordance with their reconciliation. Furthermore, the analysis highlights the other shifts in the paradigm that Paul makes, most significantly that the offended party takes the initiative for reconciliation.

Conclusion

The argument put forward in this paper was that beginning with his own radical experience of reconciliation with God on the Damascus road, a particular vision of reality started to emerge for Paul. In addition to his reconciliation, that event changed Paul's identity which determined, in turn, a totally new life for Paul due to a radically new understanding of reality brought about by the death and resurrection of Christ. Paul's vision of reconciliation was radically shaped by, and grounded in, the story of Christ: a world of new possibilities and radical innovations is opened up now "in Christ", with serious implications for all those living within this new reality. We have seen that there is in Paul's theology an understanding of reconciliation that is linked to a vision of reality that transcends the natural possibilities and which offers a different set of values from those of this world, and produces different results. This vision inspired him throughout his life and ministry and gave him the impetus to be constantly engaged in *reconciling practices* – between Jews and Gentiles, between various individuals and groups within the churches, between Christians and outsiders. It was the same vision worked out in Paul's life that offered an incentive for his congregations to think and act likewise and, indeed, it also inspires us to continue to build on that vision.

References

Baum, G.and H. Wells (eds.). 1997: *Reconciliation of Peoples: Challenges to the Churches*. Geneva: WCC Publications, 1997.

Constantineanu, C. 2010 *The Social Significance of Reconciliation in Paul's Theology: Narrative Readings in Romans*, London/New York: T&T Clark Continuum.

Donaldson, T. L. 1997: *Paul and the Gentiles: Remapping the Apostle's Convictional World.* Minneapolis: Fortress Press.

Everts, J.M. 1997. Conversion and Call of Paul. In: G. F. Hawthorne, R. P. Martin & D. G.Reid, eds. *Dictionary of Paul and His Letters.* Downers Grove: Inter Varsity Press.

Dunn, J. D. G. 1998. *The Theology of Paul the Apostle*. Grand Rapids: Eerdmans.

Fitzgerald, J. T. 2001. Paul and Paradigm Shifts: Reconciliation and Its Linkage Group. In: Troels Engberg-Pedersen (ed.) *Paul Beyond the Judaism/Hellenism Divide*. Louisville: Westminster John Knox Press.

Fitzmyer, J. 1967. *Pauline Theology*. Englewood Cliffs, NJ: Prentice-Hall.

Gager, J. G. 1980. Some Notes on Paul's Conversion. In: *NTS* 27, pp. 697–704.

Gunton, C. E. 2003 Towards a Theology and Reconciliation. In: Colin Gunton ed. *The Theology of Reconciliation*. London: T & T Clark.

Hodgson, P. 1998. Constructive Theology and Biblical Words. In: F. Segovia and M.A. Tolbert (eds.) *Teaching the Bible.* Maryknoll: Orbis Books.

Kim, S. 1981. *The Origin of Paul's Gospel*. Tubingen: Mohr.

Kraftchick, S. J. 2002. Death's Parsing: Experience as a Mode of Theology in Paul. In: Janice Capel Anderson, *et al.* (eds.), *Paul's Conversations in Context: Essays in Honor of Calvin J. Roetzel,* JSNTS 221 (Sheffield: Sheffield Academic Press), p. 145.

Longenecker, R. N. (ed.). 1997. *The Road from Damascus: The Impact of Paul's Conversion on His Life, Thought and Ministry.* Grand Rapids: Eerdmans.

Malherbe, A. 1998. Conversion to Paul's Gospel. In: Abraham J. Malherbe, Frederick W. Noris and James W. Thomson (eds.), *The Early Church in its Context: Essays in Honour of Everett Ferguson*, Leiden: Brill.

Martyn, J. L. 1997. Epistemology at the Turn of the Ages: 2 Corinthians 5:16. In: *Theological Issues in the Letters of Paul*. Edinburgh: T & T Clark.

Oakeshott, M. 1985. *Experience and its Modes*. Cambridge: Cambridge University Press.

Roetzel, C. 1998. *Paul: The Man and The Myth.* Columbia: University of South Carolina Press.

Schwöbel, C. 2003. Reconciliation: From Biblical Observations to Dogmatic Reconstruction. In: Colin E. Gunton (ed.), *The Theology of Reconciliation*, London: T & T Clark/ Continuum.

Wolff, C. 1989. True Apostolic Knowledge of Christ: Exegetical Reflections on 2 Cor. 5.14ff. In: A. J. M. Wedderburn (ed.) *Paul and Jesus: Collected Essays.* Edited. JSNTS 37. Sheffield: Sheffield Academic Press.

RECONCILIATION AND CONFESSION IN THE THEOLOGY OF DIETRICH BONHOEFFER

Wilhelm Guggenberger, Innsbruck

Reconciliation is an interactive process which could not be realized by one agent alone, at least two persons or groups are involved. Customary culprit and victim will be distinguished even if in real conflict-scenarios all agents involved are mostly culprits and victims at the same time.

However the twofold nature of the phenomenon - two different roles and two perspectives connected with these roles - is essential. According to this, there are two pillars upon which reconciliation has to be built: Confession or repentance respectively and forgiveness. These two elements are complementary parts of the same occurrence. If one of them is missing reconciliation never will happen.

Discussions about reconciliation in social and political contexts in particular are focussed on the element of forgiveness for the most part. They are interested in questions like: How is it possible to forgive? Which psychological preconditions have to be given to enable a victim to forgive? Which setting do we need to facilitate forgiveness? What is the effect on victims if they are not able to forgive? And so on. Though these questions are of unquestionable importance we should not succumb to the temptation of undervaluing the element of confession and repentance. It is not enough to locate and to state guilt as a fact, so to speak from outside. The objective assessment of guilt may be a first and sometimes necessary step, but the confession of guiltiness by the culprit remains indispensable if reconciliation should succeed. As Francis Cardinal Arinze - former president of the papal council for interreligious dialogue - wrote in his 2002 book *Religions for peace* real and lasting peace is impossible, where own mistakes are not recognised and people are not ready to self-criticism (cf. Arinze, 2002: 85).

From this point of view the question why it could be helpful to take the theology of Dietrich Bonhoeffer into account, considering the topic of reconciliation seems not hard to be answered to me.

As I have to be short, I want to focus on one central argument of the Lutheran theologian. In his manuscripts on ethics, which remained uncompleted when Bonhoeffer was imprisoned by the German Gestapo in April 1943, he wrote:

"The place where this acknowledgement of guilt becomes real is the church. This does not mean that the church, alongside other things it is and does, is also the place where guilt is genuinely acknowledged. Instead, the church is that community of people that has been led by the grace of Christ to acknowledge its guilt toward Christ. It is tautological to say that the Church is the place where guilt is acknowledged. If it were otherwise, the church would no longer be church."[1] (Bonhoeffer, 2009: 135)

I will try to unfold some reflections on this quote in the following. The quote is part of a chapter on guilt, justification and renewal in Bonhoeffer's text. First we have to consider what Bonhoeffer means by acknowledgement of guilt, and then we have to ask why he identifies this acknowledgement with being Church. A third step then will be to reflect about the duties and chances of current churches in reconciliation-processes.

1) Acknowledgement of guilt

I have insisted that reconciliation requires confession of guilt. But of course there will be no confession without the recognition of being wrong or having been wrong at least. Everyone knows that it is anything but easy to reach such recognition much less to make it public, even if the public in question is very limited.

Bonhoeffer refers to a special kind of guilt in the quoted sentences: guilt towards Christ. So we are reminded that there is a difference between guilt and sin; not a material difference but one concerning the acknowledgement of what's going wrong. Sin is guilt in front of God. To speak about sin means to realize that the root of all our failures is a violated relation to God even if the outcome of this are particular offences against the social order, against other people or the created nature for example.

Thus guilt in Bonhoeffer does not mean any "occasional mistake" that could take place now and then. It also does not mean the "breaking of an abstract law" but only the "the falling away from Christ" (Bonhoeffer, 2009: 135). The term "defection from Christ" (Abfall von Christus) describes the attitude of a human

1 I want to give you the German text of this crucial passage too: "Der Ort, an dem diese Schulderkenntnis wirklich wird, ist die Kirche. Das darf jedoch nicht so verstanden werden, als ob die Kirche neben anderem, was sie ist und tut, auch noch der Ort echter Schulderkenntnis ist. Sondern die Kirche ist eben jene Gemeinschaft von Menschen, die durch die Gnade Christi zur Erkenntnis der Schuld an Christus geführt worden ist. Dass die Kirche der Ort der Schulderkenntnis ist, ist also eine tautologische Aussage. Wo es anders wäre, wäre die Kirche nicht mehr Kirche." (Bonhoeffer, 1998: 126)

being failing his or her essential nature by trying to create, to judge and to restore himself. The attempt to be his own creator, his own judge and his own restorer seems to be a perfect portrait especially of modern man. It is crucial now that nominal Christianity is no guaranty at all to differ from this way of life. Otherwise it would not make sense to define the church as place where acknowledgement of guilt in the mentioned meaning has to be practiced. In fact there is no church faithfully following Christ in opposition to a rotten world. The only difference between church and not-church, church and world is that the church of Christ is the community where recognition of guilt takes place.

Such recognition can be called a real one in so far it avoids any sidelong glance at the fellow offenders (cf. Bonhoeffer, 2009: 136). We are far beyond questions of mere justice here. To decide how much guilt one agent has compared to another or to excuse oneself by arguing that other offences are much worse than the own ones is absolutely meaningless in this context. The decisive fact is that the relationship between God and man is broken, which causes pain and violence among us. To acknowledge the own causal involvement in this disunion means to admit being responsible for everything going wrong even if no one of us could take responsibility in the literal sense for each transgression taking place. Even the most insignificant sin or omission has to be acknowledged as source of poison for the community. What is considered by Bonhoeffer thus is the recognition of being part of a web of sin, violence and disaster without longing for cheap excuses.

2) Acknowledgement of guilt and the church

Why does Bonhoeffer identify the mentioned acknowledgement with being church? To understand this in the right way we have to understand the church as servant; not only a servant of God but primarily a servant of the world. To explain this approach not only to be found in Bonhoeffer but also in the theology of the Second Vatican Council (cf. Hennecke, 1997: 137–142). I have to go far afield a little bit in favor of showing some components of Bonhoeffer's understanding of a Christian ethic.

Secular ethics, particularly the best of secular ethics, confronts us with demands which are too much for us. According to Bonhoeffer secular ethics formulate the contrast or gap between reality and the imagination of what should be. This gap never will be bridged in a sufficient way. In contrast to that a Christian ethic formulates the relationship between reality, which means the reality of Christ and their realization within our world, which has to be understood as becoming more and more like Christ, being conformed to him guided by the Holy Spirit (cf.

Bonhoeffer, 2009: 49–50; 93). Therefore norms are not the most important thing in Christian ethics. The experience and further more the witness to this experience of a liberating relationship is rather crucial. Christian ethics is not focused on a behavior in order to (um zu), which characterizes our common functional considerations but on a behavior because of (deswegen weil). This of course is not Bonhoeffer's formulation but my own - to be honest it is a formulation I owe to my wife - but nonetheless the idea is essential in Bonhoeffer's theology. Because I have experienced grace and love I am urged to follow a particular way of life now. That means in our context: Because the church is witness to God's forgiveness it is compelled to recognize and confess its guilt.

Christian ethics which does not mean to ask: "What do I have to do to become good?", but to ask: "What is the will of God?", is quite impossible without the experience of grace. The church's service to the world is to prepare the way (Wegbereitung) for such an experience of grace (cf. Bonhoeffer, 2009: 161–163). What it could mean to fail according to this service in a specific situation is mentioned by Bonhoeffer in very concrete terms. In his manuscripts on ethics he formulates a catalogue of the sins following the Decalogue committed by his church during the first decades of the twentieth century. He concludes: "The church confesses itself guilty of violating all of the Ten Commandments." (Bonhoeffer, 2009: 140) An example out of this catalogue is that the church is considered guilty in the violation of the day of the lord because its preaching was weak and its worship was limp. Furthermore it is said that the church is guilty because it stayed silent while countless innocent people were oppressed and murdered. Or finally the church desired for security, tranquility, property and honor in an inappropriate way which made it guilty of being unable to tame human covetousness. To get to the heart of the problem: the church is guilty since she does not witness God's grace to the world. Consistent to his own theology Bonhoeffer did not criticize the Catholic Church or the Lutheran Church of the so called Deutsche Christen in this way but the community of the Confessing Church (Bekennende Kirche) he himself adhered to. Concerning this fact Bonhoeffer asked 1943 in one of his letters from prison: Are we still of any use, of any use as Christians, of any use as Church? (Cf. Bonhoeffer, 2010: 52) Are we still of any use if we do not prepare the becoming of God's reality among his creatures? Among other things preparing the way means to be a sign of the presence of God's grace in our world. This does not require to be morally perfect but to risk acting even if we know it is likely to fail and to confess the own failure (cf. Prüller-Jagenteufel, 2004: 509). What enables us to do so is quite the experience of the forgiving grace of the Father. To decide, to act within the twilight of human history, which means to live a responsible life is only possible because we know that we do not have to be perfect. We are able to venture acting even if we can't be sure of its goodness, since guiltless Jesus bore our guilt already (cf. Bonhoeffer, 2009: 233–235).

3) Church and reconciliation

What is the result of that in the context of reconciliation?

Imagine the confrontation of victim and culprit with each other which is branded as well by the fact of their violated relationship as by the fact of their respective broken biography. The victim will expect the culprit to take a first step. That means the victim needs a kind of confession or at least acknowledgement of fault by the offender to overcome anger or even fear. Otherwise resentment and accusation will remain the only reaction possible to the suffered insult. Forgiveness usually will not take place if there is no contrition testified by the culprit. But on the other side the offender fears the consequences of his confession. How will the violated and angry person vis-a-vis react? There is no automatism for forgiveness even if confession took place. Thus the culprit will be likely to be frightened by the imagination of increasing and even public accusation that could wreck him. Therefore distrust, prejudice, aversion, anxiety, resentment and finally new violence will be fixed as inescapable facts. Although the given analysis of very complex phenomena is inappropriately superficial, it should be comprehensible that a vicious circle arises in such situations caused by agents who orient themselves by the behavior of the opponent. "Then people handed over to one another's judgment mercilessly, living together becomes an endless circle in which they seek one another's recognition, but cannot satisfy each other's expectations, and break down under one another's judgment. The result is a merciless society that only demands and does not give anything, because it cannot for-give anything either." (DeLange, 2004: 167)

Such paralyzed cycles do not offer much hope of change. That is why Hannah Arendt called forgiveness the only active - not merely re-active - human action but also the one furthest beyond expectation and calculation. "In contrast to revenge, which is the natural, automatic reaction to transgression and which because of the irreversibility of the action process can be expected and even calculated, the act of forgiving can never be predicted; it is the only reaction that acts in an unexpected way and thus retains, though being a reaction, something of the original character of action." (Arendt, 1989: 240–241). What Arendt missed to answer is the question how such an unexpected "miracle" could come true.

For the most part an impulse from outside could give the sole chance to break the cycle and trigger new motion. Concerning interpersonal conflicts we will think of different forms of mediation which turned out to be very helpful if not indispensable many times. Also in social conflicts between national, ethnic or religious groups mediation could be a proper means even if it is much more difficult to use it in the right way. Sometimes the churches have the chance to do such mediation-work.[2] In this case it could be one of the most important approaches to motivate culprits to confess. If victims are expected to grant forgiveness, which argumentation could convince them to come up to this expectation? It only will be possible to ask them to excuse the culprit by complying with a commandment that frequently will ask too much of them. But if culprits are expected to confess, forgiveness can be offered. At least the churches have the chance to do this. In the instance of the South Africa's Truth and Reconciliation Commission 1996–1998 even forgiveness in the meaning of legal amnesty was possible. The commission was empowered to grant amnesty to those people who committed even grave transgressions during the apartheid era under the condition that the crimes were politically motivated and there was full disclosure by the person seeking amnesty. This is quite an extraordinary case although it is not unique and has been imitated several times. Also the Federal Republic of Yugoslavia tried to install a Truth and Reconciliation Commission in 2002 based on the model of South Africa, which unfortunately did not succeed. But the church has a kind of forgiveness to offer aside legal amnesty and the forgiveness by the victim. Let us use the term sacramental for this kind of forgiveness, which should not be underestimated. Of course sometimes it will not suffice, especially if culprits do not have any religious background. Then it will be necessary to find a substitute for full reconciliation.[3] But if the chance is given to motivate real acknowledgement and confession of guilt by getting the transcendent dimension in the process it should be used.

The biblical text itself gives us examples of situations prepared to reconciliation by the offer of forgiveness. One of them is the experience of the earliest Christian community as it is reported in the Acts of the Apostles. The trial and the crucifixion of Jesus could have become the source of bitter revenge among

2 A collection of examples is given in Weingardt, 2007 and also in Brocker, 2008.

3 The essay of G. Prüller-Jagenteufel in this volume is concerned with the possibility and necessity of such a substitute in Bonhoeffer's approach.

his disciples. And indeed there has always been the temptation to abuse the cross to rectify feelings and actions of vengeance, for example against Jews. However the behavior of the community in Jerusalem is completely different. Peter for example addressed his audience in his Pentecostal sermon by saying: "You have taken Jesus by lawless hands, have him crucified and put to death." (Acts 2,23) Straight afterwards he invites the same people to join the Christian community saying: "For the promise is to you and to your children." (Acts 2,39). This seems to be quite astonishing.

I suppose this behavior springs from what had happened before. Peter had become aware of his own guilt concerning the death of his master. He even had been forced by Jesus' gaze to acknowledge his fault. But this guilt had been forgiven to him on the Easter morning without any claims or demands. What's more there is no accusation or reproach. I think the assumption is justified this experience of unconditional forgiveness granted by the denied, abandoned and killed Lord enabled the young church to practice a new way in dealing with guilt and failure. According to the gospel of John the community of Jesus' disciples received the Holy Spirit just at the same moment, when Jesus spoke his forgiving Easter-shalom. Thus forgiveness has to be estimated to be the origin of a new spirit.

Frits DeLange concludes: "In the eyes of the Christian tradition, human beings are before everything else receivers of forgiveness, who offer forgiveness (Matthew 18:21–35). This view is no longer very popular in our liberal culture - if it ever was popular." (DeLange, 2004: 162) Is there any reason for a decrease of the popularity of this view? May be one reason is that liberal, modern people do not like the idea of being dependent on anything which is beyond their control. In fact forgiveness is something we cannot demand or acquire. Thus I am dependent on the placatory attitude of the person whose debtor I am. But since we have experienced unconditional forgiveness and have been able to accept it we get the capability to confess and to give a push to faltering processes of reconciliation. Received forgiveness is a strong encouragement that even makes us capable of offering forgiveness.

That is exactly what is meant by Bonhoeffer writing: "Acknowledgement of guilt is based only on the grace of Christ, because of Christ's reaching out for those who have fallen." (Bonhoeffer, 2009: 135)

Within conflict-scenarios usually the church itself will not be the culprit who has to confess. But it will be more convincing in motivating others to confess if the witness of forgiving grace does not remain hypothetically. The most compelling case for forgiving grace is the sincere acknowledgement of its own faults by the church. Thus it is of enormous importance - not only for the church itself

- that the Christian community asks forgiveness in public. John Paul II. said in his prayer in front of the Western Wall in Jerusalem on 26th March 2000: "We are deeply saddened by the behavior of those who in the course of history have caused these children of yours to suffer, and asking your forgiveness we wish to commit ourselves to genuine brotherhood with the people of the Covenant." This is one example of the realization of the acknowledgement of guilt mentioned by Bonhoeffer, another one is the request for pardon of the church at the beginning of Lent 2000. Such steps have to be taken also in the future because only a church confessing guilt can be a credible witness of the experience of forgiveness in advance.

References

Arendt, H, 1989. *The Human condition*, Chicago: University of Chicago Press.

Arinze, C. F.A. 2002. *Religions for Peace. A Call for Solidarity to the Religions of the World*, Michigan: Doubleday.

Bonhoeffer, D. 2009. *Ethics*. Ed. by Clifford J. Green (Dietrich Bonhoeffer Works English, Volume 6), Minneapolis: Fortress Press.

Bonhoeffer, D. 2010. Prologue: An Account at the Turn of the Year 1942–1943: After Ten Years. In: Bonhoeffer D. *Letters and Papers from Prison*. Ed. by John W. de Gruchy (Dietrich Bonhoeffer Works English, Volume 8), Minneapolis: Fortress Press, pp. 37–52.

Brocker, M. (ed.). 2008. *Friedensstiftende Religionen? Religion und Deeskalation politischer Konflikte*, Wiesbaden: Verlag für Sozialwissenschaften.

De Lange, F. 2004. Room for Forgiveness? A Theological Perspective. In: *Incredible Forgiveness. Christian Ethics between Fanaticism and Reconciliation*, edited by Didier Pollefeyt, Leuven: Peeters, pp. 161–182.

Hennecke, Ch. 1997. *Die Wirklichkeit der Welt erhellen. Ein ökumenisches Gespräch mit Dietrich Bonhoeffer über die ekklesiologische Perspektive der Moralverkündigung*, Paderborn: Bonifatius.

Prüller-Jagenteufel, G. 2004. *Befreit zur Verantwortung. Sünde und Versöhnung in der Ethik Dietrich Bonhoeffer's*, Münster: LIT Verlag.

Weingardt, M. 2007. *Religion macht Frieden. Das Friedenspotential von Religionen in politischen Gewaltkonflikten*, Stuttgart: Kohlhammer.

"RESTRAINING POWER" AGAINST EVIL AND "SCARRING OVER" OF GUILT. BONHOEFFERIAN REMARKS ON "PENULTIMATE" STEPS TOWARD RECONCILIATION

Gunter Prüller-Jagenteufel, Wienna

In this paper we will explore a different side of Bonhoeffer's theology, complementary to the more church-based theology of reconciliation which Wilhelm Guggenberger has presented earlier in this book.[1] Bonhoeffer's ethical theology always sees both sides: the eschatological reality of God's grace and the "this-worldliness" of our lives and our secular reality. It is clear to him, therefore, that even forgiveness and reconciliation, which are eschatological realities in the strictest sense of the word, have to begin "here and now".[2]

1. Responsibility in the penultimate

Especially in the last two years of his life Bonhoeffer's concentrated on the "this-worldliness" of Christianity and theology, without separating them from God. He considers the worldly reality, the "penultimate", as always deeply linked with God's reality, the "ultimate". And it is exactly this undissolvable connection between God and world that shapes his theological thoughts, especially his ethics. While Wilhelm Guggenberger's focus is more on the side of the "ultimate", I will focus on the penultimate, on our responsibility for "here and today". As Bonhoeffer puts it: "We are asking … about the penultimate in the life of a Christian" (Ethics, 152).[3]

As Catholics we have to be careful not to identify "penultimate" with the "natural" and "ultimate" with the "supernatural". Bonhoeffer's main effort is to show that these two realities are not separated from each other, even if they are absolutely different. His perspective is an eschatological one, but with emphasis

1 Cf. the article of Wilhelm Guggenberger in this book.

2 I have published a detailed and comprehensive study of Bonhoeffer's theology of reconciliation: Prüller-Jagenteufel, 2004. For this topic and for secondary literature cf. pp. 282–392; 555–564.

3 Since most of the quotations are taken from Bonhoeffer's *Ethics*, from here on quotations from that book will be specified by page alone.

on the fact that we already *are* in an eschatological status – even if not yet fully. The penultimate is on its way to the ultimate, to salvation:

> From this follows now something of decisive importance, that the penultimate must be preserved fort he sake of the ultimate. Arbitrary destruction of the penultimate seriously harms the ultimate. When, for example, a human life is deprived of the conditions that are part of being human, the justification of such a life by grace and faith is at least seriously hindered, if not made impossible. ... Given this fact ... it is necessary to care for the penultimate in order that the ultimate not be hindered by the penultimate's destruction. (160)

How do we connect this theology to Christian ethics? Actually Bonhoeffer's approach is incarnational:

> In Christ we are invited to participate in the reality of God and the reality of the world at the same time, the one not without the other. The reality of God is disclosed only as it places me completely into the reality of the world. But I find the reality of the world always already borne, accepted, and reconciled in the reality of God. That is the revelation of God in the human being Jesus Christ. The Christian ethic asks, then, how the reality of God and of the world that is given in Christ becomes real in our world. Ethics (55)
> Thus, especially as Christians we have to live responsibly "here and now":

> Christian life is the dawn of the ultimate in me, the life of Jesus Christ in me. But it is also always life in the penultimate, waiting for the ultimate. (168)

Even if our acting is ultimately eschatological, this does not release us from our responsibilities that our historical situation imposes on us. As he puts it in his "Account at the Turn of the Year 1942–43" (Letters, 37–52), the goal of Bonhoeffer himself is "how a coming generation is to go on living" (Letters, 42). The question for here and now is not "what is good as such, but what is good given life as it actually is and what is good fur us who are living." (246) Responsible action means sober, realistic action.

> Action in accord with reality is limited by our creatureliness. ... In our action we are bound by certain limitations from both the past and the future that cannot be leaped over. Our responsibility is not infinite but limited. (267)

Thus Bonhoeffer states the task of ethical action:

> The objective is not the application of some kind of limitless general principle. ... It cannot be our task to revolutionize the way the world operates, but at the

> given place to consider reality and do what is necessary. In so doing we must also ask what is possible, since we cannot always take the final step right away. (268)

Since we are not able to perceive our historical situation clearly but only in a kind of "twilight" (222), we can never decide between "the clearly recognized good and the clearly recognized evil" (247). Instead, we have to take the "very risk of the action itself, within the ambiguity of a historical situation" (248).

2. Restraining power against evil

Bonhoeffer understands responsible action in the penultimate as "preparing the way" (161) for Christ. This preparation has a counterpart that is mentioned only once and very briefly. It arises from Bonhoeffer's experience in the resistance against the Nazi regime: Bonhoeffer calls it with reference to 2 Thess. 2:7 (katexwn), the "restrainer"[4]:

> The 'restraining power' [das Aufhaltende] is the force that is made effective within history by God's rule of the world, which sets limits to evil. The 'restrainer' [der Aufhaltende] itself is not God and is not without guilt, but God uses it to protect the world from disintegration. (131)

The "restraining power", therefore, is limited to the area of the "penultimate"; it does not bring salvation from sin but God uses it to set limits to the consequences of sin – and by doing that he "preserves" (165) his creation for the "ultimate" salvation.

Bonhoeffer counts the restraining power among "the ordering power of the state" (131), but this does not mean that it is only found in a concrete political "government" (388). It is rather the *divine commission* to the state to act in this way, while in contrast it is the task of the church to work for reconciliation. We can see that very clearly in Bonhoeffer's own involvement in the resistance against the Nazi regime. It is not the state but the resistance which represents "'the restraining power ..., the remnant of ordering power, that still effectively resists

4 Cf. Ethics, 131–133; cf. also Prüller-Jagenteufel, 2004, 357–362; 555–564.

decay" (132). In saying this Bonhoeffer claims that the resistance movement in fact executes the "ordering power of the state" according to God's will.

As a penultimate reality, the restraining power itself is "not without guilt" (131), but it answers to the "necessities" of an "extraordinary situation" that are "beyond any possible regulation by law" (273). Bonhoeffer knew quite well that these are situations where straightforward solutions are impossible; namely where the human person has to act in a free and responsible manner – being a part of the world under the power of sin, but also being God's "ally" (132) in a world which is already reconciled by God's grace, a grace re-presented by the church, which draws together – if only implicitly – the restraining action with the "ultimate".

3. Reconciliation and "scarring over" of guilt

But responsibility is not only directed towards the future – acting out of conscience – but also into the past, meaning to take responsibility for what we have done. Thus, ethics deals on the one hand with the question of how to act rightly, and on the other hand with the question of what to do about what we have done wrongly – be it by mistake, be through our own fault, and for which we acknowledge our guilt. Bonhoeffer is very clear about the fact that the overcoming of guilt and sin is essentially the "ultimate" reality: "the justification of the sinner by grace alone" (164). But, at the same time, Bonhoeffer is quite adamant that this eschatological reality is already truly present and at work "here and now", as it is re-presented by the church, the community that follows Jesus Christ and therefore should act accordingly: making forgiveness and reconciliation a tangible reality.

Therefore we will concentrate on the question, whether or not there is an analogy to reconciliation in the "penultimate"; namely, in a political and social reality that defines itself as merely secular. Bonhoeffer discusses this question right after he talks about the "restraining power": He calls this way to overcome evil – if only penultimate and partial – the "scarring over" of guilt.[5] And just as the "restraining power" limits the consequences of guilt and sin in the here and now, the "scarring over" of guilt helps us to overcome conflict and to start anew in a cooperative way. Of course, this is not true and full reconciliation. That would depend on acts of confession, penitence and forgiveness, a process which can only be realized

5 Cf. Ethics, 142–145; cf. also Prüller-Jagenteufel, 2004, 358–362; 555–564.

through Christ. In the penultimate however, especially in politics, there has to be another way. This is because reconciliation is dependent on the good will of all parties, while “scarring over” is more easily initiated by the parties involved.

> The nations bear the heritage of their guilt. Yet by God’s gracious rule in history it can happen that what began as a curse can finally become a blessing on the nations, that out of usurped power can come justice, out of rebellion order, and out of bloodshed peace. (143)

Thus the wounds of the past “gradually ... scar over and heal” through a “slow turning toward justice, toward peace, even toward happiness for those once violated” (143). But one thing is clear:

> To be sure, the guilt is not justified, not removed, not forgiven. It remains, but the wound that it inflicted is scarred over. For the church and for individual believers there can only be a full break with guilt and a new beginning, through the gift of forgiveness of sin. But in the historical life of nations there can only be a slow process of healing. ... Something of forgiveness takes place, though it is only a weak shadow of the forgiveness that Jesus Christ gives to believers. (143–144)

This difference is clear and profound: While conversion and reconciliation are a radical break and a new beginning, “scarring over” involves a slow and gradual process of healing, with the effects of past guilt lessening but the “continuity with past guilt” (144) remaining. Even if a certain degree of (penultimate) justice is reached, there is no way to create (ultimate) justice in this way. What is more, we must not believe that this “scarring over” is automatically achieved in time alone. There are certain conditions: the most important being that no one can expect ultimate justice to be reached in this way. On the contrary:

> Here the claim to full atonement by the guilty for past injustice is renounced; here it is recognized that what is past can never be restored by human power, that the wheel of history can no longer be rolled back. ... This means giving up any illusion that one can, by punishment, undo what has been done. (144)

The critical part, therefore, is that those, who have suffered injustice have to renounce vengeance or retaliation, since this would lead to nothing but further injustice. “Not all wounds that were made can be healed; but it is critical that no further wounds be inflicted.” (144) On the other hand, we should not simply renounce our demands for justice. The minimal condition is that those who have acted unjustly cease to do so and truly start to act according to the principles of justice and peace:

> Where this does not happen, where injustice rules unchecked and inflicts ever-new wounds there can certainly be no talk about such forgiveness. Instead, our first concern must be to resist injustice and to convict the guilty of their guilt. (144)

Since society, especially the state, is not a subject that can make an act of faith in Christ, it is not able to carry out forgiveness and reconciliation in the full meaning of the word. Instead we see a profound difference between "scarring over" and reconciliation, which is why scarring over itself is not able to overpower sin but only its effects. On the other hand, these two processes are not incompatible. The "scarring over" is to bee seen rather as an analogy to the "restraining power": Both are "preparation" and therefore connected to God's grace – but in regard to preservation and not salvation; that is, on the level of penultimate, not ultimate reality.

4. Bonhoeffer's participation in the resistance against Nazism

It should be noted that Bonhoeffer himself knew quite well what he was talking about. He understood his participation in the political resistance against Hitler as making his own life part of the "restraining power"; on the other hand he also tried to promote the "scarring over" of the evil the Nazis had done. He wanted to participate in the building of a new social and political basis for Europe. He knew that any form of adequate retribution was impossible and that vengeance would not lead anywhere. He saw that the most important task was to remove the structures of injustice and build new institutions that would guarantee justice. Bonhoeffer's notion that "out of usurped power can come justice, out of rebellion order, and out of bloodshed peace" (143) is not to be seen as metaphysical romanticism[6] but rather as a justification of the resistance fighters' attempt to seize control over Germany by bringing about Hitler's death. The notion also points out the direction that Germany ought to take after the war.

6 This I state in contrast to Barbara Green. In Green, 1996.

5. Consequences for resolving political conflicts

What significance has Bonhoeffer's concept for us now? I will make a few comments with reference South African reconciliation processes.[7] I will also refer to Bonhoeffer's theology of reconciliation as presented in the article of Willhelm Guggenberger already mentioned. Many ideas between the two approaches are similar but significant differences between the two different perspectives should be underlined.

First of all, the "core grammar" (Daye, 2004, 7) of forgiveness is built on *truth*; thus the naming and articulation of the all the harm done is absolutely necessary. It is a big mistake to try to start with "forgetting", or at least "not talking about it any more". Rather "forgiveness begins with memory, in particular memory that contains a moral judgment of wrong, injustice, and injury" (Daye, 2004, 20).

This is also true for collective responsibility. The only adequate way to talk about guilt is not in the modes of accusation nor apology but of true confession and taking over of responsibility. The problem in our case is that there is not simply one guilty person who relates to one other person but usually a whole group, maybe even a nation, where guilt and innocence are distributed in a complex manner. Not every member has assumed personal guilt, but in being part of the group he or she is still to a certain extent responsible. So how can confession be undertaken? It would not do to look for the few who have committed the most heinous crimes to use them as scapegoats so that all others could feel innocent. This would be mere self-deception and would make true reconciliation impossible. What has to be done is to find a representative who is able to express the collective guilt, and to do this in a way that all the members can participate in the process doing this, thereby confessing in a symbolic way their own share of responsibility.

A famous example can be seen in one of the iconic photographs of the twentieth century: Willy Brandt, bending his knees in front of the Warsaw Ghetto. Here we also see the deep meaning of representation: It is not Brandt's personal guilt but the responsibility of the German people that is shown and recognized in a symbolic way. It underlines that no German could further deny what happened during the occupation and that all Germans should take on the burden of

7 The following part mainly refers to Daye, 2004.

responsibility – not only their personal one, but the shared responsibility of the German people.

A *second* step in such a process of reconciliation is the building of a *transitional justice framework*. This means, on the one hand, *restorative justice*; on the other hand; also *retributive justice*; namely the punishment of those who bear personal responsibility for war crimes (cf. Daye, 2004, 9). Even if full retribution cannot be realized, reconciliation cannot be reached without doing justice (at least symbolically) to the victims of injustice. Nevertheless, those victims have to be prepared to renounce full compensation, because this could well lead to even more injustice.

To give an example: After World War II and in so many other wars of past and present times "ethnic cleansing" has taken place. Although we consider the expulsion of an ethnic group as unjust, after some decades, it is practically impossible give the land back to the former owners; after one or more generations, it would only lead to a new act of injustice. What can and should be expected is the acknowledgement that the expulsion was unjust and that such an act will not be committed again. At least a symbolic retribution is indispensible. If such gestures express the true will to repent, they might prove to be the bases of a new relationship between former adversaries. The long path from "scarring over" to forgiveness, however, still has to be walked.

The *third* step on this scale would be to find *ways to heal*. Both parties are challenged to abandon their desire for vengeance and to arrive at a certain degree of "empathy for the humanity of the enemy" (Daye, 2004, 21). Empathy, however, does not mean sympathy. It rather means the acknowledgement that the adversary is likewise a human person. On this basis, it might be possible to start a new relationship and less conflict-ridden social coexistence.

Of course, all this is not yet full reconciliation; but it is at least a process that leads us towards a more peaceful and more human social life together. In our world today, this is a step whose healing power we should not underestimate. But we must all share in the efforts to bring it about; we must not leave it to the ruling class alone. Especially as Christians and as church people we are called to promote the necessary steps.

References

Bonhoeffer, D. 2005. *Ethics*. Ed. by Clifford J. Green (DBWE 6), Minneapolis: Fortress Press (quoted as: Ethics).

Bonhoeffer, D. 2010. *Letters and Papers from Prison*. Ed. by John W. de Gruchy, (DBWE 8) Minneapolis: Fortress Press (quoted as: Letters).

Daye, R. 2004. *Political Forgiveness. Lessons from Africa*, Marynoll: Orbis.

Prüller-Jagenteufel, G. 2004. *Befreit zur Verantwortung. Sünde und Versöhnung in der Ethik Dietrich Bonhoeffer's* (EthD 7), Münster: LIT.

Green, B. 1996. Die politische Dimension von Schuld und Versöhnung bei Dietrich Bonhoeffer. In: Huber W. (ed.): *Schuld und Versöhnung in politischer Perspektive. Dietrich-Bonhoeffer-Vorlesungen in Berlin*, Gütersloh: Kaiser, pp. 11–20.

RECONCILIATION IN CHURCH AND SOCIETY: CHURCH'S MINISTRY AS GOD'S RECONCILIATION AGENCY

Daniel G. Oprean, Osijek

Introduction

There is much talk in the world today about reconciliation. Yet in a global perspective the world looks more and more divided and unjust with every hour of the contemporary time. The thesis of this paper is that reconciliation is not only a topic to be spoken about, rather it is to be shown in a practical way. Addressing the captivity of the concept of reconciliation in its vertical dimension or in its limitation to the church's internal business horizontal dimension, this paper argues that we would be able to explore possible ways for the church to become a model of reconciliation, only if the Church will overcome the artificial limitations of reconciliation both in its thinking and its theology, not only in theory but also in practical action in society. The church has to mirror the example of Christ being an embodiment of the three cardinal virtues: faith, love and hope.[1]

The proposal of this paper is that the three cardinal virtues are the basis and motivation for the threefold reconciliation ministry of the Church to the world, namely, education, social care, and prophetic ministry. The framework and lens for the perspective of this paper is Christ event, his *kenosis* in incarnation being the model for the Church's identification with the world.

Captivity of Reconciliation in its Vertical Dimension

The first aspect under scrutiny is the captivity of reconciliation in its vertical dimension, namely, the reduction of reconciliation to the relationship of the one with God.[2] It is clear from the Bible that reconciliation starts at the individual level

1 John R.W Stott, *The Message of Thessalonians: Preparing for the coming King* (Illinois: Inter-Varsity Press 1991), 29.

2 Miroslav Volf, "The Social Meaning of Reconciliation," in *Religion in Eastern Europe*, Volume XVIII, Number 3, June 1998, 23. He says: "There are two basic ways in which the social agenda

(Ro. 10: 9, 10, 13), yet it is equally true that it does not stop at this level. Apostle Paul emphasizes in his theology this equilibrium between the individual and corporate or communal aspects of reconciliation. Still it is necessary to speak of the other danger in which the church can be trapped, the isolation from the world, considering reconciliation a possibility only for the "insiders." This attempt was described rightly by Dietrich Bonhoeffer in *The Cost of Discipleship*, as a form of worldliness,[3] inappropriate for a disciple of Christ. Therefore this captivity of reconciliation in its short horizontal dimension will be discussed in the next section.

Captivity of Reconciliation as only an Internal Practice of the Church

The church could be trapped in a more subtle form of captivity of reconciliation, namely, to consider reconciliation only as an internal business of the church.[4] A good illustration of this kind of mentality concerning God's love is the case of the prophet Jonah, in the Old Testament. Many times in its history the church suffered by the so called "Jonah syndrome." Jonah, even if he was a prophet of God, was a rebel,[5] not listening to the call of God that was very clear: "Go to the great city of Nineveh and preach against it, because its wickedness has come up before me" (Jnh. 1: 2).

Even if his disobedience could be motivated by his love for his country and people,[6] it is still disobedience and misunderstanding of God's character as God

of the church has been isolated from the message of reconciliation. The first way reduces the doctrine of reconciliation to the *reconciliation of the soul with God* and is favored by pietistic or socially conservative evangelicals."

3 Dietrich Bonhoeffer, *The Cost of Discipleship* (New York: SCM Press Ltd, 1959), 48. "The attempt to flee from the world turning out in being a subtle form of love for the world"

4 Joon-Sik Park, "Ecclesiologies in Creative Tension: The Church as Ethical and Missional Reality in Richard Niebuhr and John H. Yoder" in *International Review of Mission,* vol. XCII, No. 366, July 2003, 341–342. He says: The Church must be constantly reminded of its solidarity with and mission to the universal community, lest it fall into the danger of 'church-centricity' and introversion. Being a fallible community itself in need of grace, it is to remain humble, and not to slip into self-exaltation and false pride."

5 William M. Pickard, *Rather Die Than Live – Jonah* (New York: Education and Cultivation Division Board of Global Ministry, 1974), 23. For a psychological profile see Andre Lacocque and Pierre-Emmanuel Lacocque, *The Jonah Complex* (Atlanta: John Knox Press, 1981), 126.

6 Frank E. Gaebelein, *Four Minor Prophets: Their Message for Today* (Chicago: Moody Press, 1970), 72.

of the entire world not only the private God of Israel. Here is the first parallel with the church. The church too has received a call from God: "Go and make disciples of all nations..." (Mt. 28: 19a). In Jonah's case the disobedience to the call of God led to lethargy, expressed in his sleep during the storm on the sea: "the Lord sent a great wind…and such violent storm…But Jonah…lay down and fell into a deep sleep" (Jnh 1:4–5). Here is the second parallel to the church. Not obeying God's command and isolating herself in the privacy of its worship of a God who has a part in each believer's life, the church could fall into the same lethargy as Jonah.

The sleep of disobedience can be seen in many cases through the silence of the church and of its "silent saints,"[7] in many times of its history, in the vital issues of the society around, and in its comfortable narcosis of a theology of pharisaic[8] self – righteousness.[9] Back to Jonah, if the first symptom of his syndrome was lethargy, the second symptom was pride. When he was asked by the sailors, about his identity he proudly tells them the following: "I am a Hebrew and I worship the Lord, the God of heaven, who made the sea and the land" (Jnh 1: 9). The parallel with the church is obvious.[10] When the church sleeps on/in her theology, tradition, or worship it is possible even blindly to be proud of her activism.

In conclusion, the church will overcome her rebellion, lethargy, and pride only by the way of her repentance which will lead to resurrection, a resurrection as the one of Jonah who was three days and three nights under the waters. The resurrection of the Church is to be the starting point of a fresh understanding of God's incommensurable love for the world (*cosmos*). The repentance of the church will

7 John R. W. Stott, *Our Guilty Silence* (Michigan: Grand Rapids, William B. Eerdmans Publishing Company, 1967), 9.

8 Gaebelein, 70. In this context is worth to be mentioned the fact that "instead of going five hundred miles northeast to Nineveh, Jonah set out on a journey of two thousand miles due west." This reminds the admonition of Christ addressed to the Pharisees in Matthew 23: 15: "You travel over land and sea."

9 Don W. Hillis, *The Book of Jonah: Jonah Speaks Again* (Michigan: Grand Rapids, Baker Books House, 1967), 43–45. He says: "Beyond question one of the great weaknesses in the church today is the presence of Jonah's spirit – that self-righteous spirit which puts doctrine and dogma ahead of compassion for the souls of men is evident on every hand….It is altogether possible to become indignant at the sin of the world and yet do nothing to reach the sinner with the only message of deliverance that will help him."

10 Pickard, 39. He says: "Jonah was as many of us today: professing a great faith while living by small concepts."

lead to the recovering of the "hermeneutics of humility,"[11] acknowledging anew that to be a Christian in relation to the world, is to be as D.T Niles said: "a beggar telling another beggar where to find bread."[12] These considerations lead us to the discussion of the Church as God's reconciling agency in and to the world.

The Church as God's Reconciliation Agency

The status of the church as an agency of reconciliation in and to the world is defined and validated, as discussed in the sections above, by her understanding and practice of reconciliation within internal life. One of the areas with direct correspondence to the practice of reconciliation in and to the world is the practice of authority within the church. The illustration for this is the way in which Moses and Christ used the authority given to them by God.

Moses was a man of great authority. Yet he disqualified himself through the misuse of authority.[13] He is challenged to use his authority (expressed in the presence of the staff in his hand[14]) to serve people. It was the purpose of God to teach Moses and his people the power of love and of service. Moses had to serve them the water as a demonstration of his self-sacrifice and love for the people loved by God, to show mercy instead of judgment. [15]

11 Kevin J. Vanhoozer, *Is There A Meaning in This Text?* (Michigan: Grand Rapids, Zondervan Publishing House, 1998), 463.

12 Pickard, 53. Also, Robert J. Schreiter, C.PP.S. *The Ministry of Reconciliation: Spirituality & Strategies* (Maryknoll, New York: Orbis Books, 1998), 116.

13 The Lord said to Moses, "Take the staff and, and you and your brother Aaron gather the assembly together. Speak to that rock before their eyes and it will pour out its water. You will bring the water out of the rock for the community so they and their livestock can drink." (Nu. 20: 7–8)

14 Aaron Wildavscky, *The Nursing Father: Moses as a Political Leader* (USA: The University of Alabama Press, 1984). He says: "The rod represents a power that may be wielded but, like the name must not be abused." 38

15 B. Maarsingh, *Numbers: A Practical Commentary* (Grand Rapids, Michigan: Eerdmans Publishing Company, 1987). "This was God's intention, a change from his attitude in the case of earlier rebellion: here mercy was over judgment." 71.

Unfortunately, instead of this demonstration of love, Moses demonstrated unbelief,[16] unkindness[17] and by substituting "force for faith" [18] as a way of solving the problem, replacing God's solution, he "was guilty of the worst form of idolatry – self-worship."[19] God said to Moses to speak to the rock but he spoke to the people, and struck the rock twice.[20]

The Gospels are witnessing about the second Moses, Jesus Christ, who demonstrated that love, belief and kindness were a reality in his life, in a practical way. One of the most expressive texts in this concern is in the gospel of John.

> Jesus knew that the Father had put all things under his power and that he had come from God and was returning to God; so he got up from the meal, took off his outer clothing and wrapped a towel around his waist. After that, he poured water into a basin and began to wash his disciples' feet, drying them with the towel that was wrapped around him (13: 3–5)

The Church has always been between these two theologies: the theology of staff and the theology of towel, and both of them would be reflected in the way the church relates to the world.[21] Myron Augsburger says:

> The work of any community is to discern how its members should hold justice and mercy in common, and then pass patterns of justice and mercy onto the

16 Gordon J Wenham, *Numbers: An Introduction and Commentary* (Leicester: Intervarsity Press, 1981), 151. Also, Philip J. Budd, Numbers, in *Word Biblical Commentary,* edited by David A. Hubbard, Glenn W. Barker (Waco: Word Books Publisher, 1984), 218.

17 Irving L. Jensen, *Numbers: Journey to God's Rest Land* (Chicago: Moody Press, 1964), 184.

18 Wildavscky, 156–157.

19 Ibid. "Moses took the staff from the Lord's presence, just as he commanded him. He and Aaron gathered the assembly together in front of the rock and Moses said to them, 'Listen, you rebels, must we bring you water out of this rock. Then Moses raised his arm and struck the rock twice with his staff. (Nu. 20: 9–11)."

20 C H. Macintosh, *Notes on the Book of Numbers (*New York: The Bible Truth Press). He says: "It was a grave mistake for Moses to smite the rock a second time – a mistake to use his rod in the matter at all," 396. Also, James Philip, Numbers, in *The Communicator's Commentary*, edited by Lloyd J. Ogilvie (Waco: Word Books, Publisher, 1987), 224. This provision for their need is yet another signal evidence of the meaning of the grace of God. Water for the thirsty, bread for the sinful – this is grace, and in the story of these verses we have and illustration of something that is fulfilled and magnified in the gospel of Christ.

21 Karl Barth, *Against the Stream* (London: SCM Press, 1954), 70.

> future community. Justice that is punitive without reconciliation is little short of tyranny. Authentic justice seeks to correct the problem.[22]

Regarding the question of how the mandate of *diakonia* is to be fulfilled to and in the world, in a practical way, and some of the areas where the church should develop a strategy, will be the subject of the next section.

Threefold Ministry of the Church to the World

If the church succeeds to overcome the captivity of reconciliation in its vertical and short horizontal dimensions, and if she recovers the kind of attitude and spirit that Christ had in his relationships with humankind, then and only then will the church be prepared and equipped to do the best in her social involvement in society. In this section, therefore, it will be argued that there are three domains in which the church should concentrate her attention and efforts in regard to her ministry of reconciliation in and to the world: education, social care and prophetic ministry.

The Education of Faith Ministry

This education of faith is showing faith working in real life in such a way that the convert can enter himself in a life of faith with God, having the word of God as his mirror (Ja. 1: 22–25). The task of the church is to live out the faith in the context of togetherness which is the real *koinonia* of the church and then the Lord will "add." For the early church this did not come out of any evangelistic strategy, rather it was totally the work of the Holy Spirit, through the Word of God embodied in the message of the church's life.

The Diakonia Ministry

Once the church is clear about her theology concerning her social role, she will be able *to see* the needs. When she sees the needs, she can start to elaborate strategies

22 Augsburger, *The Robe of God: Reconciliation, the Believers Essential* (Scottdale: Herald Press, 2000), 98.

for social assistance. Especially in the Third and Fourth World countries,[23] the Christian Gospel should mean actions not merely words, food in soup-kitchens not merely prayers, shelters for homeless not merely sermons, social programs for development not merely evangelistic strategies. All of this would be true expressions of Christian love.

When the church has the conviction that when she does all these to the poor, oppressed, homeless, sick, she does it all for Christ, then truly the church is the embodiment of God's Kingdom. Christ himself said that at his return people will be separated by the way they acted concerning the "least brothers" of Him, with whom he fully identified (Mt. 25: 31–46).[24]

Prophetic Ministry

The prophetic ministry of the church is to promote hope in the world. The church in herself, as presence and embodiment of the values of the Kingdom of God, is a sign of hope for and in the world. Yet besides her presence the church is to point to the One in whom all things are possible. Pointing towards God and to what He has done in Christ means bringing hope in the midst of world despair. The prophetic ministry of the church is based on the all-encompassing work of Christ to reconcile humankind to God (Ro. 5: 3–8).[25] To be a community of hope also means for the church to let people of the world know that they are with God and not without him.[26] Of course humankind is fallen, but in Christ, God overcomes the power of sin over humanity and restores human beings.

23 Ronald J. Sider, *Rich Christians in an Age of Hunger: A Biblical Study* (Illinois: Inter-Varsity Press, 1977), 33.

24 Augsburger, *The Peace Maker* (Nashville: Abington Press, 1987), 50: "For I was hungry and you were obese, I was thirsty and you kept filling your swimming pools, I was naked and you were discussing fall fashions, I was sick and you said, 'Let him call a doctor,' I was in prison and you said, 'It serves him right."

25 Bela Vassady, Gleanings in *How Karl Barth Changed My Mind,* Edited by Donald K. McKim (Michigan: Grand Rapids, Eerdmans Publishing Company, 1986), 33. "The beachhead mission of the church, its role as a prophetic critic, should always be subordinated to its mission as a bridge, that is, as agent of reconciliation."

26 Karl Barth, *The Word of God and the Word of Man* (New York: Harper& Brothers Publishers, 1928), 169.

Conclusion

Reconciliation is God's initiative towards humankind. As such it is not only for the church but for the entire world. To reduce reconciliation to one's relationship with God or with his community of so-called "saved ones "means actually to deny God's eternal plan of reconciliation, powerfully displayed and revealed in the Christ event.

When the church understands that reconciliation has not only an individual but also a corporal dimension, not only a vertical but also a horizontal dimension - that Christ is the center of the church and as such He is also the center of the world - then the church is prepared to be God's agency of reconciliation in the world. Only when based on such understanding and acknowledgment will the church be a community of faith, love and hope.

Then the threefold ministry of the church in education of faith, in social care of love and in prophetic ministry of hope will open the possibility for the world to acknowledge "now, through the church, the manifold wisdom of God…according to the eternal purpose which he accomplished in Christ Jesus our Lord" and that "in him and through the faith in him we may approach God with freedom and confidence." (Ephesians 3: 10–12).

Bibliography

Augsburger, M. S. 1987. *The Peacemaker.* Nashville: Abington Press.

________________2000. *The Robe of God: Reconciliation, the Believers Essential.* Scottdale: Herald Press.

Barth, K. 1928. *The Word of God and the Word of Man.* New York: Harper& Brothers Publishers.

__________1954. *Against the Stream.* London: SCM Press.

Bonhoeffer, D. 1959. *The Cost of Discipleship.* New York: SCM Press Ltd.

Budd, P. J. 1984. Numbers. In: *Word Biblical Commentary.* Edited by David A. Hubbard, Glenn W. Barker. Waco: Word Books Publisher, 1984.

Gaebelein, F. E. 1970. *Four Minor Prophets: Their Message for Today.* Chicago: Moody Press.

Hillis, D. W. 1967. *The Book of Jonah: Jonah Speaks Again.* Grand Rapids, Michigan: Baker Books House.

Jensen, I. L. 1964. *Numbers: Journey to God's Rest Land.* Chicago: Moody Press.

Lacocque, A. and Lacocque, P.-E. 1981. *The Jonah Complex.* Atlanta: John Knox Press.

Maarsingh, B. 1987. *Numbers: A Practical Commentary*. Grand Rapids, Michigan: Eerdmans Publishing Company.

Macintosh, C. H. *Notes on the Book of Numbers.* New York: The Bible Truth Press.

Park, Joon-Sik. 2003. Ecclesiologies in Creative Tension: The Church as Ethical and Missional Reality in Richard Niebuhr and John H. Yoder. In: *International Review of Mission,* vol. XCII, No. 366, July 2003.

Pickard, W. M. 1974. *Rather Die Than Live – Jonah*. New York: Education and Cultivation Division Board of Global Ministry.

Philip, J. 1987. Numbers. In: *The Communicator's Commentary*. Edited by Lloyd J. Ogilvie. Waco: Word Books, Publisher, 1987.

Schreiter, R. J. 1998. *The Ministry of Reconciliation: Spirituality & Strategies.* Maryknoll, New York: Orbis Books.

Sider, R. J. 1977. *Rich Christians in an Age of Hunger: A Biblical Study*. Illinois: Inter-Varsity Press.

Stott, J. R. W. 1967. *Our Guilty Silence.* Grand Rapids, Michigan: William B. Eerdmans Publishing Company.

_____________.1991. *The Message of Thessalonians: Preparing for the coming King*. Illinois: Inter-Varsity Press.

Vanhoozer, K. J. 1998. *Is There A Meaning in This Text?* Grand Rapids, Michigan: Zondervan Publishing House.

Vassady, B. 1986. Gleanings. In: *How Karl Barth Changed My Mind.* Edited by Donald K. McKim. Grand Rapids, Michigan: Eerdmans Publishing Company, 1986.

Volf, M. 1996. *Exclusion and Embrace: A Theological Exploration of Identity, Otherness, and Reconciliation*. Nashville: Abingdon Press.

____________.1998. The Social Meaning of Reconciliation. In: *Religion in Eastern Europe*, Volume XVIII, Number 3, June 1998.

Wenham, G. J. 1981. *Numbers: An Introduction and Commentary*. Leicester: Intervarsity Press.

Wildavscky, A. 1984. *The Nursing Father: Moses as a Political Leader*. USA: The University of Alabama Press.

FORGIVENESS ALLOWS A NEW CREATION

Mari Jože Osredkar, Ljubljana

Our goal in this paper is a theological argument for the concept of forgiveness. Because the essential element of Christian doctrine is Jesus' call to exercise forgiveness, this paper will base on the text of the Gospel. Jesus' command to forgive others is seen in the Gospel of Matthew: "When someone slaps your right cheek, turn and let that person slap your other cheek. If someone sues you for your shirt, give up your coat as well" (Mt 5, 39–40). For many critics of Christian doctrine, however, Jesus' request for unconditional forgiveness leads to the position that Christianity in its design is doomed to collapse. So the question explored here becomes: Is forgiveness a sign of victory or a sign of defeat?

The search for this answer divides our presentation into two parts. In the first part, we will show that forgiveness is renunciation of one's self. In the second part, we will see that forgiveness allows a new creation of subjects which find themselves still in relationship, one to the other.

Forgiveness is renunciation of one's self

The first concept of forgiveness we find in the opening pages of the Bible. Here is a beautiful example of God's forgiveness: "The Lord called out to the man and asked: 'Where are you?'" (Gn 3, 9). This text defines that "to forgive" means looking for the other and calling out his name. In fact, this kind of forgiveness expresses the fact that can be realized in the relationship; and at the same time, it expresses the desire to conserve the relationship with the other. God always forgives man and repeatedly searches for him and calls him by name, although man has proven himself bad in turning away from Him. The Bible text encourages man to become like God; in order to become as God. In a biblical context, this instance of "forgiveness" equates to becoming holy. In Leviticus we read: "I am the Lord your God, and you must dedicate yourselves to me and be holy, just as I am holy" (Lv 11, 44). So man models himself on God when he forgives another, looks for that person, and waits for him to return.

In the Gospel of Luke we have the inspirational story of the father and the prodigal son[1]. The former awaits a son, who has disappeared, to return. The father had handed over an inheritance to this son who squandered everything. He returned to the father, poor and beaten down. In spite of his son's condition, the father can forgive him and welcome him home because the father had already renounced all that had belonged to himself. On the other hand, a second son, who kept his inheritance intact, begrudged his sibling's return. He was unable to forgive him because he was unable to renounce the property his father had given him. Unlike the father, second son cannot express forgiveness for the estrangement.

We can say thus, that to forgive means to renounce one's own property, one's own rights, one's own will. Forgiveness is renunciation of one's self. In fact, each of our relationships with others is always an abandonment of our own sovereignty. Man forgives, when, in spite of a conflict, he still wants to keep a relationship with his partner. Forgiveness should not thus be considered only in the context of disagreement. Forgiveness, as the renunciation of one's self, is in the broad sense of the word already one's accepting another as a partner in the relationship.

But, we must be aware that taking the other for a partner means to accept responsibility. Anyone who is linked to another is consequently obligated. To say "you" to another, to look into his face, requires a decision and the responsibility for it (Lévinas, 1982, 1992). So we come to the conclusion that: to forgive the other means to adopt the other as a partner in the relationship and thus not to be alone. It also means to accept responsibility for him and, at the same time, to renounce one's own self. So, forgiveness is not easy. The easier route to follow is not to take another for a partner in the relationship and remain alone. Forgiveness with its process involving the other can be truly more difficult. Why, therefore, does one forgive the other? This is because one always needs the other, because one is incomplete. Mutual acceptance or affiliation is insurance for the achievement of both partners. The partner in relationship to you joins you as yet another in the place of incompleteness.

Let's consider now the notion of "human imperfection". At first glance imperfection reflects a failure of man. It points to a major flaw in an individual's development. Whereas the sovereignty of the individual is considered as the highest value, the dependence on the other is often perceived as a less than preferred

1 Lk 15, 11–32

value. Perhaps the praise acknowledged in completeness or wholeness is also the origin of the notion that forgiveness is viewed in its negative connotation. Perhaps it is precisely this reason why many thinkers have represented salvation as something or as Someone who is able to transform the incomplete being into perfection. However, by this logic, the man who resolved his failures does not need anything more, even salvation. Expressed in biblical language, we can say that a saved man would no longer need a God. But this is complete nonsense. To be saved actually means to live with God. In such a situation it is possible to have two options: attempt to resolve one's own failures with no need of another man or God; or accept imperfection and seek God's help and close human proximity.

We see these two positions when we consider Jesus' words: "If you want to save your life, you will destroy it. But if you give up your life for me and for the good news, you will save it" (Mr 8, 35). The person, desirous of leaving his imperfection, desirous of leaving the connection with the other, is destroying his life. The only veritable life is offered to those who accept their own imperfection and acknowledge the imperfection of those persons in close proximity to them as a value. By the renunciation of one's self and one's own sovereignty when accepting a relationship with another, the individual in fact finds life. When we talk about veritable life, we don't think about the quantity of days lived, but the quality of life lived. And because we intend to live means to be in a relationship, the realization of the individual is not dependent on the number of relations, but on the way all the relations live or play themselves out. Man can "raise himself up" only if he accepts his status as incomplete. The greatest human weakness would be, therefore, his perfection. Just the "imperfect man" identifies his status with its "shortcomings" as something good; because of his limitations, he finds himself related to others.

In fact, forgiveness is not renunciation of one's superior position, but recognition of the reality of equality with others. Forgiveness is not the renunciation of independence but recognition of the need to be with the other. The person seeking perfection for the salvation of his life lives an illusion; and he does not recognize his own status of imperfection. His mistake is, to be sure, that he can become perfect.

Why do people imprison themselves in their own egoism? The passage from the illusion of perfection to the reality of imperfection is similar to the transition from the quantity to the quality of relationships. It seems that those, who are not active in relations, have not been able to implement this transition. The man, who lives in the illusion that he is perfect, makes selections from the "others". He chooses those who, in his opinion, could help him in his development, the rest of the world does not exist for him; thus he strives for the elimination of "non useful" persons. That individual is not aware that he is already in relationships with both kinds of partners, persons who he assumes (falsely) can assist him to grow and others whom he does not yet recognized who would be able to assist him. In the case of the "imperfect" man, however, the dynamic is opposite. Connecting with others, with whom he is found to be linked in life, is an opportunity for the development of himself. Relationship does not represent completeness for him, but acceptance of the imperfection of others, or in other words, he recognizes and acknowledges that he cannot live otherwise than in connection with others. "The other," in fact, does not complete him, but leads him to deeper knowledge of his status of imperfection. A partner therefore is not "exploited" with the intention that the subject himself becomes perfect, but that the relationship helps him in the progression toward the attitude of humility or deeper knowledge of one's own imperfection. This is possible only in the case, if and when, "the other" as a partner remains the "other"; when the other is not "one of the others", but he is unique.

How therefore does the subject realize the transition from quantity to quality of relationships? The person, who uses others for his interest, finds himself in the relationship of the order of quantity. The relationship is of the order of quality, when the subject does not have any specific interest with the partner and the other is not exploited for the survival of the subject; his relationship to the other of the order of quality is in reality the same as his relationship to God. Forgiveness, understood in this way, is very close to the Gospel's call for self-denial. Jesus says to his disciples: "If any of you want to be my followers, you must forget about yourself. You must take up your cross and follow me" (Mt 16, 24; Mr 8, 34; Lk 9, 23).

Forgiveness allows a New Creation

Relational theology[2] posits the axiom that subjects are born in relationship. To live means to be in relationship with another. In fact, subjects are repositioning themselves constantly in the relationship, because this situation is never static, but is always changing due to the two dimensions in the relationship: the presence and the

2 By the expression "relational theology" we refer to the thinking of the French theologian Guy Lafon and his disciples.

absence (Osredkar 2008). The change in relationship results in an ever-fluctuating "change distance" between subjects, who encounter each other always in a new light. So, we can speak about the always-new relationship and the always-new subjects. Specifically we shall focus now on how forgiveness alters the relationship and how it impacts the positioning of subjects in relationship. Forgiveness can promote the continuation of the relationship and of life because, as we know, to forgive is to denounce self-sufficiency. The relationship underscores the searching for the partner; and the man, who forgives another, recognizes at the same time his partner in a new light. The seeking out of the other enables him to change, experiencing a new birth. Anyone who does not forgive does not lead his brother to a new birth, so the other is left unchanged when "this anyone" leaves him alone. In that light can be understood well the words of Apostle Paul when he says: "Anyone who belongs to Christ", you could say, anyone who forgives and asking forgiveness, as teaches Christ "is a new person" (creation) (2Cor 5, 17–21). To be a new man means that he recognizes that he cannot be alone – it means a search for the father, or for the brother or for the sister. In this sense can be understood also Jesus' answer to Nicodemus, that you must be born from above (Jn 3, 3–8). The first is the birth of the individual; the second is the birth of communion with others.

As a life and a relationship, forgiveness is a gift too. As no one has earned his existence, so also no one has merited forgiveness or the new birth. The lost son in the Gospel text did not earn the forgiveness of his father. It was a gift. God forgives man at all times. In fact He allows him to be every time a new person, a new creation. Every time He forgives him, He creates him as a new being.

We can find a parallel also between God's forgiveness and God's creation. God creates a being that can answer him. This means that this being is created free. Freedom is an essential condition of the person that can say "you" to the "other". God's creation gets real meaning if it is understood in the context of the relationship, i.e. a commitment between God and human beings. Christians believe in "God the father, the creator of heaven and Earth" and under these terms we understand first the diversity between us and God, but also the dependencies (Ocvirk 1990, 10). God does all out of love. If, therefore, God created beings equal to himself, this would be just love of himself. However, love between individual beings exists only in diversity. Therefore, creation is not a duplication or an effusion of the Creator. "Love enables others to be. If God does not renounce being all things, He would not be love. The creation must be different from the creator and it must be free, not just his reflection, his extension or his satellite. Love wants the other "to be" and "to come" from him, but not to be his slave" (Ocvirk 1990).

Let us consider a theological interpretation of God's forgiveness to support our argument. God gave man a life, a world, and everything on it for his use. He concluded with a commitment that He will protect and defend him. He but asks of man that he would return the love, that he respect and listen to Him. In essence, this is not required, but again a gift. With this commandment, God told him how he can survive. And what does man? He breaks the commitment with God. He breaks the link to the origin of life. And yet he does not die. He receives a new gift: a new commitment and a new life.

The French language affords us a wonderful translation or explanation of the English "forgiveness." The word "pardonner" consists of "par" meaning "over", while "donner" means "to give". Pardonner means to give again, to give more, to give over. This then is the essence of forgiveness: when you make a mistake; nothing is over or complete. In fact, everything is incomplete. One, who asks for pardon, should be incomplete to be able to receive a new gift, that is, continuation. And in God's forgiving, He offers man an even greater gift: God approaches man and accepts him again (Lc 15, 11–32).

Conclusion

In the beginning of this paper we pose the question: Is forgiveness a sign of victory or a sign of defeat? In order "to love your enemies and pray for anyone who mistreats you" (Mt5, 44), one really may find, at first glance, that that Christianity in its design is doomed to collapse. However, we showed the opposite: Revenge is but a "Pyrrhic" victory. The destruction of one's opponent or partner in a relationship essentially means one's own self-destruction. Anyone who thwarts the other also thwarts himself, because for his own subsistence one requires the other. Forgiveness permits the continuation of life for both the subject and the other. Now we can answer that the real victor is the one who is able to forgive the other and not seek revenge. More emphatically speaking, the real winner is the one who is able to respond with goodness to the evil he confronts.

To forgive the other or not forgive the other, that's the question now. God's Revelation gives a final answer: "Today I am giving you a choice. You can choose life and success or death and disaster. I am commanding you to be loyal to the Lord, to live the way He has told you, and to obey His laws and teachings. You are about to cross the Jordan River and take the land that He is giving you. If you obey Him, you will live and become successful and powerful. On the other hand, you might choose to disobey the Lord and reject Him. So I'm warning you that if you bow down and worship other gods, you won't have long to live" (Lv 30, 15–18).

References

Lafon, G. 1964. *Essai sur la Signification du Salut*. Paris: Cerf.
Lafon, G. 1982. *Le Dieu commun*. Paris: Seuil.
Lafon, G. 1987. *L'autre Roi*. Paris: Nouvelle cité.
Levinas, E. 1982. *Ethique et infini*. Paris: Fayard.
Levinas, E. 1992. *Totalité et infini*. Paris: Kluwer Academic.
Ocvirk, D. 1990. Stvarjenje je odnos. In: *Nedelja*, 1st of April 1990.
Osredkar, M. J. 2008. *Il est important d'être ensemble*. Paris: Editions franciscaines.

RELIGION, CULTURE, HISTORY AND SOCIETY

JESUS – NEITHER A HAND OF RECONCILIATION NOR AN APPLE OF DISCORD BETWEEN CHRISTIANS AND MUSLIMS

Drago K. Ocvirk, Ljubljana

> Sheikh Ibrahim, your metaphors erase boundaries, deprive the world of clear principles, turn justice into fantasy, equate jar and man, elephant and an ant, day and night, reality and farce. The world built of metaphors and seen through them soon becomes a mess in which any boundary is known. Right knowledge does not make the boundaries blurred. The right knowledge shows them as sharp, clear, sensible.
>
> Enes Karić, *Songs of wild birds* (2009, 73–74)

Jesus of Nazareth has been interesting for many people already from the times of his public life to today. During his public life he was for some one more prophet in the long line from the times of King Saul; some saw in him re-apparition of this or that late prophet; for political and religious establishments he was a dangerous troublemaker; and for sure this list is not exhaustive. After his disappearance there were a real explosion of different perceptions and explanations concerning his identity, function and mission. He was adopted and adapted by movements such as Gnostics, Jewish-Nazarenes, Jewish-Christians and – for sure – by the movement of his immediate disciples and followers soon christened as Christians. These Christians perceived and attested Jesus as a Messiah or Christ. It took several centuries of discussions, disputes, polemics and divisions about the meaning of Christic function of Jesus before the mainstream orthodox Christianity emerged from the councils of Nicaea (325) and Chalcedon (451).

This orthodox position was not unanimously accepted. It was contested by many Christians of that times who become known as Nestorians and Monophysites and was also fiercely attacked, criticized and deconstructed by the messianic movement of Jewish-Nazarenes. This movement was at that time well established in the Palestine, Syria and Northern Arabia and spread among nomads – Arabs. When it got these warring tribes for their cause, which was the conquest of Jerusalem, a new movement of "believers" emerged that would finally take the shapes and name of Islam in 9th century (Donner 2010). This new movement recycled surrounding Jesus' narratives and recreated its own in tune with its own logic, needs and horizons. This new Jesus' narrative is found in Koran – as it is known today – and is absolutely normative in the predominant Sunni Islam. Nonetheless, this "official" or "orthodox" narrative has been paralleled and further developed by different Islamic traditions and movements also influenced by Christian and other Jesus' narratives spread all over the Mediterranean and Middle East areas. In Muslim narratives Jesus is christened Isa, which is somehow strange, because the old Arabic Christian name for him was and still is Jasu, meanwhile Isa comes probably from the name Esau (Gallez 2005; Jourdan 2008).

As Jesus has been adopted and adapted by many religious and ideological movements in the past the same happens today. There are different versions of Jesus' narratives in rabbinic Judaism and other religions such as Hinduism and Buddhism. Indeed, everywhere Christianity has come in contact with other religions Jesus has been in some way accepted, recycled and integrated by them (Merrigan and Haers 2000; Barker and Gregg 2010). Something similar has happened even when secular or antireligious ideologies have been met, that why there is also a Jesus of contemporary agnostics and atheists (Machovec 1977).

1. From love of Jesus to persecution of his followers

In these ongoing re/interpretations and recycling of Jesus' narratives the Christian and Muslim ones are of special importance when we deal with the questions of possibilities and meanings of reconciliation and peaceful co-existence.

Indeed, these two religions represent a half of humanity and there is a lot of tension and suffering, even persecution, in many places in the world also because of their different Jesus'/Isa's narratives. To avoid and over-come these destructive attitudes many Christians and Muslims strive to find a possible common ground for dialog, peace-making and cooperative coexistence. For some of them Jesus of Nazareth is an apple of discord between two religions, for some others, just on the contrary, Jesus is a hand of reconciliation. Therefore, it is possible both either to quarrel about the question whose narrative is true and whose false or to try to adjust and harmonise these two different narratives by finding a concordant narrative with the smallest common denominator, which purposely ignores the differences between the two established and official traditional narratives. As respectful as they may be I believe that either of these antagonistic positions is finally incapable to achieve its proclaimed goal: better mutual understanding, reconciliation and peaceful coexistence.

Let us look first at the "conciliatory" position that mainly comes from some Muslims in Western countries where they feel to be members of minority. A large publicity spot in Herald Sun, a Melbourne's leading newspaper, informed during several days at the end of October 2011 that "*We love Jesus too*". At the first glance I thought it was an evangelical charismatic love declaration, but I was wrong. Indeed, it was a publicity of Muslim organizations, which endeavour to earn better fame for Islam in Australian public opinion (We love Jesus too 2011). It is not news that Muslims love Isa/Jesus, whom the Qur'an presents as one of the main prophets and messengers. What is more surprising is that they advertise it in a highly secularised society. If they had not wanted to miss a target it would be better to spread among Australians a clear message: "*We love each human being*" – Muslim and no-Muslim alike, believer and no-believer, women, men or gays etc. This – and not religious declarations – is the message that attracts hearing, esteem and support in a secular society.

But there is another more important thing! The message encapsulated in the statement "*We love Jesus too*" might be highly misleading, because Jesus of Christian narrative is not the same as Isa of Qur'an. Whom they love is Qur'anic Isa, not the Gospel's Jesus. The Qur'anic revelation rejects, indeed, both: the presentation of Jesus in the four Gospels and his Christian perception. By Chalcedonian Council Jesus is defined as follows: "One and the same Christ, Son, Lord, only begotten, to be acknowledged in two natures, inconfusedly, unchangeably, indivisibly, inseparably". What characterises the Qur'anic Isa's narrative is, in reality, above all a total deconstruction of this kind of Christology. "O followers of the Book! do not exceed the limits in your religion, and do not speak (lies) against Allah, but (speak) the truth; the Messiah, Isa son of Marium is only an apostle of Allah and His Word which He communicated to Marium and a spirit from Him; believe therefore in Allah and His apostles, and say not, Three. Desist, it is better for you; Allah is only one God; far be It from His glory that He should have a son, whatever is in the heavens and whatever is in the earth is His, and Allah is sufficient for a Protector" (Qur'an 4,171). This deconstruction is done in the name of the divine indivisible and simple unity – *tawhid*. This doctrine of *tawhid* does not allow any complexity or relationship inside Godhead. Due to such a representation of God as a compact simplex without any differentiation inside itself nothing can matche or be compared to God or be at the same level as the Creator. For this reason some Muslims have seen the Aryanism as a quite correct understanding of Jesus, meanwhile some Christians look at Islam as a more radical heir of Aryanism. Regardless whatever might be correlation between Qur'an and Aryanism, the fact is that Isa – son of Marium and Muhammad's forerunner – is in this optics only a human being, the penultimate prophet and messenger.

Isa's mission was on the one hand to show Allah's sovereign power trough his miraculous life and deeds and on the other hand to foretell someone greater than him to come: the last prophet Ahmad, i.e. Muhammad. Because it is assumed that all of Allah's prophets reveal his omnipotence, such a great prophet as Isa surly could not suffer and be crucified. How he could do so through any weakness or even failure!? "And their saying: Surely we have killed the Messiah, Isa son of Marium, the apostle of Allah; and they did not kill him nor did they crucify him, but it appeared to them so (like Isa) and most surely those who differ therein are only in doubt about it; they have no knowledge respecting it, but only follow a conjecture, and they killed him not for sure. Nay! Allah took him up to Himself; and Allah is Mighty, Wise" (Qur'an 4,157–158). The idea about a special protection of God for his prophets and messengers is so deeply rooted in Sunni Muslim consciousness that any doubt about or negation of it is often seen as a blasphemy.

Christian and Qur'anic narratives concerning Jesus'/Isa's end reveal the impossibility to concord and unite these two narratives and their heroes. As long as this dream is dreamed we are driven between Scylla of a cheap concordism and Charybdis of perceiving an irreducible difference except by violence. This is a turning point because it becomes obvious that Jesus/Isa cannot be a Hand of Reconciliation between Christians and Muslims but he might be an Apple of Discord. Alas, many events in the past and today in different places in the world have shown how difficult it is for Sunni Muslims to stand a Christian representation of crucified Jesus. When Sunnis confound the crucified Jesus with the Qur'anic Isa, what usually they do, then they consider it as a very grave offense of Allah's prophet. Indeed, they treat it as a blasphemy that must be either punished if possible or, at least, disappear. Let us illustrate this by two cases.

The state of Pakistan has an anti-blasphemy law which persecute everyone who threats the Islamic nature of state. It is manly oriented against Christians and some Islamic non-Sunni groups such as the Ahmadya. "According to the available statistics, in Pakistan 1,274 people have been charged with offences under the blasphemy laws from 1986 to 2010 with none of them tried to the end or convicted, warranting the framing of a comprehensive law to protect the rights of a complainant and accused equally" (Mujahid 2011). Among many cases of blasphemy I picked out the case of two nursery students. They hanged in February 2009 a photo of the crucified Jesus on the wall in their faculty. According to the law this is a double blasphemy: on the one hand such a representation contradicts

Qur'anic version of Isa's end and on the other it violates the interdiction to represent the prophets of Islam. This incident might as many other blasphemy offences end with imprisonment and theoretically even with capital punishment (Fourest 2009).

The second case dates from October 2011. John Banzhaf, an attorney, sent to the Washington, D.C. Office of Human Rights a complaint against Catholic University. He alleges that Catholic University has violated the human rights of Muslim students by not allowing them to form a Muslim student group and by not providing them rooms without Christian symbols for their daily prayers. Banzhaf said some Muslim students were particularly offended because they had to meditate in the school's chapels "and at the cathedral that looms over the entire campus – the Basilica of the National Shrine of the Immaculate Conception. It shouldn't be too difficult somewhere on the campus for the university to set aside a small room where Muslims can pray without having to stare up and be looked down upon by a cross of Jesus." The Fox News commentator said about this incident: "This attorney is really turning civil rights on its head. He's using the law for his own discrimination against the Catholic institution and essentially saying Catholic University cannot operate according to Catholic principles." (Fox News 2011).

It must be repeated that such either "conciliatory" or "violent" positions manly occur in Sunni mainstream interpretation of Qur'anic revelation. Shiite, Sufi or other Muslim minority communities have not had an exclusivist triumphant understanding of Isa because they have been persecuted by Sunnis and suffered under their domination (Amir-Moezzi 2011). It is possible to overcome the dilemma about Jesus/Isa as either a Hand of Reconciliation or an Apple of Discord if we swap a will to indivisible and simple unity for a will to unity in diversity. For the achievement of a better mutual understanding, reconciliation and peaceful coexistence at least three main steps have to be done. First, there is a need for a real knowledge on both sides about their respective narratives; it must be followed, secondly, by a sincere acceptance of their differences and therefore their incompatibility; hopefully – and this is the third step – it leads both sides to the unity in diversity that respects respective singularities, due also to different Jesus'/Isa's narratives.

2. Acceptance of various Jesus'/Isa's narratives

There is no peaceful co-existence in any state-society if there is not at least a minimal acceptance and accommodation of differences of thoughts, opinions, and beliefs. In a global and open world it is no more possible for a state-society to be a monolithic with either a mono-religious or mono-ideological worldview. It is possible and maybe unavoidable in a tribal society, but no more in a state-society unless it is either dictatorial or totalitarian. Among other it means that state-society has to admit diversity and pluralism as a constitutive of itself. States, which call themselves "Islamic", are in reality Sunni with few exceptions. In them it is already difficult to be a no-Sunni Muslim and even more difficult to be a Jew or Christian; for other religious people and non-believers there is no place. Among many reasons for these difficulties I emphasise here two that concern religion and its relationship to religiously others: the first is a refusal of right to exist to alternative and competitive narratives and, the second, is a deliberate refusal of sciences as a way to better understanding of religion in this case of Sunni Islam.

As long as there is a privileged or unique allowed religious community the other religious narratives, sayings and believes have big difficulties to be presented and known correctly. They are perceived, appreciated and judged trough the eyeglasses of a dominant religion. In this case the others cannot be more than either heresy or falsification of the true religion. Therefore, there is no need to listen to and learn from others and to be eventually ready to question the claim to an absolute value of one's own narrative. As long as others do not have any possibility to tell and explain their own Jesus'/Isa's narratives and be well heard in their difference there is no real dialogue and equal treatment. If in many environments where Sunnis are in majority even other Islamic communities have no equal rights it is quite difficult to expect that no-Muslims, i.e. Jews or Christians would be treated better. But where Sunnis and other Muslims are minority there is much more possibilities for the change of mentality and be ready to accept religiously others with their own narratives. So, a historian Richard W. Bulliet wants "to highlight the comparative potency of the developments on the edge in conditions of weakly institutionalized religious authority. The center in Islam has a frequently expressed horror of innovation (*bid'a*) in matters of faith and practice. This position buttresses the widespread impression that Islam is an unchanging religion. The vitality of Islam's edge communities has developed in the face of this theoretical abhorrence and given rise to remarkable diversity under the name of Islam. Confrontation between the conservative center and the creative edge will surely continue in the future as the current crisis of authority in Islam plays itself out" (2004, 140–141).

As any other religion Islam changes because of different inner and outer factors. To switch from exclusivist to pluralistic and dialogical position concerning Isa's/Jesus' narratives presupposes an effort to learn what others narrate and believe. To get today complex and satisfactory knowledge of these narratives it is not enough to carefully listen to others' narratives but we have to pay attention also to sciences that work under the guide of reason. Without it religious self-understanding and inter-understanding is one-sided and deficient. Malek Chebel, an anthropologist, in his work *A Manifesto for an Islam of the Enlightenment* affirms the need to acknowledge "the superiority of reason over all other forms of thought or belief" (2004, 29–36). It is interesting that the same author in a later book *Islam Explained* pretends that Qur'anic Isa is same as a Christian Jesus. "The Christ' message is mainly *ne varietur* included in the holy text of Muslims. (...) Jesus (Isa), whose name is preceded by the term *Sidna – Our Lord*, is associated with Adam and other prophets. Because he was anointed, he is Messiah (Al-Massih), a Greek meaning of Hristos. Because of this title he is one who foretells the arrival of a prophet named Ahmed (61,6), i.e. Muhammad« (2007, 103). Chebel is a pious Sunni and a great expert in Islam and humanities but it seems he has not yet found time to read carefully the Gospel and penetrate the spirit of Christianity. Even though he is critical to his own Sunni beliefs still he looks at Christianity uncritically through his Qur'anic narrative. Something to be avoided even by experts in humanities! Hasan, a philosopher, in Enes Karić's novel quoted at the entrance of this paper, points to the necessity of reason and right knowledge to expose boundaries, differences, singularities and nuances to avoid a mess.

Sunnis who learn and know narratives of others and accept that they have right to stick to and spread them become agents of a pluralistic society respecting unity in diversity. Muslim personalities from all major communities/denominations and from across the world proposed in 2007 to Christian leaders a text "*A Common Word between Us and You*". In it they stated that the common ground between Islam and Christianity is: "The Unity of God, the necessity of love for Him, and the necessity of love of the neighbour". Dialogue and cooperation are unavoidable because: "With the terrible weaponry of the modern world; with Muslims and Christians intertwined everywhere as never before, no side can unilaterally win a conflict between more than half of the world's inhabitants. Thus our common future is at stake. The very survival of the world itself is perhaps at stake." At the end they made following appeal: "So let our differences not cause hatred and strife between us. Let us vie with each other only in righteousness and good works. Let us respect each other, be fair, just and kind to the other and live in sincere peace, harmony and mutual goodwill" (Common Word 2007).

Bibliography

Amir-Moezzi, Mohammad A.. 2011. *Le Coran silencieux et le Coran parlant. Sources scripturaires de l'islam entre histoire et ferveur*. Paris: CNRS Editions.

Barker, A. G. and Gregg, E. S. 2010. *Jesus beyond Christianity. The Classic Texts*. Oxford: University Press.

Bulliet, W. R. 2004. *The Case for Islamo-Christian Civilization*. New York: Columbia University Press.

Chebel, M. 2004. *Manifest pour un islam des Lumières. 27 propositions pour réformer l'islam*. Paris: Hachette.

---- 2007. *L'islam expliqué*. Paris: Perrin.

A Common Word. 2007. http://acommonword.com/index.php?lang=en&page=option1 (28.10.2011).

Donner, F. McGraw. 2010. *Muhammad and the Believers: At the Origins of Islam*. New York: Belknap Press of Harvard University Press.

Fourest, C. 2009. Chrétiens et "blasphème" au Pakistan. In: *Le Monde* 27.02.

Fox News. 2011. Do Crosses at Catholic University Violate "Human Rights" of Muslims?. In: http://radio.foxnews.com/toddstarnes/top-stories/muslims-want-catholic-school-to-provide-room-without-crosses.html (04.11.2011).

Gallez, E.-M. 2005/I. *Le messie et son prophète. Aux origines de l'islam. De Qumran à Muhammad*. Paris: Ed. de Paris.

--- 2005/II. *Le messie et son prophète. Aux origines de l'islam. De Muhammad des Califes au Muhammad de l'histoire*. Paris: Ed. de Paris.

Jourdan, F. 2008. *Dieu des chrétiens, Dieu des muslimans. Des repères pour comprendre*. Paris: L'œuvre.

Karić, E. 2009. *Pjesme divljih ptica*. Sarajevo: Tugra.

Machovec, M. 1977. *Jezus za ateiste*. Celje: Mohorjeva družba.

Merrigan, T. and Haers, J. 2000. *The Myriad Christ. Plurality and the Quest for Unity in Contemporary Christology*. Leuven: University Press.

Mujahid, Z. 2011. The Thin Red Line – the Blasphemy Law and Concept of Defamation. In: *The Express Tribune*, 06.01. http://tribune.com.pk/story/99784/the-thin-red-line-the-blasphemy-law-and-concept-of-defamation/ (04.11.2011).

We love Jesus too. 2011. http://welovejesustoo.blogspot.com/ (04.11.2011).

RECONCILIATION AS A BASIS OF ESTABLISHING POLITICAL COMMUNITIES. ATHENS AFTER THE THIRTY TYRANTS – CENTRAL EUROPE AFTER ITS POCKET-TYRANTS[1]

Béla Mester, Budapest

Reconciliation Based on Oblivion – the Instance of the Amnesty of Athens

Reconciliation as a process of political community, distinguished from the personal relationships of the private life, can be based both on the collective remembrance and on the collective oblivion. The composite commemorative structure of the identity of the political communities is clearly shown by the ambiguous words used for the processes of amnesty. It is a long tradition to engrave important historical turning points into the collective memory by granting a large amnesty, with an act of *Bill of Oblivion*. This juridical term mirrors the ambiguity of our relationship concerning the collective memory; the oblivion of *personal* crimes establishes the *common* memory of a political community. A classic case of this method of foundation of a working political community is the history of the ancient Athens after the cruel and utopian rule of the board of *synographeis* of the ancient lows, usually called *the thirty tyrants*. (For the utopian intellectual background of the rule of the thirties; see Németh 1996.) In the cultural heritage of Athens were known in that time both, the art of memory and the art of oblivion, in the story of Simonides who could remember everything, and Themistocles who could not forget anything. Xenophon and Aristotle wrote well-formed narratives of the rule of the thirty tyrants. By the words of Xenophanes, reconciliation was started by the speech of Trasybulus, leader of the triumphant Democrats to the followers of the failed regime: "I advise you, [...] men of the city,[2] to know yourselves. And you would best learn to know yourselves were you to consider what grounds you have for arrogance that you should undertake to rule over us. Are you more just?"

1 Supported by the research project *Early Enlightenment on the Threshold of 18th Century* (OTKA-67798).

2 In the last weeks of the civil war, the thirty occupied the city of Athens, and Piraeus was under the rule of the Democrats. They were usually called "men of the city" and "men of Piraeus".

(Xenophon 1918–1921, *Hellenica*, II. 4, 40) After a democratic argumentation against the difference between the civic virtues of the aristocrats and commoners, he offered an *oath of oblivion of the crimes* that happened in the time of the civil war. It meant both, the amnesty and a *taboo* of remembering them, at least in the public utterances. The citizens of Athens "pledged as they were under oath that in very truth they would not remember past grievances, the two parties even to this they live together as fellow-citizens and the commons abide by their oaths" (Xenophon 1918–1921, *Hellenica*, II. 4, 43). By the words of Aristotle, "never [...] has anybody broken the amnesty, but the Athenians appear both in private and public to have behaved towards the past disasters in the most completely honourable and statesmanlike manner of any people in history" (Aristotle 1952, *Athenaion Politeia* XL, 2). We must remember this oath of oblivion, and it will be the basis of the identity of our renovated political community. It is the essence of the *taboo* of speech; we must clearly remember *what* must be forgotten. This mental structure of the surviving state of Athens has satisfied our sources of the greatest authority. Both Xenophon in his *Hellenica*, and Aristotle in his *Athenian Constitution* finished this narrative with a happy ending. Commons and aristocrats of the *polis* were faithful to their oaths, and they were managing the public affairs of Athens together since the act of reconciliation. This reconciliation was the basis of the constitution of the city in the time of the publication of *Hellenica* and *Athenian Constitution*; and this constitution was evaluated optimal by Xenophon and Aristotle.

It is interesting that the double role of one of the fathers of the *Act of Oblivion* did not appear in this context in the ancient text; it is a novelty of the recent interpretations. It is the history of *Anytos*, the founder of the *Act of Oblivion*, and the accuser of Socrates. Based on the newest interpretation of the texts concerning the trial of Socrates we can describe the ambiguity of the story of Anytos in the following way. The amnesty act created a working political community after the civil war, and the rigid *literalism* of the dogmas of taboo of public utterances, rooted in the same act, made Anytos a killer, and marked the margins of his politics of oblivion. Anytos could be described by the mental contents of fear and *amathia* (shameful ignorance, see *Apologia* 29b), because of the refusal of the rational discourse about the public affairs. Later, this ignorant and emotional closeness of the political thinking proved to be unsustainable; and the survival of the community was possible by the forgetting of the act of oblivion, and the *taboo* of remembering. In this reading, Socrates was not guilty in *asebeia*, but he transgressed the *taboo* of public speech about the crimes of time of tyranny.[3] Socrates wanted to rethink the meaning of the concept of *politeia* after the civil war in a concrete *politeia*, Anytos wanted to save the same particular *politeia*, Athens, based on its real and imagined moral tradition, and on the prohibition of rational discourse on the roots of this political community. It was not possible for both of them to have influence on their community, and survive at the same time. The ambiguity of our antique sources is eloquent. Xenophon, a disciple of Socrates, and Aristotle, a disciple of the disciple of Socrates, when speaking about the personality of Socrates, admire his endeavour for rethinking the morality of *politeia*. When they speak about the history of the political institutions of Athens, they recognise the importance of the act of oblivion, and the merits of its founders. Reading their works, we can hardly observe that the topics and the agents of the two stories are partly identical. This oblivion of the connection of the memories of Socrates and the amnesty act mirrors the authors' ambiguity in the question of the foundation of a political community in the minds of its citizens, both by the tools of the collective memory, and the collective oblivion.

Cultural Memory and Oblivion in Modernity

In this antique instance there was equilibrium between the personality of individual oblivion, and the structure of collective memory; citizens' enforced oblivion was a foundation of the collective memory, and of the collective identity, based on it. When the same problem emerged seriously, again, in the 19th century, as a question of the new discipline of historiography, this equilibrium disappeared. For the 19thcentury scholars, the meaning of history changed from reliable reports of *histors* (witnesses) to the discovering of the unknown past, or a conscious or unconscious construction of historical narratives. Both these, scientific discovery of the unknown past and the use of the narratives produced by it are signed by the same word like in the ancient case of *historiographers*; that is historical memory.

3 By this reading of the *Apologia*, the crucial point of Socrates' trial was the prohibited remembrance of the story of the executed Leon from Salamis (*Apologia* 32c). However, the connection of the *Act of Oblivion* with the trial of Socrates was not unknown in the previous interpretations; its significance has become clear nowadays. This part of my essay is based on the results of the new Hungarian edition of Plato's oeuvre with commentaries; see especially Mogyoródi 2005, 145 sqq.

An inevitable instance of the theoretical reflections in this epoch is *Vom Nutzen und Nachteil der Historie für das Leben* of Friedrich Nietzsche. Nietzsche in this essay recognises the needed equilibrium of memory and oblivion, speaking about the equal need of historicity and a-historicity for the mental health of individuals, peoples and cultures, or about the need of oblivion of the past for the sake of the future. Nietzsche's utterances show for us the parallel of the individual memory and oblivion with the collective one, and the personal mental health with that of a political community. It is partly a characteristic of the 19th century discourse, and partly it is rooted in the role and the epistemological position of the historian as a scholar. This second aspect will be analysed by the case of a highly influential philosopher of history in the 20th century, Robin George Collingwood.

Collingwood summarised his opinions on the meaning of history in his posthumous work, entitled *The Idea of History* (Collingwood 1946). In the network of the universalism of the ideas of Collingwood, the reflection of the community on the history, and the use of the collective historical memory in the cultural and political life of the present are not discussed as important questions. The central figure of his epistemological point of view is an individual historian who works as a detective, using the scientific methodology developed by the discipline of history. This conception mirrors an interpretation of the history of humankind made by an individual scientist, regardless to the use of this interpretation in the present life. In the line of ideas of his book, reconstruction of the past has gradually become purely rational, and has lost the emotionality of the collective memory, rooted in two connected features of his thinking. From the metaphysical construction of the British idealism, the ontological fundament of Collingwood's thought follows the existence of an eternal truth, which can be known by the correct methodology of the scholars of history. In this system of ideas, Reason is the ruler of the history; and we can understand it by *rethinking* the thoughts of the winners of the history as a historical truth. In this conception, because of the possibility of one, unique historical truth only, there is no place for the understanding of victims, and for interpreting the plurality of the contested narratives of the same history, which is a typical situation between and within political communities, at least in Europe. A sign of this unconscious rationalisation is the change of crucial terms. Collingwood in the first chapters speaks about the *reacting* the past, which implies the reconstruction of whole life with its aesthetical and emotional phenomena; later he discusses the *rethinking* of the winners from the historical agents, in the study-room of a historian, only. In this point we should use the German term *Erlebnis*, and its equivalents in the Central-European languages, to avoid the reduction of the historical experience to rationality. We can see by the instance of Collingwood that a rational system of historical ideas, which excludes the possibility of concurrent narratives of the same history, cannot be a basis of rethinking of identities of political communities, and that of reconciliation as a part of this renewed identity. A new influential theory of the cultural memory has emerged partly because of this insufficiency. It is the thought of Jan Assmann explicated in his *Cultural Memory* (Assmann 1992, 2011),[4] and a reflection on it written by Harald Weinrich in his *Lethe* (Weinrich 1997, 2004).

The theory of Assmann is focussed on the history of the signs of memory, or, by other words, the structure of the memory of a community as a part of its identity. However, it is another theory developed by an experienced historian; it is not concerned to the concept of historical facts or to the idea of history, but to the facts of history of ideas. The central topic of this system of ideas is the economy of collective memories, with regard to its role in the present life of the same community, and the emotional elements of this commemorative process. However, Assmann's intention is to emphasise the structure of collective commemoration as a special genre of the remembrance, the roles of personal and collective memoirs are not clear in every detail. It is not an accident reaction that Weinrich's counter-theory could be based on the individual remembrance, speaking about the same cultural phenomena, and reflecting to the influential masterpiece of Assmann. In the contemporary applications of Assmann's theory is an important element the presence of the micro-history and oral history on the scientific horizon of the interpreter. In this context the horizons of the individual and collective thinking can be easily fused. Maybe, this intention is connected with the Central-European historical experiences, and structure of the collective political identity. In this point I can offer several recent Hungarian experiences of the economy of the symbols of memory as a Central-European instance.

4 However, I have added the data of the English edition to the list of references; it was not available before the deadline of the present volume. It is interesting that Assmann's masterpiece was published in English as late as 2011, later than its versions in several Central-European languages, amongst them the Hungarian one (1999). I suppose that one of its reasons was a different interest of the Central-European and English audiences in the structure and history of the collective memory.

Epilogue: a Hungarian Instance of the Dysfunction of the Cultural Memory

I had the opportunity to analyse the Hungarian economy of cultural memory in several recent researches. I can offer here several conclusions from those analyses. At first, it is remarkable that, however public places in Hungary are abundant in haphazard visual elements of collective identity, the cultural memory in Hungary has lost its pictorial characteristics. I called it recently *image-less memory* (Mester 2010). One of the causes of this image-less collective memory is the structure of strata of the collective memory. I have described it in the visual symbols of the commemorative events such as the reburials of the prime ministers of the revolutions of 1848 and 1956, and in the patterns of the theoretical reflections on the Hungarian history from the middle of the 19th century to nowadays. The symbol of 1989 was the reburial of the Prime Minister of 1956, following the cultural pattern of the reburial of the Prime Minister of 1848 in 1867. All these events had their importance in the original context, later every strata of this commemorative structure covered the previous one, and made shadow to the newer one. Conclusively, it was formed a special commemorative structure from the elements of the collective oblivion and remembrance. Historical symbols have transformed remembrance of nothing, and everything, making an empty collective remembrance, full of memorial symbols, but without working memory. These strata of the cultural memory cause an always-repeated structure of our cultural memory. All the significant historical events mean the same, and at the same time they mean nothing, have become empty topics of a meaningless memory. In this context, the numerous archives of oral history, and the large volumes of microhistory has remained the part of historiography as an academic discipline, in spite of their original intention to bring the history closer to people. All new historical facts will be a part of old structures of a-historically expressed identities, their patterns are useful in every memorial events from the memorial day of King Saint Stephen to the memorial day of the revolution of 1848, and 1956. (They are non-religious national Holidays in Hungary.) This a-historical structure of the Hungarian cultural memory has had two connected consequences in the public speech in the recent years. The first one is a denying of the fact of the changed political and social system in 1989, combined with the promise of a new, radical social and political turn. However, this rhetoric of "missing the real change of the political system" has existed continuously from 1989, and it was regarded as an extremist opinion, and nowadays it has chance to be the mainstream idea with its counterpart, the topic of "1989 was an error of the Hungarian history". However, almost all the elements of the artificial collective remembrance in this dysfunctional, a-historical system of the cultural memory can be a basis of collective political identities, these identities will be far from personal experiences, and from the structure of personified remembrance. Under the circumstances of this empty collectiveness of an a-historic cultural remembrance system, the abundant personal historical data are insufficient for the often recommended *talking cure*, as a prerequisite of any reconciliation process; because all the experiments for a *talking cure* will use these repeated, empty elements of political rhetoric instead of the remembrance of personal sufferings.

A recent interpretation developed within the framework of the Intellectual Workshop "István Bibó", which is a free research group dealing with the Hungarian history of ideas, has described this situation in the conceptual framework of *competition among victims* of the recent cruel Hungarian history, mainly that of the Nazism and Communism.[5] However, it is true, nowadays this concurrency has lost its connection with personal experiences, and it has become a part of the historical data in the role of the crude material of political rhetoric. This haphazard instrumentality and emptiness of the values of politics has achieved the heart and central concept of the political community, today. A symbol of the emptiness of this cultural memory is the new official name of our country, valid from 2012. The leadership of a political community in the form of a republic, having republican institutions as the President of Republic and so on, ritually has omitted the word 'republic' from the name of the same political community. Today this *hiatus*, an empty space in the former place of the word 'republic' can be a symbolic name of our political community. It is the point when the a-historic destruction of the collective historical memory jeopardizes the very roots of identity of our political community.

References

Aristotle. 1952. Athenaion Politeia [Athenian Constitution]. In: *Aristotle in 23 Volumes*, Vol. 20, translated by H. Rackham. Cambridge/MA – London: Harvard University Press – William Heinemann Ltd.

5 The concept of the *competition among victims* is the expression of a French scholar, Jean-Michel Chaumont (Chaumont 1997, 2001). It was applied for the Hungarian case in the researches of Iván Balog; see especially Balog 2010, 45.

Assmann, J. 1992. *Das kulturelle Gedächtnis. Schrift, Erinnerung und politische Identität in frühen Hochkulturen.* München: H. C. Beck.

Assmann, J. 2011. *Cultural Memory and Early Civilization. Writing, Remembrance, and Political Imagination.* Cambridge: Cambridge University Press.

Balog, I. 2010. *Bibó István recepciója. Politikai átértelmezések [The Reception of István Bibó. Political Misinterpretations].* Budapest: Argumentum Kiadó – Bibó István Szellemi Műhely (*Eszmetöréneti könyvtár*, 12)

Chaumont, J-M. 1997. *La concurrence des victimes. Génocide, identité, reconnaissance.* Paris: Editions la Découverte.

Chaumont, J-M. 2001. *Die Konkurrenz der Opfer. Genozid, Identität und Anerkennung.* Lüneburg: zu Klampen Verlag.

Collingwood, R. G. 1946. *The idea of history.* Oxford: Clarendon Press.

Mester, B. 2010. Pamięć bez obrazów [Image-less Memory]. In: *Res Publika Nowa*, September 20. Retrieved November 21, 2011, from http://publica.pl/teksty/pamiec-bez-obrazow/

Mogyoródi, E. 2005. Utószó Szókratész védőbeszédéhez és az Euthüphrónhoz [Epilogue to Apologia of Socrates, and to Euthyphro]. In: *Euthüphrón; Szókratész védőbeszéde; Kritón*, translated, notes and commentary by Alirán Gelenczey-Miháltz, Emese Mogyoródi, Budapest: Atlantisz Kvk. (*Platón összes művei kommentárokkal*, 8), pp. 121–151.

Németh, Gy. 1996. A zsarnokok utópiája [Utopia of the Tyrants]. In: *Antik Tanulmányok / Studia Antiqua*, 40, pp. 11–39.

Xenophon, 1918–1921. Hellenica. In: *Xenophon in Seven Volumes*, Vol. 1–2, translated by Carleton L. Brownson, Cambridge/MA – London: Harvard University Press –William Heinemann, Ltd.

Weinrich, H. 1997. *Lethe. Kunst und Kritik des Vergessens,* München: Beck.

Weinrich, H. 2004. *Lethe, the art and critique of forgetting*, translated by Steven Rendall, Ithaca–London: Cornell University Press.

RECOLLECTION, FORGETTING, RECONCILIATION – THE HUNGARIAN CASE

Gábor Kovács, Budapest

In the following paper I am going to discuss the relation of the above-mentioned notions, *recollection, forgetting and reconciliation* concerning Hungary. It is intended to be the first draft of a prospective case-study about the history of Hungarian collective mentality in the 20th century. It is my obligation to mention that such kind enterprise wouldn't be imaginable without the pioneering work of István Bibó (1911–1979), the great Hungarian political thinker, whose inspiring and thought-provoking writings concerning historical impasses and political hysterias of Central-Eastern Europe furnish a foundation to my paper. I am greatly indebted to Bibó whose seminal achievement is unavoidable for everyone dealing with the problems of the history of Hungarian political-communal mentalities. I have been inspired as well by the theory of Wolfgang Schivelbusch whose book *The Culture of Defeat* on national traumas, mourning and recovery has proved very serviceable when I was looking for the proper frame of the reference for my paper.

It is very bookish, I am aware of it, to start with history, but, I am afraid, it cant' be saved. Without a rough sketch of the changes of Hungarian historical situations in the 20th century, put in a nutshell, my train of thought would be incomprehensible for foreigners even they are interested in the topic of this paper.

The causes of the present state of Hungarian collective historical-political consciousness can be partly traced back to the national trauma of the Trianon Peace-Treaty imposed on Hungary after the lost First Word War. It was a part of the package of the Versailles Peace Treaty closing the first total war of the 20th century. The Austro-Hungarian Monarchy was the ally of Germany and as one of the losers it had to give penitence for its war activities. The fact that, as the consequence of the war defeat, Hungary lost two thirds of its territory and a half of its population was, both for Hungarian political elites and masses, a traumatic experience. Hungary which, before the war, had been the co-tenant of one of the European major powers, the Austro-Hungarian Monarchy, now diminished to one of the small states of Central-Eastern Europe. The country became a dwarf with the consciousness of a giant. It was a situation in which arose the necessity of a many-layered reconciliation. Hungary should have reconciled the tension between the past and the future; the Hungarian nation should have reconciled the fact that one third of Hungarian ethnicity had become citizen of the successor states encircling

Hungary. Hungary should have reconciled with its new geo-political situation in this area. And last but not least Hungarian national community should have reconciled with itself; it should have avoided the temptation of searching scape-goats.

The first question emerges for us: to which extent was the enormous task of this multi-dimensional reconciliation a success? Putting forward the conclusion of my paper it must be said that the adaptation to the new situation was just partly successful; in many respects it was a failure. The disintegration of the Greater Hungary, after the First World War, was a trauma for the national consciousness, which, using the term coined by the abovementioned István Bibó, had evoked some kind of political hysteria lingering to our time. (On Bibó see: Berki 1992, Kovács 1999, Kovács 2010) Hungary, after 1920, became a deeply divided national community with two parties opposing sharply to each other. On one side there were the *westernizers* (urbánusok) [meaning urbanites] who wanted to complete a western-style modernization emulating western political and cultural models, on the other side there were the *Hungarian populists* (népiek) who feared for the loss of 'Hungarian national character' and preferred a self-contained development.

The split of the Hungarian political-cultural elites into antagonistic fractions opposing each other was not a new phenomenon neither in Hungarian nor in East-European history. Its most renowned variant was the 'Narodnik' vs. 'Zapadnik' opposition in Russia. The problem, in Hungary, emerged in the first half of the 19th century when the modernization seemed more and more to be an unavoidable constraint for the ruling elites. Before the revolution of 1848, in the thus called *reform age,* the twin slogan of *fatherland and progress* had been formulated by the contemporaneous reformers, referring to this dilemma. What was new, after the defeated First World War, it was the previously unknown intensity of the opposition involving mutual intolerance between the opposing rivals. The situation was encumbered by the historical fact that among the westernizers the Jewish origin persons were over-represented in the sociological meaning. The historical explanation of it is relatively simple; the traditional Hungarian elites, being not mobile enough to be the vehicles of capital accumulation, alone were not able to launch modernization; the Hungarian Jews, in the lack of an organically developed bourgeoisie of Hungarian origin, had to play the role of the capitalist entrepreneur indispensable for a modern society.

The main consequence of the war defeat, apart from the social-historical constellations of the post-war situation, was a radical change of the dominant political discourse. The prewar Hungary had been a multi-ethnical entity in which the domineering political discourse was that of assimilation imbued with liberalism as the ruling idea of the second half of the 19th century. After the war, as the consequence of shock caused by the defeat, the *liberal-assimilationist* political discourse was replaced by an *ethno-protectionist, dissimilative* one. The purge of the so called Hungarian national character from the foreign influences became one of the main problems for the conservative and the populist segments of the Hungarian cultural-political elites. It was some kind of a paradox; ethnical pureness emerged as a plank of different political programs at the time when, as a consequence of the post-war partition of the 'Saint Stephen's Empire', Hungary, apart from the above-mentioned Jewish origin intelligentsia and bourgeoisie, had practically become a mono-ethnical political entity. The political mal-development concluded in the anti-Jewish legislations of the late 30s and the early 40s. (1938, 1939, 1941, 1942) Those laws gravely restricted the civil and political rights of the Hungarian Jews; they were scapegoated and expelled from the Hungarian national community. This terrible process consummated after the German occupation of 1944 when almost all Hungarian Jewry was carried by freight-trains to the Nazi extermination camps. Only a fragment of them returned back alive after the war.

István Bibó writes without flattery and in a very self critical-way about the special Hungarian situation which emerged after the First World War. Hungarian nation failed as a problem-solving community, he concludes; it was unable to cope with the task addressed by the historical situation. The challenge proved to be too great for evoking a proper response. Hungary, because of outer and inner causes, Bibó argues, had run into a historical deadlock involving some kind of communal or political hysteria:

"Political hysteria always starts out from a traumatic historical experience in the life a community, particularly one the members of the community believe to be intolerable, and think the solution to the problems it gave rise to outdoes the abilities of their community. Much like a healthy individual, a community capable of putting to good and safe use its abilities, however great or small, is strengthened when encountering catastrophe, because it makes reasonable assessment of the causes of its troubles, draws lessons from them, bears what it deems elemental calamity, assumes the moral responsibility it recognizes as its own fault, finds redress for the injustices committed against it, resigns itself to what cannot be undone, renounces dreams impossible to attain, and defines and performs its duties. For all its vehement or feverish reactions, a balanced community will thus finally solve its problems; in other words, it will not fall into hysteria, because hysteria per se means shunning the problem." (Bibó, 2011: 6)

It is conspicuously that the notion of political hysteria has been borrowed from the terminology of psychoanalysis by Bibó. He describes the symptoms of this illness as follows:

"Real community hysteria occurs when all its characteristic symptoms are present together: an entire community's loss of touch with reality, an inability to resolve the problems that life creates, an insecure yet over-blown self-assessment, and an unrealistic and disproportionate response to the impacts of the outer world."(Bibó, 2011:5)

It is essential, Bibó strongly emphasizes, that communal-political hysteria is the ill of the whole community; it can't be cured once and for all by punishing the persons committed vile acts evoked by their hysterical psychic states:

"Plans seeking to cure hysteria by destroying, isolating or casting out its carriers who can be grouped on whatever basis, will not help at all. Community hysteria is the condition of the community as a whole, and there is no use of eliminating the visible carriers of hysteria when its conditions and grounds remain untouched, its initial traumas are unrelieved, and the make-believe situation it is actually founded on is unresolved. There is no use of eliminating all "evil" men; the delusions and false responses of hysteria will live on in peaceful patresfamilias, in mothers of six, in clear-headed persons who would not hurt a fly, in noble, lofty, exalted minds, and the community will bring forth the madmen, the beneficiaries and thugs of hysteria in a generation." (Bibó, 2011:6)

However, Hungarian culture emerged after the First World War was, borrowing the term of Wolfgang Schivelbusch, the culture of defeat. Its attitudes, symbols were deeply determined by the shocking experience of the lost war. However, the Hungarian case was different of the model elaborated by the German cultural historian. Schivelbusch's theory has been based on the comparative typology of the American, French and German history; his frame of reference focuses for the connection of the winner and defeated communities. His reference relations are those of the South and North in the American Civil War (1861–65) and those of Germany and France from Sedan (1870) to the German defeat in 1918. France in Sedan was forced to act of the uncomfortable role of the vanquished nation while, with the rotation of the wheel of fortune, in Versailles it became winner, while Germany was enforced to the position of the vanquished party. However the aforementioned societies, the American South and North and the French and German ones were able, going through the painful process of healing of the collective psyche, for recovery. Schivelbusch's theory, at least to some extend, runs parallel, with Bibó's one. He, using psychoanalytic terms, supposes some kind of analogy between the individual and collective psyche but, contrast to Bibó, explains that the phases of a pathological collective consciousness ensuing each other are the necessary stations to the permanent regeneration of community:

"What neurosis is to the individual, the creation of myths is to the collective. Our three losers' myth – the Lost Cause, the dream of revanche, and im Felde unbesiegt (undefeated on the field of battle) – all deny that the nation has been defeated and postpone the settling of accounts (most explicitly revanche and most obliquely in the Lost Cause) – to an undefinite, messianic future. Such myths (or, in the Freudian term, fantasies, arising from frustrated desires for revenge), are the psychological mechanism for coming to terms with defeat. Moreover, they are not merely neurotic fictions of the imagination but also healthful protective shields or buffer zones – emotional fortresses – against a reality unbearable to the psyche."(Schivelbusch, 2001: 26)

Now, let's return to Hungarian history! After the German occupation there came the Russian army, carrying the only marketable product of bolshevism; the bolshevism itself. While in the previous period they were the Hungarian Jews who had been transported by freight trains to Auschwitz and Birkenau, now they were the Hungarian war prisoners, later the real and alleged enemies of communism who were enforced to share the similar fate; they were carried by freight trains to the camps of the Gulag.

It is beyond doubt that reconciliation is one of the most frequently used terms in Eastern-and South-Eastern-Europe. The cause of the repeated reference to this notion lies in the history of this region. Communism is a common heritage in this part of Europe. Historical recollection here has been burdened with the tragic experiences of genocides, massacres and deportations. Hungary is not an exception to the rule; remembrance to the past was forbidden, the events of the 20th century, especially the shock of the disintegration of the preceding Greater Hungary was suppressed to the collective unconsciousness. Similar fate befell the anti-totalitarian revolution of 1956; it was amongst the severe taboos to talk about it. Collective amnesia was one of the most conspicuous phenomena of Hungarian national consciousness during the decades of Hungarian communism.

The fact that Communism in Hungary brought with itself a low-standard modernization, made the situation even more complicated. It came soon to light, after the collapse of the communist regime, that the bringing of the suppressed past from the social sub-consciousness to the social consciousness, is a necessary but not satisfactory precondition. After the political transformation of 1989 everyone can talk about the historical injuries which afflicted his/her family and everyone can construct his/her narrative concerning the past, but reconciliation seems to be more far away than it was ever. It became evident that the talking cure or 'chimney sweep' which relieves the symptoms of the individual patient kas not functioned properly in societal dimensions; at least it has not worked in Hungary after the political turn of the velvet revolutions of Eastern Europe of 1989. It can be traced back to many reasons. It was one of the most significant among them that nobody has wanted to bear the responsibility for the vices committed during the years of Jewish persecution and in the ensuing decades of communism. Among the survivors of Shoah and Gulag and among the descendants of them emerged a strange phenomenon which is can be called a *concurrence of victims* (Chaumont, 2001). It means a nonsense debate about the question that which side is able to enumerate more dead and humiliation; we are witnesses of a strange card-game, played in societal dimensions, in which the quantity of suffering presents itself as a winning card in this sad poker-game. Another problem, putting one from the array of unsettled ones, is that there was no real intent for the clarification of the role played by the secret police during the decades of communism. From time to tome different lists of the informers of the secret police are published but mostly without consequences; such leaking outs are mostly motivated by the desire to denounce the political opponents.

The fruitless inter-war debate of the westernizers and populists has revived in Hungary; it seems to be a paradox phenomenon after the joining EU but it is a fact; Hungary is in the state of a permanent cold civil war.

Conclusion

It has came to light that reconciliation needs a delicate balance of recollection and forgetting, moreover a common set of basic values accepted by the whole national community; these preconditions are missing in Hungary. The task of reconciliation, outlined by one of the greatest Hungarian poets, Attila József in his poem 'By Danube' written in the 30s, is yet an unsettled one for Hungary:

> [...] "I am the whole-all that which was and is;
> The many generations transient,
> Each yielding to the next; the next; the victories
> Of long dead conquerors; and the lament
> Of vanquished peoples live in me. Magyar,
> Turk, Tartar, Slovak and Rumanian
> Flow in this heart's blood, debtor to this far
> Past for a gentler future age for man.
>
> I wish to work; it is sufficient
> Struggle avowal of the past to make

To the great Danube in whose waters blend,
Past, present, future through time's limit break;
By memory to solve through peace the war
Waged by our ancestors, at length to bring
A righteous settlement for all to share –
This is our work, and it is no small thing.
/Translated by J.C.W. Horne/

References

Bibó, I. 2011. *The German Hysteria*, translated by P. Pásztor, manuscript.

Berki, R. 1992. The Realism of Moralism: The Political Philosophy of István Bibó. In: *History of Political Thought*, vol. XIII., (3), pp. 513–534.

Chaumont, J. M. 2001. *La concurrence des victimes.* Paris: La Découverte.

Kovács, G. 1999. Can Power Be Humanized? The Notions of Elite and Legitimation in István Bibó's Political Philosophy. In: *Studies in Eastern European Thought*, 51 (4), pp. 307–327.

Kovács, G. 2010. Region of Deformities? – The Image of Central-Eastern Europe in the Political Philosophy of István Bibó. In: Jurova J., Jozek M., Kiepas A., Machura P., (eds.), *Central-European Ethos or Local Traditions: Equality, Justice*, Boskovice, Czech Republic: Albert, pp. 133–140.

Schivelbusch, W. 2001. *The Culture of Defeat. On National Trauma, Mourning and Recovery*. New York: Henry Holt and Company.

SLOVENIA AND THE CRIMINAL BURDEN OF TITOISM

Jože Dežman, Ljubljana

Slovenians also experienced the short 20th century as the age of extremes.

After the dissolution of the Austro-Hungarian Monarchy in 1918, Slovenians fought for land with Hungarians (gained Prekmurje in 1919), Italians/Friulians (Rapallo, 1920 – Italy gained a third of Slovenian ethnic territory, Paris, 1947 - Slovenia gains Primorska, London 1954 – Yugoslavia gains Zone B, Osimo, 1974), Austrians/Germans (lost Austrian Koroška, 1920).[1] The border between Slovenia and Croatia, which is being resolved by the International Court, is mostly the border between the Austrian and the Hungarian parts of the Monarchy.

Slovenian nation was successful in its struggle for land. Divided into Austrian duchies and Hungary, it received a part of the territory in First Yugoslavia (1918–1941), and most of its national territory and limited republic sovereignty in the Second Yugoslavia (1945–1991). The highest rise of the Slovenian nation was the processes of democratization in the 1980's, the creation of the independent Republic of Slovenia and a bloodless departure from the Yugoslav Federation in 1991.

Totalitarianisms

Into the Alps-Adriatic regions the agitated nationalisms triggered intensive totalitarian movements after the dissolution of Austria-Hungary. Border fascism in Italy and National Socialism in Austria, puppet governments of Nazi Germany in Croatia and Hungary, Stalinism of Yugoslav communists were extremely aggressive.

Slovenia is the only member of EU, which has (as a victim and as a perpetrator) experienced three totalitarian regimes: fascism, national socialism and communism.

On the third of the ethnic territory that was awarded to Italy after the First World War, Slovenians suffered extreme pressures of Italian nationalism and fas-

1 Slovenia 1941: 15 849 square kilometres.
Slovenia 1954: 20 255 square kilometres.

cism from 1920 onwards. The Slovenian minority in Austrian Carinthia was also exposed to German nationalism and National Socialism, especially after Austria joined the Third Reich in 1938.

Slovenian Stalinism is born with the creation of the Communist Party of Slovenia in 1937.

Following the plan of world revolution, Yugoslav communists triggered civil wars against their own nations. Their man goal was to win these wars. Communists ensured a monopoly on the leadership of the resistance against the occupiers by subjugating non-communist allies and prohibiting any resistance outside of the communist partisan movement.

The proof that the civil war was more important than the resistance against the occupier is in the fact that more than 97,000 Slovenians (6.5 % of the population) were victims of war, revolution, civil war, but the occupying units did not lose more than a few thousand men in the fights with Slovenian partisans. More than 25,000 Slovenians died as direct victims of the civil war.

Titoism - violation of human rights and state terrorism

The list of human rights that were systematically violated in Socialist Yugoslavia is long. To each we could add a list of systemic measures that targeted large groups or even the majority of the population, primarily because of the permanent civil, class and religious war.

The system of maintaining and developing revolutionary traditions was an ideological mechanism that, with the help of cult forms, concealed the crimes and failures of the Yugoslav Communist Party and the League of Communists of Slovenia/Yugoslavia.

Rather than liberation, the end of the Second World War denoted the continuation of the Bolshevik aggression, manifested in class, ethnic, religious and cultural "cleansing". More than one percent of the entire Slovene population was murdered in May and June 1945.

The Communist Party tried to monopolize the truth. Intolerant militarization and caste differentiation of the living and the dead ruled in the name of brotherhood, unity and equality. The Bolshevik 'gods' divided the world of the dead into Party heaven and Party hell. The acknowledged dead were accepted into the party cult of the dead, the graves and memories of the suppressed (ignored) were erased. Almost one half of Slovene victims of war and revolution were denied their own grave and the right to be remembered.

The living were divided in the same way as the dead. The partisan survivors, their relatives and the relatives of the celebrated fallen received commendations and rents. Surviving partisan opponents, their relatives and the relatives of the despised dead were forced to keep silent, were despised and deprived. Their property was confiscated, they were shamed, refused help, their relatives, especially children, were disadvantaged in education, employment, promotions. They were identified as the so-called national traitors, collaborators and so on.

Today we know that the discriminated dead were all the way until the end of the regime registered in the dossiers of the secret political police. These records were used to control their relatives. And despite that the defenders of Titoism claim that they "did not know" about the crimes.

Class struggle

Similarly to masquerading the revolution as an 'independence' war, they also hid the goals of the class struggle. E.g. in the brochure *On Questions of Property, Order and Lawfulness* (1944) they stated: "They know the statement given in 1943 by chief commander marshal Tito and president of Antifascist Council dr. Ribar about the integrity of private property and full potential of personal initiative in industry, trade and agriculture."

In the brochure *Communism – our Final Goal* (1943), intended to educate communists, they reveal their real goal: "The private property will be abolished and replaced by a collective social property."

After the War, the civil war continued as a class struggle. Let us mention the war against private property and entrepreneurship and the war against farmers.

The basis of the class struggle was confiscation of private property and preventing private entrepreneurship. Between 1945 and 1952, at least 27,000 confiscations of property occurred. Confiscations continued with the three nationalizations. The first nationalization, in December, 1946, included the most important industrial, construction, forestry, agricultural, bank and insurance, trade, traffic and transport companies. The second nationalization, in April, 1948, included around 690 companies, warehouses and wine cellars, traffic, cultural and health institutions, and real estate of foreign nationals and establishments. The first and the second nationalization witnessed the nationalization of all industry, trade, banking and insurance, major parts of traffic and catering industries and all cultural, educational and health enterprises. In the third nationalization, in December, 1958, around 19,000 buildings and around 113,400 building plots, with the area of almost 12,000 hectares, were confiscated.

For almost a decade after the War, farmers suffered from a long line of exploitative and repressive measures: prescribed quantities of produce, compulsory delivery and sales of goods, high taxes, collectivization and cooperatives. Farmers were exploited through high prices of industrial products and low prices of agricultural products. In 1953, land ownership was maximized (10 hectares of arable land) and thus it was impossible for the farmers to become a socially stable and wealthy class. Thousands of rebellious farmers were dealt with by the secret political police who engineered numerous 'kulak' processes.

In fact, the destruction of the middle classes as bearers of culture and businessmen as the foundations of economic development is a tragic long-term consequence of the communist revolution. No less damaging for the survival potential of society, its sustenance and for the Slovenian cultural landscape in the long term are the consequences of the destruction of farmers and forced industrialization.

The war against religion and the Church

The communist government considered the Catholic Church to be the 'backbone of the opposition'. For more than a decade after the Second World War, they resorted to extreme measures to destroy it.

After the war 62 theologians and 275 priests emigrated to escape the communists. Until 1950, more than 30 priests had been murdered or had died because of the consequences of torture.

Between 1945 and 1961, 429 priests (out of a total of around one thousand) were prosecuted, nine death sentences were passed and four were carried out.

They confiscated Church property, levied high taxes and financial punishments, forbade religious education in schools, expelled the Faculty of Theology from the Ljubljana University, and forbade religious newspapers. To subjugate the church, they created a special priest association, which was full of secret political police co-operators.

Numerous religious objects, especially churches in the Kočevje region were demolished, along with many chapels and signs. They changed names of places named after Catholic tradition. There were many attacks on priests and disruptions of religious rituals. Catholic holidays were no longer work free days; they tried to appropriate some Catholic traditions.

The planned discrimination of religious people began, they were not allowed to perform a number of jobs; even children attending religious education were mocked in schools.

Iron Curtain and the Cold War – emigration and immigration

The Iron Curtain towards the West was deadly for more than a decade, hundreds of people were killed on the Italian and Austrian border (a refugee from Sri Lanka was shot on the Austrian border on the 17th of June, 1991, a week before Slovenia became independent). Between 1945 and 1965, more than 65,000 people escaped from communism, either because of political persecution or poverty. More than 30,000 were arrested before they managed to escape or while attempting to escape and sentenced to prison with forced labour. Adding to that number the 50,000 members of the German and Italian minorities, who were killed, exiled or choose Italy, Slovenia lost more than a tenth of its population.

After Stalin excluded Yugoslavia from the Soviet Bloc in 1948, the iron curtain towards the East rised, restricting Yugoslavia from the Slavic world.

When Yugoslavs were allowed to work in the West in the 60s, more than 200,000 people left Slovenia. A similar number of workers from other Yugoslav states arrived to Slovenia.

Despite the dependence on the West, Yugoslavia persisted on the ideology of anti-western politics and exportation of the revolution.

Lawlessness

Court-martials, Courts of National Honour and other courts sentenced people to prison, forced labour, confiscation of property, loss of voting rights... In numerous political trials, orchestrated by the secret political police, almost 25,000 people were sentenced. These processes were a part of nationalist, class and political cleansing, or of the fight against the church; they used them to break the resistance of farmers against collectivization. Numerous processes ended with confiscation of property, death penalty or a long prison sentence.

Police state – the rule of the secret political police

The secret political police led a civil war by using all available means to attack political opponents as the enemies of the people at home and abroad. All-powerful and omnipresent, it restricted the freedom of thought and completely established a totalitarian regime. In 1946 there was 1 member of Udba per 1200 inhabitants of Slovenia (including the active informers, there was 1 member of Udba per 282 inhabitants). Hundreds of thousands of people were affected by the constant spying and denunciations, creating an atmosphere of general distrust.

Exploiters - the new class and partisan veterans

The absolute power in Tito's Yugoslavia was in the hands of the Communist Party (after 1952, The League of Communists).

The Party members held all leading social positions. A typical party member was a man, with a good job or a leading function, with a good pay and access to other advantages. That is why the highest percentage of Party members was among the officials, and the lowest among manual labourers and farmers.

The governing Party was at the same time a magnet and a source of disappointment. From 1950 to 1977 almost 124,000 members were accepted into the League of Communists of Slovenia; 68,000 left the Party or were suspended.

In Slovenia in 1948, when it was formed, the League of Veterans' Associations had 120,000 members in 792 local branches. Data from 1953 reveals than less than 45,000 were soldiers, others were members of political organizations of the partisan movement. The number of members of the League of Partisan Veterans' Associations rose to 157,000 by the year 1973, and 86,000 had their years of participating in the partisan movement officially recognized towards their retirement funds, some had the pension years doubled. In 1996, more than 50,000 partisan veterans received bonuses with their pensions; in 2007, around 27,000 partisan veterans received around 61,000,000 € of bonuses to their pensions.

The system of privileges, developed all throughout Titoism, gave partisan veterans access to numerous benefits, from assuming leading positions without adequate education, advantages in schooling, employment, apartments, to numerous local and republic rents, decorations, free transport. There was a special parallel health system in place for them.

Through Slovenian transition, the Titoistic elites managed to keep their privileges and significant part of political power.

Detabooisation

All crimes and consequence of state terrorism were concealed with numerous taboos and forgeries. The criminal burden of Titoism is so great that it will require international cooperation, especially when the countries of Western Balkan begin the European intergration.

For example the problem of concealed killing and burial sides, we now know that in Slovenia there are more than 600 concealed graves with estimated 100,000 victims, in Croatia around 600 concealed graves with estimated 90,000 victims and in Serbia around 200 concealed graves with tens of thousands of victims.

Taboos were also maintained with extreme measures. For example, in 1947, 33 year old Elza Premšak was sentenced to death and shot because she reported to the English about the mass killings of prisoners and civilians taking place in 1945 in and around Celje.

The taboo crimes also burdened the perpetrators. When the Communist Party started to prepare measures to protect the failing taboos in 1984, they called Milan Venišnik, an important Yugoslav diplomat, who was the chief of the secret political police in Celje in 1945, to the Central Committee of the Communist Party of Slovenia. Venišnik was so disturbed by this that he described in letters how guilty he felt because of a group of women that shouldn't have been killed back then. At the end of 1984, he shot himself in Ljubljana.

With democratization, the taboos started falling. Reveals of killing and burial sites were followed by the lists of victims. Anti-communist veterans and their adherents erected many parish memorial plaques for more than 13,000 victims. All victims of war and revolution are recorded by the Institute of Contemporary History. Numerous concealed fates and events are publicized.

Especially intense is the process of de-mythicization of the persona of Josip Broz Tito, as data on his cooperation in the crimes in the Spanish Civil War, about betraying Yugoslav communists in the Stalinist purges in Moscow, about negotiations on cooperation with Germans against the Allied landing in the Adriatic and so on have become public knowledge.

Transitional justice

The acts implemented by the Republic of Slovenia to manage issues of transitional justice: Denationalization Law (1991), Act on the Victims of War Violence (1995), Act on Repatriation of Wrongs (1996), Act on War Burial Sites (2003).

Numerous issues remain open, connected mostly with the package of these so-called war laws.

According to decision of the Constitutional Court in 2006 the Slovenian parliament changed the Law on Victims of War Violence in 2010 so that also the persons, who were killed by the partisans without their guilt being proven and without proper procedure, would be awarded the status and the rights of the victims of war violence.

The property of victims of Titoist terror was as a rule confiscated, so an important part of transitional justice processes is connected to denationalization. The restitution of confiscated property is now being concluded. Out of 39,656 filed denationalization demands, 39,261, or 99 percent, were legally concluded.

Law on the Restitution of Injustices has been active since 1997, but because of Titophillic extremists' activities it remained very marginal for the first few years. During the mandate of the government of Janez Janša, it was finally enabled to work effectively. The Committee has so far resolved more than 23,000 applications with more than 30,000 applicants.

Instead of 858 applications per year, which was the Committee's average between 1997 and 2004, it resolved on average 4,731 applications per year between 2005 and 2008.

The invalidations of Titoist show trials are ongoing according to the Act on criminal proceedings. So far, the courts and prosecutions withdrew or invalidated around 4,000 sentences. Restitution is given for any prison time.

In the police actions Reconciliation, a huge amount of data was gathered, more than a thousand interviews performed and two persons were indicted.

The Slovenian media, printed and electronic, played a great role. Documentaries had a huge impact. The database of articles on Titoist terror (since 1990) will include more than 20 000 pieces.

There are numerous historical researches. Let us mention the international import of the 'reconciliatory' science, as we have had successful cooperation in historical commission with Italy and also Austria and Croatia.

Reconciliation

The ideology of Slovenian process of reconciliation initiated by liberal activists was: We will build the monument for all victims and that is reconciliation. However, that initiative did have a huge and important resonance in the Slovenian society.

But reconciliation is not wordless and senseless pacification; it is a painful and long-term process of individual and social change.

Reconciliation is not possible without forgiveness, regret, sorrow, penance …

Detabooisation, truth, justice, compassion

The process of confronting Titoist totalitarianism is very dynamic in Slovenia.

For example, 2009, on March 5th there was a press conference about the discovery of the concealed mass grave of victims of Titoism in tunnel of St. Barbara in Huda Jama.

2009, on April 20th in the Slovenian capital, Josip Broz Tito was honoured by renaming a street into Titova cesta – Tito's street.

2011, on October 3th the naming of Tito's street was reversed by the decision of the Slovenian Constitutional Court, according to which such names have no place in current time, because they are contrary to the principle of respect for human dignity which has its basis in the Article One of the Constitution and falls into the very core of the constitutional system of the Republic of Slovenia.

The above can help us to understand how important the stance towards the crimes of Titoism is, as they are the basis of transcending the traumatic burden of Titoism.

When comparing Slovenian transitional processes with processes in other societies trying to transcend the criminal heritage of totalitarian and authoritarian regimes, we can see that it is likely that the bearers of the totalitarian Titoist regime and their descendents will not be punished because of the long-term rule of taboos and impunity of the criminals, they will not regret their crimes or sympathize with the victims. However, their version of history must not be accepted.

Table 1: The pros ant the cons in Slovenian dispute about Titoism and democracy

Tabooisation	Detabooisation
Murder, steal, lie	Don't kill, don't steal, don't lie
Hatred and revenge	Reconciliation and forgiveness
Genocide, eliminationism, totalitarianism	Rule of law, democracy, human rights
Militarisation, state terrorism (civil war and class struggle as a normal state of affairs)	Demilitarisation, nonviolence, tolerance
So called reconciliation as avoidance of rule of law	Processes of transitional justice
Special war operations: keeping secrets, misinformation, relativization, media and "professional/expert" pressure	Process of truth, justice, reconciliation
Racist discrimination/segregation of the victims of Titoism (and partly of fascism and national socialism)	Victim centered approach
Racist discrimination, segregation of the relatives of the victims (murdered, imprisoned, persecuted)	Compensation for the relatives of the victims

Victims and crimes are erased from collective memory	Victims and crimes are registered in collective memory
Extrajudicial war and postwar slaughter is taboo, concealed and pushed into the unconscious mind	Investigation, unveiling, awareness of the crime
Victors can not be sentenced	Extra-judicial crimes (crimes against humanity) don't fall under statute of limitation
Prolongation of conspiracy of silence	International public is informed about crimes of Titoism
Destruction of archives	Tracing archives, collection of supplementary sources (topography, oral histories)
Ban on the burial of the murdered, destruction of graves	Concealed graves and killing sites are researched and curated
Political and police blockade of killing sites and graves	Erection of parish memorial plates, monuments, memorial ceremonies
Glorification of war criminals (for instance majority of so called national heroes)	The criminal police investigation Sprava (Reconciliation) is ensuring that the crimes are investigated and criminals pursued
Suspects give false evidence, lead investigators astray, lie to criminal investigators and investigation commissions	After discovery of the victims in shaft of St.Barbara in Huda Jama (2009) for the first time dozens of witnesses came to the investigators
Import of publications and other information of victims, perpetrators, concealed graves and killing sites in Yugoslavia from abroad (political emigration in West) is prohibited	Domestic public is informed about prohibited publications and information
Obstruction to research and conservation of memorial sites	Professional and programme standards are defined for research and conservation of memorial sites

Literature

Dežman, J. 2007. *Slovenia 1945–1960*. Celovec: MD.

Dežman, J. 2008. Communist repression and transitional justice in Slovenia. In: Peter Jambrek , (ed.), *Crimes committed by totalitarian regimes : reports and proceedings of the 8th April European Public Hearing on Crimes Committed by Totalitarian Regimes*. Slovenian Presidency of the Council of the European Union.

Dežman, J. 2012. Tabuizacija in detabuizacija (Tabooisation and detabooisation). In: *Poročilo 3 – resnica in sočutje*, Komisija vlade RS za reševanje vprašanj prikritih grobišč 2009–2011. (Report 3 – Truth and compassion, Commission of the Government of RS for Solving the Questions of Concealed Mass Graves.) Ljubljana: Družina, 2012, pp.131–248.

INDEPENDENT SLOVENIA AND CONCEALED MASS GRAVES

Mitja Ferenc, Ljubljana

One of the least known and explored chapters of the Second World War are the events that took place immediately after its completion. This was the time of closing battles for liberation of the country and expulsion of foreign occupying forces. This, however, was also the time of merciless vengeance of the victors against the loosing side and actual and alleged opponents of the new government. This was a time of executions of thousands of people, in majority of cases without judicial trials and verdicts. Extrajudicial executions were taking place in other parts of Europe as well, but nowhere as extensively as in Slovenia, if we consider the total number of population.

The exact number of victims lying in secret graves will probably never be known. The Republic of Slovenia has in the past few years succeeded in preparing a name-list of all residents of Slovenia who died a violent death in the Second World War and immediately after. Judging by the available data, around 15 % – that is around 13,960 (of those 12,587 Home guards, 160 Slovene Chetniks, and 1,127 civilians) – of about 84,000 people who died by January 1946 were individuals killed after the war ended.[1] Trying to answer the question of how many Croats and people of other nationalities were killed in Slovenia and where their remains could be found is even more difficult. As there is almost no primary archive material about the killings, mass graves or the number of victims as well as due to very rare excavations of the posthumous remains, to estimate or even to determine such a number could all too soon become a subject to manipulation and reach unprecedented levels.

I've been examining mass graves of soldiers and civilians from final days of second world war and the post-war era for many years. I'm mainly interested in concealed mass graves – graves, that weren't supposed to be there, that had to remain hidden, that the general public was not supposed to know about. Yugoslavian secret services OZNA and UDBA and their successors were driving relatives

1 *Slovenska novejša zgodovina*, 790–795.

of the victims from the scenes of alleged crimes.[2] For the last ten years I've been heading the project of registering and probing of concealed mass graves. We've documented over six hundred locations.[3]

With the fall of Party regime and onset of democracy, many people, especially relatives of the victims, expected the state to commemorate these victims and attend to these swamps, meadows, mineshafts – locations of mortal remains, that weren't supposed to exist. It turned out that we, the people, charged the state with a burden that it wasn't able or didn't want to cope with.

In the first decade of democracy, from 1990 to 2000, Slovenian state carried out only a few symbolic acts, but refrained from doing anything concrete about the mass graves. Shortly after the first democratic elections, there was a reconciliation ceremony in Kočevski rog for the Home Guard militia members killed after the war. Many of them found their graves in pits at Kočevski rog. This name became a synonym for post-war executions in Slovenia, and the reconciliation ceremony a symbolic burial of the victims. A monument in Kočevski rog, that was selected in a public tender, was erected as late as 10 years after the selection and 14 years after the ceremony, and was preceded by another monument, that was actually built without permits. We now have two national monuments at the most notorious mass grave site in Slovenia – each built by different governments.[4]

Another example of only symbolic management is the Teharje memorial park at the site of a concentration camp, from which the prisoners were being taken to their deaths. Slovenian state unveiled a monument there in 2004, that still hasn't

2 OZNA = Division for the Protection of the People; the Yugoslav service fighting the so called interior enemy of new Yugoslavia, established in 1944 and subordinate to the Supreme Commandant of the Partisan Army Josip Broz Tito or his deputy Aleksander Rankovič and the Leaderships of individual federal units. The executive armed body of the OZNA was the Army of State Security (VDV) and afterwards the units of the Corps of National Defence of Yugoslavia (KNOJ). After the end of the war OZNA and KNOJ have, by order of the Yugoslav Centre, carried out the so called purification (out-of-court killings of arrested or, by the English authorities from Austria returned, members of anti-Partisan formations and other opponents of the new Yugoslav authorities).

3 The problem of secret mass graves was presented in more detail by the author at the exhibition *Hidden and Concealed. Hidden graves 60 years after the end of World War II* in Celje in May 2005 and later in larger Slovene cities as well as in the homonymous monograph; Ferenc, M.: *Prikrito in očem zakrito.*

4 Ferenc, M. 2006: Poklon slovenskim žrtvam.

been completed. The repair costs are already sky high. I should also note that people were playing golf above the mortal remains for many years at Teharje. Nowadays access to the monument is limited due to vandalism.

The third example of only symbolical management is a parliamentary resolution, that all concealed mass graves shall be marked with uniform monuments with a uniform inscription. In stead of confirming or at least marking the grave sites in situ, we were waiting for a uniform monument to be selected. When it was finally chosen after years of public tenders, only five were constructed. A controversy regarding the contents of the inscription arose. In 2003 the Slovenian National Assembly decreed, that the monuments shall carry the text "Victims of war and post-war executions". [5] This became a subject of numerous controversies. The politicians couldn't agree on a new text for seven years and no new monuments were built. There was a general public belief that the inscription is the main obstacle, preventing the state to start settling mass graves. But even after the politicians agreed on a new text, "Victims of war and revolutionary violence", only a single memorial tablet was erected at the (barred doors of/ entrance to) Huda jama mine.

The lack of legislation prevented or at least limited any attempts to start the settlement of mass grave sites. Everyone was waiting for an act on this subject to be passed, there was a general belief that such an act would deal with this problem by itself. Seven years after the Act has been passed, we can safely say that its implementation depends upon the political will of the current government or minister.

The state didn't take up investigating and settlement of concealed mass grave sites unless it was forced to – mostly due to coincidental findings during construction works. The most disdainful thing about this is that the mortal remains of soldiers from Germany and Italy, the occupying countries, were taken care of – their remains are being exhumed and buried at appropriate sites.[6]

5 Official Gazette RS, no. 65/2003.

6 Agreement between the governments of the Republic of Slovenia and the Italian Republic on the management of wartime graves, Off. Gaz. RS, International Agreements, no. 10/1997; Agreement between the governments of the Republic of Slovenia and the Federal Republic of Germany on wartime graves, Off. Gaz. RS, International Agreements, no. 6/1999; MD, Agreement between the governments of the Republic of Slovenia and the Republic of Croatia on management of wartime graves, Draft.

The first investigation and actual settlement of a mass grave site took place in Slovenska Bistrica municipality. Local authorities decided to inspect and confirm or disprove the suspicions that two abandoned shelters were actually mass grave sites. They started work in 2001 at their own expense and soon found the victims. There were 431 men and women.[7] This stirred the public and forced the government to act . The mass grave was inspected by state prosecutor general and director general of the police, while the government pledged to begin settling the mass grave sites, which initially meant that it would enable registration of mass grave sites.[8] A criminal investigation of the killings was also renewed. This final attempt to find the culprits of these war crimes eventually came to a standstill and concrete settlement of mass grave sites wasn't possible for many years. Only registration of alleged mass grave sites was permitted, actual research and probing were not possible.

The site in Slovenska Bistrica was settled in 2004. An ossuary was built and a monument was built. After a tiresome effort, the costs were reimbursed to the municipality by the state. But unfortunately there are only two more such municipalities as Slovenska Bistrica; these are Kamnik and Škofja loka, where they marked the grave sites or exhumed the victims on their own accord.

Between 2006 and 2008 it seemed we'll be able to start with concrete investigations and settlement of mass graves in the field. A government commission, led by Jože Dežman, established the methodology of probing, that is, field research to confirm and determine the existence and size of mass grave sites. We analyzed around 130 sites.[9] We confirmed that the anti-tank trench in Tezno in Maribor is the largest mass grave site in this part of Europe with around 15 000 victims.[10] We managed to move victims from a karstic abyss for the first time. We started geodetic measurements of known mass grave sites, we settled and marked the first mass grave sites in Kočevski rog, an ossuary for the mortal remains was built. Despite a slow response by governmental agencies there was hope that this would become part of their regular activities.

7 Ferenc, M. 2009: Usodna odločenost Bistričanov.

8 Statement of the government of the Republic of Slovenia about a wholesome plan to manage mass graves of post-war mass killings and at the passing of the Law on War-time Mass Graves, 22. 11. 2001.

9 Dežman, J. 2008: *Poročilo Komisije*.

10 Ferenc, M. 2008: Verborgene Grabstätte Maribor : der Wald Tezenski Gozd.

In 2008 the Commission for the settlement of hidden graves decided to investigate a potential mass grave site in the shaft of Huda jama mine near Laško. After eight months of excavations the mining crews removed 400 square meters of gangue and breached 11 barriers Criminalists, historians and miners found a white bulk of 427 non-decomposed corpses.

The work in the mine shaft continued, after the investigative judge decreed an exhumation of mortal remains of the victims, but only to the depth of 5 meters. They found 346 corpses of men and women. As the mine shaft is 48 meters deep, we presume there are over 2000 victims in the shaft. The government decided to leave them there. One could say the state failed the test of maturity in Huda jama exhumations.[11]

The temporary ossuary in one of the mine shafts, that now holds 773 victims, is too small for proper preservation of all mortal remains from the mine. Expectations of numerous relatives and majority of Slovenians were not met – a Christian burial and proper settlement of a burial field above the mine were not conducted. The funds for completion of the work were substantially reduced at first and later practically cancelled.

Huda jama is a symbolic and concrete example of our relations towards the victims of post-war executions. It proves the inability of Slovenian state to properly address these cases, concretely or symbolically. No short or long term decisions that would appease the victims and their relatives were adopted. Charting of concealed mass graves has been cancelled – probably because someone decided that 600 registered hidden mass graves was enough and that there aren't any more. Unfortunately new reports of grave sites locations are still coming – they should be investigated. Probing of the sites also ceased. A high representative from Ministry of labour, family and social affairs said that "they shouldn't dig through whole Slovenia like moles and that all mass grave sites were already investigated". Geodetic surveys of the sites have been stopped, already confirmed locations are not being marked any more. Due to terrain changes and overgrowing we can't find some sites any more. Exhumations and relocations of mortal remains from unsuitable locations, such as landfills and refuse dumps, have stopped. The largest mass grave, the anti-tank ditch in Tezno remains unsettled, overgrown and inaccessible, despite the government pledges to transform it into a memorial park.

11 Ferenc et al.: *Huda jama*, 49–264.

While it is quite understandable that these crimes and graves were concealed during 45 years of a totalitarian regime, one has to wonder why so little was done in 20 years of democracy.

A quick glance at official state representatives responses shows a considerable discomfort regarding mass grave sites discoveries. Efforts of granting the victims' rights to proper remembrance and decent burial are being disregarded. Zealous academic work is quickly given political connotation. In stead of proper pieta, pain, anguish and reflection, that should result in reconciliation, we are responded by questions as: "Why are "bone collectors" bothering us again? We should finally let go of the past and focus on the present and the future!" Researchers are reproached as trying to sow dissention and rewrite history. But killing grounds, turned into landfills, sealed mines, filled up and polluted karstic pits ("foiba"), full of human remains, are not the past. They are reality that all democratically elected Slovenian governments are turning a blind eye to.

Slovenian government decided to erect a common monument for all victims in Ljubljana. This is supposed to mark the completion of reconciliation. We obviously still fail to realize that symbolic gestures are not enough, they do not diminish the sorrow, grief, anger and anguish of the relatives.[12]

We are drawn to a conclusion, that Slovenia failed to fulfil its civilisation obligations in the area of settlement of concealed mass graves and failed to contribute to appeasement and reconciliation among its people.

20 years after reconciliation ceremony, more than 20 years after democratic regime change, after 20 years of living in independent state, thousands of Slovenians, relatives of the victims, still have nowhere to light a candle for their loved ones. They do not have a place where they could shed their tears and remember their missing fathers, mothers, grandparents, brothers, sisters. Even if they discover the location of their graves, they are faced with numerous bureaucratic obstacles and difficulties, imposed by the democratic Slovenian state. After 40 years of Party regime, that prosecuted even mentioning this, let alone marking of the graves, exhumation or removal of mortal remains, relatives expected the new regime will

12 http://www.rtvslo.si/slovenija/noveli-vojnih-zakonov-sprejeti/211777 ; http://www.rtvslo.si/slovenija/spomenik-vsem-zrtvam-vojn-bo-na-kongresnem-trgu/255516

at least mitigate their situation, if not conduct civil and pieta actions by itself. How are people supposed to comprehend reconciliation talks of the politicians, if the state wouldn't even mark the hidden graves of their relatives? They encounter first obstacles at acquiring permits for identification of a concealed mass grave, which is followed by further difficulties in getting permissions to exhume the mortal remains, remove and identify them. There are just too many obstacles to believe the state apparatus and its leaders are sincere in their statements.

In my field work I frequently come across relatives, who wish to exhume the remains of their loved ones and properly bury them at the local graveyard, or at least inspect the grounds for potential proofs of a mass grave. They are prohibited to do this as individuals, while the state is not prone to conduct this continually, systematically and expertly. And the years go by. My wish is that we could, especially considering the appalling magnitude of these phenomena, complete this task as soon as possible, as the number of those, who would find solace in proper burial and marking of the graves, is diminishing with the passing of time.

References

Cowgill, A., Brimelow, T., Booker, C.1990. *The Repatriations from Austria in 1945. The Report of an Inquiry*, London: Sinclair Stevenson.

Dežman, J. (ed.) 2008. *Poročilo Komisije Vlade Republike Slovenije za reševanje vprašanj prikritih grobišč: 2005–2008*, Ljubljana: Družina.

Ferenc, M., Kužatko, Ž. 2007. *Prikrivena grobišta Hrvata u Republici Sloveniji / Prikrita grobišča Hrvatov v Republiki Sloveniji / Hidden croatian mass graves in the Republic of Slovenia*, Zagreb: Počasni bleiburški vod.

Ferenc, M. 2008. Verborgene Grabstätte Maribor : der Wald Tezenski Gozd = Prikrito grobišče Maribor : Tezenski gozd. In: *Signal : Jahresschrift des Pavel-Hauses : Winter/zima 2008/2009 = Letni zbornik Pavlove hiše*. Laafeld: Pavel-haus = Potrna: Pavlova hiša, pp. 223–251.

Ferenc, M. 2005. *Prikrito in očem zakrito. Prikrita grobišča 60 let po koncu druge svetovne vojne*, Celje: Muzej novejše zgodovine.

Ferenc, M., Alić, M., Jamnik, P. 2011. *Huda Jama. Skrito za enajstimi pregradami*, Ljubljana: Družina.

Ferenc, M. 2009. Usodna odločenost Bistričanov: o raziskavah prikritih grobišč na Zgornji Bistrici. In: *Zbornik občine Slovenska Bistrica,* 3, Slovenska Bistrica: Skupščina občine, Kulturna skupnost, pp. 333–347.

Ferenc, M. 2006. Ministry of culture and the register of hidden burial-grounds in the Republic of Slovenia : analysis of work completed between April 2002 and October 2004. In: *Varstvo spomenikov,* 41, pp. 100–128.

Ferenc, M. 2006. Poklon slovenskim žrtvam na napačnem kraju zločina. In: *Mitsko in stereotipno v slovenskem pogledu na zgodovino,* Zbirka Zgodovinskega časopisa, 32. Ljubljana: Zveza zgodovinskih društev Slovenije, pp. 153–164.

Griesser – Pečar, T. 2004. *Razdvojeni narod: Slovenija 1941–1945 : okupacija, kolaboracija, državljanska vojna, revolucija,* Ljubljana: Mladinska knjiga.

Jambrek, P. (ed.) 2008. *Crimes committed by totalitarian regimes : reports and proceedings of the 8 April European Public Hearing on Crimes Committed by Totalitarian Regimes.* Ljubljana: Slovenian Presidency of the Council of the European Union, pp. 155–160.

Mlakar, B. 2003. *Slovensko domobranstvo: 1943–1945. Ustanovitev, organizacija, idejno ozadje,* Ljubljana: Slovenska matica.

Pučnik, J. 1988. Množični povojni poboji. In: D. Jančar (ed.), *Temna stran meseca. Kratka zgodovina totalitarizma v Sloveniji 1945–1990,* Ljubljana, pp. 39–52.

Prcela, J. Živić, D. 2001. *Hrvatski holokaust,* Zagreb.

Slovenska novejša zgodovina. Od programa Zedinjene Slovenije do mednarodnega priznanja Republike Slovenije. 1848–1992, 2005, 1, Ljubljana, pp. 790–795.

URBAN DEVELOPMENT, GRASSROOTS AUTHORITARIANISM AND THE PROBLEM OF RECONCILIATION IN POST-SOVIET RUSSIA

Mark Kleyman, Ivanovo

Violence as a global issue: case Russia

On 22 July 2011 seventy-six persons were killed in Norway, and many of them were under the age of 18 years old. A certain man decided that the practices founded in the ideas of tolerance and multiculturalism threatened Europe, and a "right" end of defending European culture would justify any means of reaching it. News of the mass murder left Norway in shock. For many decades Norwegians have been tending to believe that their nation presented an example of the most humane social system ever created worldwide. At the same time, they preferred to ignore numerous problems that increasingly challenged the development of the country (Pollestad, 1987). For example, in depicting the economic and social transitions, as Norway moved from an agricultural culture to an industrial, and then to a post-industrial society, Kjartan Fløgstad insisted on that in the mid 1970s many people, especially the young ones, started to experience identity crisis. In turn, to cope with that, they often began to think that violence was the only way to solve any problem (Fløgstad, 1981). As a result, already in the1980s national and local elections saw gains by fringe parties running an openly xenophobic platform (Einhorn and Logue, 2003: 46). In either case, perhaps the tragedy in Norway shows that the emphasis on violence in solving every problem is increasingly becoming a global issue, and even the most affluent and advanced democracies cannot escape that (Enzensberger, 1993).

Like that of any other country, the history of Russia provides many examples of violence, but this problem became extremely acute after 1917. The Russian Revolution led to seizure of power by the Communist Bolsheviks. Their leaders emphasized violence as the proper way to abolish social inequality worldwide, since the revolution in Russia was considered just as the beginning of the world socialist revolution. As a result, the Communist ideal was becoming discredited. According to Nikolai Berdyaev, by the mid 1930s Joseph Stalin's regime had become quite similar to that in Nazi Germany (Berdyaev, 1937), though the Nazis pursued in regarding Marx's communist ideal in terms of the "Jewish-Bolshevist conspiracy theory".

However, the analysis of the Soviet politics and policies is beyond the scope of this paper. Indeed, it aims to focus on examining some processes that provided mass support for the regime. Without such a support the long-standing rule of the Communist Party would be hardly possible. It became even more evident after the death of Stalin, when the repressive policies became somewhat less visible, and the authorities gradually took a tolerant attitude toward a slack work ethic and a growing black market second economy. By the late 1980s the Communist leaders embarked on major reforms, which led to the fall of the totalitarian regime and produced many optimistic prospects upon the future. But the further events showed that the democracy in Russia failed. Yet, it is now widely accepted that before a country can be classified as a "consolidated democracy", democratic institutions must be established and adopted at the local community level. Grassroots democracy means not only policy making, but rather everyday practices. These practices might give way for reconciliation that is so crucial for the Russian society nowadays. But the question is whether the moral climate within the particular community is favorable for that. A moral climate is defined by the shared perceptions of how moral issues should be addressed and what morally correct behavior is (Victor and Cullen, 1988; Novikov, 2003). The paper presents an attempt to provide some groundwork for studying these issues, while developing a multidisciplinary approach, based on the perspectives of cultural and community psychology, as well as that of urban anthropology.

Urbanization and the emergence of grassroots authoritarianism in Russia

The fact that the Marxist-Leninist movement was distinctly urban-oriented is relevant to understanding the nature of the subsequent urbanization that occurred in Russia during the Soviet era. The leaders of the Communist party had a philosophy regarding the 19th century capitalist city that was heavily influenced by the *Communist Manifesto*, written by Marx and Engels in 1848 decrying the degradation of the proletariat in large, industrial cities. The irony of the situation lay in the fact that Russia was an agrarian society at the time of the Revolution, and urban squalor was not nearly at the level of other European metropolises. Yet, the new leaders believed that industrialization was the wave of the future and would legitimize the new state to the rest of the world. The aggressive pursuance of economic development via industrialization was largely responsible for an explosion of urban growth (Iyer, 1997).

Moral climate within the most of urban communities in Russia was produced by these trends. The non-defense single-enterprise town defined as a city with population 100,000 or more where 30% of the population is employed in one enterprise, became prevalent in Soviet Russia. The extensive development of the centrally planned economy, in the way of the dawn of the industrial era, required many low-skilled workers from the countryside who were forced to move in the cities because of the collectivization of their lands. A large and sudden invasion of new people inevitably awakens a strong sense of community (Freudenburg, 1984: 697–705). To replace the traditional sense of community found in rural areas, these people often restored principal traits of face-to-face social relations. The elements of local traditions were mixed with official ideological patterns (it would be possible to define this phenomenon as *quasi-traditionalism*). The Soviet ideology encouraged the traditional collectivism typical for a small rural community (Russian: *obshchina*). It was incorporated in the urban environment in numerous modifying forms, such as, for example, those of communal apartments.

Since the Soviet model of industrialization required, first of all, low-skilled labor force, the underclass put together the majority of population. As a result, some traits of the culture of poverty became prevalent within the urban communities. Oscar Lewis (2002) gave some seventy characteristics that indicated the presence of the culture of poverty. *The people in that culture have a strong feeling of marginality, of helplessness, of dependency, of not belonging.* Despite decades of the criticism of that idea by prominent sociologists, anthropologists and other academics (Ember and Ember, 2004: 210), the culture of poverty concept persists in popular culture. We refer to this concept, while assuming that its scope might give an opportunity to understand the origins of some values that were propagandized by the Soviet ideology, e.g., those of *personal unworthiness and dependency on the party and state leader (Russian: vozhd').* The official propaganda presented these values as the principal elements of the "proletarian culture". The Communist Party purported to rule in the name of the urban working class (proletariat), while initially claimed to have created socialist state that was "dictatorship of the proletariat" (Fitzpatrick, 1993). The nominally favored class status of proletarians was a guarantee to provide opportunity for social advancement. For example, the fact that one's parents were "proletarians", while being not ever persecuted as "politicals", or "enemies of the people", was regarded as crucial upon his or her application for a privileged position within the ruling class of *nomenklatura* (Djilas, 1983).

But in reality proletarians generally lived in cramped apartment complexes, spent hours each day standing in line to buy food and other necessities and attended frequent obligatory sessions of political indoctrination. As a result, moral climate within many urban communities in Soviet Russia was tended to produce grassroots authoritarianism featured with populist envy, intolerance and strong belief in state power, directed against any form of (O)otherness. The breakdown of the Communist regime in the beginning of the 1990s did not mean the end of these processes.

Shock therapy without reconciliation: Soviet ideology in post-Soviet Russia

While briefly summarizing the results of the development of Russia after 1991, Anders Åslund argues that market reform succeeded and democracy failed (Åslund, 2007). In fact, in the winter of 1991 -1992 the team of the reformers lead by Yegor Gaidar had a clear idea of how to build the market economy in Russia. President Boris Yeltsin supported this idea and presented it with a set of policy actions. These actions were motivated by the opinion that the market economy *per se* could inevitably produce democracy, and there was no need of reconciliation and coping with the totalitarian past. As a result, the failure of the shock therapy of the 1990s impacted the emergence of Putin's scenario of authoritarian modernization, founded in the Chinese experience in combining the liberal economic model with many traits of the Communist regime. In fact, many elements of the Soviet ideology and policies have been restored, while being interlinked with the officially supported Orthodox fundamentalism. State-controlled media and politicians increasingly present an image of the declining and "hostile" West, and oppose it to that of "prosperous" Putin's Russia. They tend to consider Russia to be culturally closer to Asia than to Europe, and, in this sense, their ideology is somewhat close to the neo-Eurasianism that was initially popularized by Lev Gumilev (1990). At the same time, the history of Russia is presented as "glorious", and the ideas of reconciliation and coping with the totalitarian past are often regarded as "antipatriotic" ones.

At the same time, we increasingly observe the situation marked with a paradox: while opposing Russian idealism to Western materialism, the official propaganda encourages consumerism and materialism. Private ownership is presented as useful while it "conforms to national interests". In practice, the officials mean that any private business has to be subdued to state bureaucracy. As a consequence, Stalin's practices in governance are often advocated as an "effective management strategy" in terms of the economy of state capitalism.

As high oil prices initially drove the economic growth in Russia in the 2000s, there is a steady increase in the standard of living. Consumerism, or a social and economic order that is based on the systematic creation and fostering of a desire to purchase goods and services in ever greater amounts, is increasingly propagandized in terms of a socially desirable lifestyle of "never-sleeping Moscow". It seems that the state-controlled media and some officials offer the only one way for Russia to solve the numerous problems caused by globalization, that is, to restore the Iron Curtain while creating a consumerist paradise behind it.

But these practices are hardly resulted only from the official policies; perhaps they are produced by grassroots authoritarianism.

Reverence for life, grassroots democracy and reconciliation

Perhaps the elements of grassroots democracy could be developed within urban communities, where the moral climate would favour the practices founded in the idea of the reverence for life (Schweitzer, 1998). In fact, tolerance toward any form of (O)otherness might be resulted from the widely accepted social norms that encourage individuals in maintaining, assisting and enhancing life. In this sense, (O)otherness include any form of life that differs from the human one. We should stop regarding ourselves as masters of nature; in reality, the human society is a part of natural environment. But the question is if the moral climate within the particular community encourages individuals to act in such a way.

The paper provides some results of studying these processes in the city of Ivanovo in Central Russia (population: 409,277; 2010 Census preliminary results). Regarded as a centre of the textile industry of Russia, Ivanovo presents an example of the non-defense, mono-industrial city and, in this sense, it may be regarded as a model of the Soviet and post-Soviet city.

The primary data has been obtained by in-depth interviews with 28 volunteers who provide food, shelters and veterinary care for homeless cats and dogs. They report that the problem of abandoned pets is becoming acute, though there is still no relevant statistics regarding their numbers. But, at the same time, the authorities oppose having the animals spayed or neutered to prevent the births of unwanted and accidental litters, or even putting the pets into euthanasia. They prefer killing them as the only way of solving this problem. The authorities practice it openly, while hiring the gunmen to hunt the pets. Very often these bloody scenes are witnessed by children. At the same time, the volunteers report that only few people openly support these atrocities while saying that taking care of homeless animals is a "waste of money", and killing them is a "really courageous" action. But the majority of people cannot still stop the violence that is crucial for the emergence of the moral climate within the city.

In this sense, grassroots authoritarianism does not always mean an open support of violence by the majority of people. But this majority does not tend to oppose violence, while perceiving it as an inevitable evil. At the same time, any form of (O)otherness is regarded as being endangered the social order. As the animal caregivers maintain the forms of life that differ from the human one, they reported that many people, though being sympathetic to their activities, regarded them as "strange people". Perhaps it results from the egalitarian attitudes which may be regarded as an outcome of the Soviet "culture of poverty". But now these attitudes are increasingly interlinked with the spread of capitalism *tout court* in every sector of public and private life, while the gap between affluence and poverty being tremendous. Perhaps the egalitarian attitudes motivate many Russian, especially young and middle-aged ones, in being imbued with the consumerist culture, as they want to look like their neighbors who owe luxurious dwellings and expensive automobiles. As a result, the identity crisis appears in its extreme forms. Perhaps the queer mixture of Stalinism, Orthodox fundamentalism and economic liberalism in Putin's ideology may be considered as an outcome of this crisis.

Many people, both in Russia and abroad, think that the authoritarian stream of Russian history provides the only way for further development. But, in reality, under this stream there was always an undercurrent, sometimes strong, of a sense of the reverence for life. For example, *zemstvo*, or local self-government instituted during the great liberal reforms of the 1860s, succeeded in solving in the proper way many problems of general education, medical service and public welfare. After the October Revolution of 1917 it was violently shut down. But, according to Alexander Solzhenitsyn (1991), this experience may be regarded as a starting point in emerging grassroots democracy in Russia, as well as a possibility for reconciliation and coping with the totalitarian past.

Conclusion

During the 20th century Russia experienced a rapid urban growth. These processes produced an identity crisis, or feeling of being marginalized. Being interlinked with the totalitarian ideology, the identity crisis became a background for the emergence of grassroots authoritarianism, or widely accepted stereotypes that produce intolerance toward any form of (O)otherness. In the post-Soviet era these trends were impacted by the rapid societal "capitalization" that was not interlinked with reconciliation and coping with the totalitarian past. As a result, the moral climate within many urban communities does not still encourage individuals in maintaining, assisting and enhancing life. These tendencies increasingly impact the emergence of the official ideology and policies.

But, at the same time, now violence features not only Russian society. It is increasingly becoming a global issue, partly due to the urbanization worldwide. For example, urbanization produced formalization of interpersonal and social relations behind an attractive façade of the welfare state in Norway (Pollestad, 1987). Perhaps these trends impacted the terrorist attack in 2011, while the attacker, just in a manner of Adolf Hitler and his Norwegian counterpart Vidkun Quisling, started regarding the mass murder as a proper way to solve any problem.

In either case, urbanization produces multidimensional and multicultural social environment, but many people still oppose that, partly due to a fear of losing their identities. The way out of this situation might be founded in the principle of *in varietate concordia*. But, at the same time, it is hardly possible unless we really start acting in accordance with the idea of the reverence for life (Schweitzer, 1998). This idea may produce a sense of oneness despite physical, psychological or cultural barriers as a starting point of reconciliation worldwide.

References

Åslund, A. 2007. *Russia's Capitalist Revolution: Why Market Reform Succeeded and Democracy Failed*, Washington, DC: Peterson Institute for International Economics.

Berdyaev, N. 1937. *The Origin of Russian Communism*, translated by R. M. French, London: G. Bles.

Djilas, M. 1983. *The New Class: An Analysis of the Communist System*, San Diego: Harcourt Brace Jovanovich.

Einhorn, E.S., and J. Logue. 2003. Modern Welfare States: Scandinavian Politics and Policy in the Global Age, Westport, CT: Praeger Publishers.

Ember, C., and M. Ember. 2004. *Encyclopedia of Medical Anthropology*, Dordrecht; Norwell, MA: Kluwer Academic Publishers.

Enzensberger, H.M. 1993. *Aussichten auf den Bürgerkrieg (Prospects of the Civil War)*, Frankfurt am Main: Suhrkamp Verlag.

Fitzpatrick, S. 1993. Ascribing Class. The Construction of Social Identity in Soviet Russia. In: *Journal of Modern History* 65 (4), pp. 745–770.

Fløgstad, K. 1981. *Loven vest for Pecos (The Law West of Pecos)*, Oslo: Gyldendal Norsk Forlag.

Freudenburg, W. 1984. Boomtown Youth: The Differential Impacts of Rapid Community Growth on Adolescents and Adults. In: *American Sociological Review* 49 (October), pp. 697–705.

Gumilev, L. N. 1990. *Ethnogenesis and the Biosphere*, Moscow: Progress.

Iyer, S. 1997. The Urbanization Transition in Russia. Available from: http://www.umich.edu/~csfound/545/1997/iye/seemapap.html [Accessed 15 November 2011].

Lewis, O. 2002. The Culture of Poverty. In: G. Gmelch and W. Zenner (eds.), *Urban Life, Prospect Heights,* IL: Waveland Press, pp. 269–278.

Novikov, V.V. 2003. *Sotsialnaya Psikhologuiya: Fenomen i Nauka (Social Psychology: Phenomenon and Science)*, Moscow: Institute of Psychotherapy.

Pollestad, K.A. 1987. *Skål for Norge (Cheers to Norway)*, Oslo: Cappelens.

Schweitzer, A. 1998. *Out of my Life and Thought,* Baltimore, MD: Johns Hopkins University Press.

Solzhenitsyn, A. I. 1991. *Rebuilding Russia: Reflections and Tentative Proposals*, translated by Alexis Klimoff, New York: Farrar, Straus & Giroux.

Victor, B., and J. B. Cullen. 1988. The Organizational Bases of Ethical Work Climates. In: *Administrative Science Quarterly* 33 (1), pp. 101–125.

THE MEANING OF CULTURE FOR RECONCILIATION: DIALOGUE, MEMORY AND COMMUNITY

Igor Bahovec, Ljubljana

1. Introduction

Reconciliation has emerged as one of the master narratives of the late twentieth century. Individuals and entire nations struggle to overcome the legacy of suffering ranging from wars, genocide, an apartheid regime, ethnic conflicts etc. In addition to the events of recent decades, there is also a call for reconciliation due to more historical injustices and oppression in relations between (and within) nations, countries and/or cultural groups.

In this paper we focus on the role of culture in reconciliation processes. We consider culture in its broader, anthropological and sociological meaning. We believe that a genuine reconciliation process should integrate all aspects of human life, including all three dimensions or aspects of human sociality: persons in interpersonal relationships, the socio-structural dimension and culture. Culture is related to the depth of personal and group identity. We believe that without the addition of cultural aspects of reconciliation, reconciliation cannot reach the deep level of human life needed for genuine co-existence and the more profound cooperation of previously hostile, conflicting or divided people, groups and cultures.

Globalisation and the global connectedness of cultures is creating another and new notion. Societies and cultures have developed various ways of reconciliation processes. These reflect the actual experience of life in these cultures and their creative potential. Some authors stress that the approach to reconciliation as developed and understood in the socio-cultural context of the West, especially in Northern Europe and the United States, is not the universal way of reconciliation. Some other approaches to reconciliation may also be appropriate – especially in non-Western cultures. Globalisation in this sense may lead to the cross-fertilised, dialogical meeting of people and their cultures. It does not lead to a single global monoculture; on the contrary, it is bringing about a transformation of all cultures. In such two-way (multi-way) communication the West can learn from the approaches to reconciliation of other cultures and civilisations.

2. Culture and processes of reconciliation

Broadly speaking, culture refers to a people's way of life. Culture includes many societal aspects: meanings and symbols, language, values, norms, beliefs, behaviours, mores and attitudes, objects, institutions, along with other characteristics common to members of a particular group or society.

Regarding the meaning and role of culture in reconciliation processes we would like to stress four points:

(1) Culture is important for communication, orientation and action.

Cultural values, habits and attitudes provide the foundation for the social norms according to which people live and act.

When people of different cultures meet, difficulties in communication and mutual understanding do not arise due to language alone. Many problems occur because they do not share the same culture. One can improve the mutual understanding of language and habits. But many parts of a culture cannot be learned. Sometimes even the experience of living in another culture (for a longer time) does not reveal all parts of a culture. We believe this can be explained through an analogy: culture is like an iceberg. 'Culture lies primarily under the surface, beneath conscious awareness' (Hooker, 2009: 59).

(2) Cultures are different.

Differences in cultures are also evident from empirical data. According to Hofstede's study in the 1980s, values that distinguish countries from each other can be statistically grouped into four clusters. They show different ways of how societies deal with differences between genders (masculinity versus femininity), power inequality (power distance), uncertainty (uncertainty avoidance), the relationship between individuals and (primary) groups (individualism versus collectivism). Later on, the fifth 'dimension of national culture' was added: short-term versus long-term orientation (Samovar et al., 2007: 140–151).

(3) Culture counts.

After the 1940s and 1950s when much attention was paid to culture as an important element of understanding societies, for decades the role of cultural values and attitudes was largely ignored in many aspects of their social life. The situation changed in the 1990s when 'a major renewal of interest in culture' appeared among the social sciences. It was then becoming clear that 'values shape human progress' (Harrison and Huntington, 2000). Culture is the theme of our time. 'Our most pressing issues are profoundly cultural in nature. We try to address them, but without an appreciation of how deeply culture determines our worldviews, we can only grope and fumble' (Hooker, 2009: 63).

(4) Cultural values and attitudes can be an obstacle to or promoter of reconciliation.

Of course, culture does not exist in a vacuum. Yet including and integrating cultural aspects into reconciliation processes seems to be both necessary and promising (Schreiter, 2002: 107).

For example, while reflecting in the post-war situation in ex-Yugoslavia Slavenka Drakulić stressed: 'When relying on the positive role of culture in reconciliation, we should keep in mind its capacity to produce ideology and propaganda', to manipulate people, even to prepare and justify murder. Culture can be a vehicle for extremist political (nationalistic) manipulations. On the other hand, 'The opposite is most likely also true [...] In a democracy, it can also enable the free circulation of ideas, which is the key to a long-term reconciliation' (Drakulic, 2011).

In short, one can easily find historical (and recent) examples of societies where a 'culture of exclusion and violence' prevails as well as societies where a culture of peace, inclusion and reconciliation prevails.

With regard to reconciliation two components of culture seem to play an especially important role: (1) symbolic narratives as stories which tell cultural groups what they need to know about themselves and how to remember what has happened to them; and (2) institutions as clusters of cultural meanings and rules associated with specific social activities. An important function of such institutions and narratives is to maintain community identity and solidarity and to shape the relationship of one group with other groups.

3. Cultural differences and the reconciliation process

Every society has developed techniques and procedures to regulate differences and conflicts. These mechanisms vary greatly from one culture to another.

In terms of the cultural specifics of Western societies one can say that Western societies are more individualistic than others. This is also evident from Hofstede's abovementioned studies. Western countries differ from all other civilisations in the indicators of individualism and power distance (see Table 1). With other indicators the differences are not so unambiguous.

Table 1 Hofstede's indicators of individualism and power distance (average values of countries group, own analysis). Source: Samovar et al., 2007: 142–147.

	Individualism Index	Power Distance Index
Western Europe	67,1	39,8
USA, Australia, Canada, New Zealand	85,0	34,3
South America	22,3	67,8
Sub-Saharan Africa	28,2	68,2
Islamic countries (North Africa and Near East)	38,3	74,9
Asia (without East Near)	26,0	72,8

Some other Western cultural characteristics are: human rights, the rule of law, democracy, a market economy with a strong welfare state. Europe is also a very secular society.

Do these cultural characteristics influence the understanding of reconciliation processes?

According to different authors who have studied reconciliation processes in African or Muslim societies, the answer is 'yes and no'. More precisely, 'yes' in certain aspects and to certain degrees, and 'no' in others. Why? One reason is that most non-Western societies are either predominantly collectivistic or predominantly communitarian. Broadly speaking, a collectivistic approach prevails in many (ex)communist countries, and a communitarian one in traditional African, Muslim and some other societies.

The approach to reconciliation taken in traditional societies of Sub-Saharan Africa is of particular interest to us. Due to wars, violence and apartheid in past decades this part of the world is trying to develop reconciliation processes to find solutions to allow a better coexistence. In so doing they employ different methods. According to Mpofu (2003), five ideologies are linked to reconciliation in Southern Africa. The main tasks in reconciliation processes are: (1) 'to convert people [...] into non-racial citizens'; (2) to improve inter-community communication and understanding, including communities with different cultures and histories; (3) to develop a new reconciled consciousness of persons, communities and society through integral 'moral reflection, repenting and rebirth'; (4) to restore the rule of law and protection of fundamental human rights; and (5) to rebuild broken interpersonal relationships and broken personal bonds at the local level.

We can see that the reconciliation process in the Southern African case includes a high level of community awareness and community building. There is a great stress on the need for genuine dialogue and dialogical processes.

4. Ubuntu: an African way of reconciliation

The specificity of the Southern African approach to reconciliation is connected with the concept of Ubuntu. This has become an integral part of the process in some African countries also because it was integral part of the reconciliation approach of Nelson Mandela and Archbishop Desmond Tutu (especially when he was Chairperson of the South African Truth and Reconciliation Commission).

The word "ubuntu" originates from one of the Bantu dialects of Africa, with the Ubuntu principle being known in most Sub-Saharan countries. It is a traditional African life-philosophy, culture mentality, and ethics. The Zulus would say: 'A person is a person through other persons.' Persons affirm their humanity when they acknowledge that of others. Some other Ubuntu sayings are: 'I am because you exist'; 'I am because we are, and since we are, therefore I am'.

Archbishop Desmond Tutu (2004: 26) described Ubuntu in the following way:

'It is the essence of being human. It speaks of the fact that my humanity is caught up and is inextricably bound up in yours. I am human because I belong. It speaks about wholeness, it speaks about compassion. A person with Ubuntu is welcoming, hospitable, warm and generous, willing to share. Such people are open and available to others, willing to be vulnerable, affirming of others, do not feel threatened that others are able and good, for they have a proper self-assurance that comes from knowing that they belong in a greater whole. They know that they are diminished when others are humiliated [...].'

Ubuntu includes several dimensions of wholeness, such as: (1) the connectedness of all people – including ancestors and the not yet born; (2) the ethics of benevolence and solidarity; (3) a message of (unconditional) hope despite inhuman living conditions; and (4) a relationship to transcendence.

The Ubuntu concept expresses strong human interconnectedness, including unconditional empathy: 'Your pain is my pain. Your salvation is my salvation.' Tutu (1999: 31) stressed: 'When I dehumanise you I inexorably dehumanise myself.'

Even though Ubuntu emphasises interconnectedness it is not a collectivist approach. There is no doubt that the Ubuntu concept runs counter to the creed of Western individualism but, on the other hand, Ubuntu includes respect for the particularity of the other (but not atomised individualism!). According to Ubuntu one cannot be human all by himself/herself. It is about the self-being strongly rooted in the community: a person's identity is defined by what he/she gives to the community.

It should be noted that individual elements of the Ubuntu concept can be misused (Moss, 2010). Ubuntu can have negative as well as positive implications. Restoring peaceful relations within the community may increase tensions in one community and others!

It seems that the positive effect of the Ubuntu concept depends on whether it is implemented in an integral way. In cases of reductions, for example where the co-responsibility of all participants involved is missing, or when the process only includes inner-group aspects and not the wider society, Ubuntu can produce bad results.

We would like to present two researches about the Ubuntu way of reconciliation; one presents the traditional Ubuntu process (Murithi 2006) and the other presents reflections on contemporary reconciliation processes in some Southern African countries (Nabudere, 2005). Both authors speak about five key stages of the process (see Table 2).

Table 2 Five stages of traditional and contemporary use of the Ubuntu way of reconciliation

Murithi, 2006	Nabudere,2005
1. After a fact-finding process where the views of victims, perpetrators and witnesses were heard, the perpetrators - if considered to have done wrong – are encouraged […] to acknowledge responsibility or guilt.	1. Reconciliation requires the creation of a consensus about the existence of the conflict. Conflict is not taken for granted for it sometimes obscures underlying stakes, which are partially expressed and which may not be clear to some of the conflicting actors, but which must nevertheless be resolved.

2. Perpetrators are encouraged to demonstrate genuine remorse or to repent.	2. Reconciliation goes beyond established normative rules, institutions and procedures, which may be inadequate to deal with the conflict. Reconciliation is therefore a creative and a flexible human activity that is undertaken for the sake of humanity as a shared community.
(3) Perpetrators are encouraged to ask for forgiveness and victims in their turn would be encouraged to show mercy.	3. Reconciliation is about accepting responsibility for wrongs committed since guilt is not the main point of the process. What is important is the recognition of the problem, acceptance of the responsibility for what has happened and the willingness to be part of the search for a solution.
(4) Where possible and at the suggestion of the Council of Elders, perpetrators would be required to pay an appropriate compensation or reparation for the wrong done (often more symbolic than a re-payment). Amnesty could thus be granted, but not with impunity.	4. Reconciliation is about the transformation of the conflict into a nonconflictual situation for the good of the larger humanity. [...] Both parties must define the stakes involved and relativise these stakes for the sake of the wider community as well as for the future of the unborn.
(5) In trying to consolidate the whole process, all parties are encouraged to commit themselves to reconciliation.	5. Reconciliation requires the performance of ritual and the explicit public verbalisation of the termination of the conflict by all parties. This may be in the form of a public oath followed by ritual such as sharing of a meal or drink, which may invoke the supernatural beings and the living-dead to intercede and assist the process of reconciliation.

We would like to stress just a few elements of the Ubuntu reconciliation process here.

1. The process of reconciliation tends to include the victim, the perpetrator and both families' members and friends. The aim is to heal the relationships among them and thus contribute to restoring harmony within the community which is a precondition of the integrity and viability of society.

2. The specific role of the institution of Elders: this institution has to play the role of a promoter or stimulator of the process – this is possible because they have the trust of the whole group that needs reconciliation and wisdom about the process. The Elders are recognised as having authority to act as arbiters and give judgement on the rights or wrongs of a dispute submitted to them and suggest a settlement, but they may have no power of physical coercion by which to enforce them.

3. The reconciliation process should include a public ritual as one of the last occurrences of the process: it is a vivid sign that the reconciliation process has led to a new, common identity. The ritual shows some kind of healing, a cleansing of memory.

4. 'The wisdom of this process lies in the recognition that it is not possible to build a healthy community at peace with itself unless past wrongs are acknowledged and brought out into the open so that the truth of what happened can be determined and social trust renewed through a process of forgiveness and reconciliation' (Murithi, 2009: 229).

5. Conclusion: truth, reconciliation and healing of memory

Despite all its diversity, we can say that all authentic and genuine reconciliation processes have some common features. One of the most important is the fact that they use a comprehensive, integrated approach that does not reduce the world and reality. Thus part of these processes involves creating a new culture, '*The Culture of Reconciliation*'. According to Schreiter (2002: 94–95), communities of reconciliation where a culture of reconciliation is present share three important aspects. They are communities of safety (zones in which victims can examine and explore their wounds), communities of memory (places where can arrive at a common memory of the past), and communities of hope. 'They are places which nurture the seedlings of a better, more just world in the future.'

One of the preconditions of such a culture is truth-telling and story-telling. This is in many aspects a difficult task. The truth can hurt. Even more difficult are situations where conflicts have happened in the past and memories are (strongly) infected by lies. In these cases, a very important part of reconciliation is the cleansing and healing of memory.

The memory of serious injustice cannot simply be deleted or forgotten. The cleansing and healing of memory is a process of seeing the past in a different way, without bitterness. In such a way a new culture is created that is less burdened by the past. This new culture keeps a memory and recognises the harsh truth, but it does not repeatedly burden new generations.

If this does not occur, there is always a danger that the unresolved memory of conflict will lead to new conflicts and wars. In this sense, we can understand the statement by the famous Croatian sociologist of religion Jakov Jukić that the war in the territory of ex-Yugoslavia was a war of centuries of unresolved memories. It is thus only in this way that one can explain the fact that in the first phase of that war symbolic cultural objects, mosques and churches were destroyed with great intensity. The destruction of culture was, similar to the displacement and expatriation of people, an integral part of an attempt to create an ethnically monolithic society, an ethnically cleansed society.

If the healing of memory does not begin and continue, this means transferring the task of healing to future generations (Stevens, 2007: 138). We may conclude that it is not 'a matter of free will' to start or not start a process that would lead to the cleansing and healing of memory: in a 'positive freedom' sense it is in fact a duty of current generations to commence the healing of memory and reconciliation process. The African concept of Ubuntu reminds us that in a reconciliation process the whole society and its cultures should be included.

References

Drakulic, S. 2011. A few "easy" steps towards reconciliation. In: *Balticworlds.com*, May 13, 2011 (orig. publ.: *Internationale Politik*, Jan/Feb 2011 in German). http://balticworlds.com/towards-reconciliation/ (Oct 25, 2011).

Harrison, L. E. and Huntington, S. P. (eds.) 2000. *Culture Matters. How Values Shape Human Progress*, New York: Basic Books.

Hooker, J. 2009. The Cultural Iceberg. In: *Intercultural Communication. A Reader* (ed. by Samovar, L. A., Porter, R.E. and McDaniel, E. R.), Wadsworth: Thomson, pp. 59–64.

Moss, S. M. 2010. The ancient African philosophy of Ubuntu: Decreasing or escalating conflicts in Africa? In: *Toronto Review*, July 18th, 2010. http://torontoreview.ca/2010/07/18/part-iii-of-ubuntu-more-or-less-conflict/ (Nov 20, 2011)

Mpofu, B. 2003. Brainstorming Racial Reconciliation in Southern Africa. Paper presented at the First International Conference on Race: Racial Reconciliation, Oct. 1–4, 2003, University of Mississippi, USA. http://www.winterinstitute.org/archives/PresentMpofu.htm (Nov 15, 2011).

Murithi, T. *2006. Practical Peacemaking Wisdom from Africa: Reflections on Ubuntu. In: Journal of Pan-African Studies*, 1, 4, pp. 25–34. http://www.jpanafrican.com/docs/vol1no4/PracticalPeacemakingWisdomFromAfrica_JPAS-vol1no4.pdf (Oct 10, 2011)

Murithi, T. 2009. An African Perspective on Peace Education: "Ubuntu" Lessons in Reconciliation. In: *International Review of Education*, 55, 2–3, pp. 221–233.

Nabudere, D. W. 2005. Ubuntu Philosophy. Memory and Reconciliation. http://repositories.lib.utexas.edu/bitstream/handle/2152/4521/3621.pdf?sequence=1 (Nov 14, 2011)

Samovar, L. A., Porter, R. E. and McDaniel, E. R. 2007. *Communication Between Cultures*. Wadsworth: Thomson.

Schreiter R. J. 2002. *The Ministry of Reconciliation: Spirituality & Strategies*. Maryknoll: Orbis books.

Stevens, D. 2007. Dealing with the Past in Northern Ireland. The Corrymeela House Perspective. In: *Healing the Memories in Europe. A Study of Reconciliation between Churches, Cultures and religions* (ed. by Brandes, D.), Cluj-Napoca: Accent Publishing House, pp. 115–143.

Tutu, D. 1999. *No Future without Forgiveness*. New York: Doubleday.

Tutu, D. 2004. *God Has a Dream: A Vision of Hope for Our Time*. New York: Doubleday.

TRAUMA AND DIVORCE

HEALING THE TRAUMA OF POSTWAR KILLINGS IN SLOVENIA

Katarina Kompan Erzar & Tomaž Erzar, Ljubljana

Our society has long been subject to strong polarization that forces us to choose one side or the other: the Partisans or the Home Guard. This dichotomy can be avoided only by putting ourselves in a position of sympathy with all victims, which, given the emotional reactivity and polarization in the current political situation, is very difficult. Who can withstand the waves of rage, blame, and shame emanating from all sides? Who can discern from them what is honest, vulnerable, and real? Despite this, anyone can understand that those who advocate respectful and compassionate burial of the victims of the killings do not necessarily approve of either the wartime cooperation with the occupying forces or the violent seizure of power and the ensuing regime's terror.

Regarding the Slovenian situation, we feel it is important to emphasize that rejecting the false dichotomy does not mean that both sides are equally guilty. Absolutely not: only the Partisan party is accountable for the killings and their long concealment, maintained by threats, imprisonments, and other forms of silencing. The long denial of the killings and concealment of the victims' graves casts the entire Partisan movement in a very bad light and has thus destroyed virtually all the credit and honest heroism one might attribute to it. It reveals an entirely different attitude: an attitude of dishonesty, antisocial vindictiveness, avoidance, and manipulation.

Today's stalemate in Slovenian society is the result of many years of unspoken grievances and long-term avoidance of responsibility: rage and dishonest evasion of responsibility by the revolutionaries, silence from the Partisan majority, and rage and the mute expectation of resolution on the part of the victims. We are all victims of this stalemate and no one can take a step forward in sincerity because the social climate is too dangerous for such a step. This lack of compassion and opportunities for mourning and solidarity is a major concern. Despite what other nations have discovered, do we really think that it is possible to overcome apathy and depression in our society merely through promises of a better future, but without a deep return back in time to the origins of most of the current feelings of helplessness, depression, passivity, self-destructiveness, and violent impassivity?

The lack of compassion and sorrow is even more frightening when we consider that both sides deserve sympathetic understanding: those who were direct or indirect victims of the massacres and also those who were forced to participate in the killings one way or another. We can assume that, apart from the rare individuals who planned the killings, all the others involved in them only more or less voluntarily agreed to participate, and, although they agreed at some point, they later regretted their loyalty or obsession with vengeance and their tacit consent. These people too are victims of cruelty and antisocial manipulation and it is immensely tragic that they have been awakened from their apathy and silence only by the voices of the other victims—victims from the other side of the rifle—who are seeking this right for themselves. Instead of sincere regret and embracing, the two groups of victims just grab each other by the hair and start a fight, which of course they cannot win and cannot stop because they do not know the real source of their pain and injustice.

In any case, the way we have dealt with the trauma of postwar killings up until now suggests that in the current situation our past wounds and injustices are very much alive and covertly active. It also suggests that the trauma was not diminished by temporal distance, as one might naively expect, but was actually increased. Until there is empathy for the victims and all those affected and as long as we all helplessly watch their agony and the hypocrisy of those in charge, their pain and our common pain will only continue and deepen. In particular, it deepens our shared feeling that things will never be otherwise, that this tragedy cannot be mourned, and that all our efforts were in vain. It is very wrong to think that trauma in a society affects only a certain population: through an increase in fear, dishonesty, and manipulation, eventually every family or every micro-community that normally generates feelings of interpersonal security loses its senses of safety and compassion.

Internalized pain

The fundamental question with which we should approach a resolution of the ongoing effects of trauma is the following: How can the flood of injustices be followed by a new kind of experience, whereby people share something unaffected by the past, something that will make them feel they are not defeated and that the horror of trauma is overcome once and for all? (Herman, 1992).

Contemporary theories of trauma and exploration of this phenomenon suggest that unresolved trauma most subtly and persistently spreads further in the victims' inner feelings. This inner feeling or voice tells the victims that "they alone are to blame for it", that "nothing can be done" in relation to it, that "it's the same everywhere", that "this is normal" and that "people have no power or resources to resolve it«, and the like. Traumatic experiences undermine or destroy our inner feeling that we deserve life in a compassionate, nonmanipulative, and benevolent interpersonal environment, and that such an environment belongs to us and that we are able to create it. Worse still, trauma reopens the wounds of insecure early attachments to our parents or caregivers, which means that it consolidates and deepens all our innermost negative and catastrophic beliefs about ourselves, others, and the world (Erzar and Kompan Erzar, 2011). Because it destroys our inner feeling of belonging and safety, after experiencing trauma we have nowhere to return to and no one to ask for help. Home in the sense of a secure base is gone, even if we did once have a home, or at least thought that we had it. This sense of lost security cannot be changed by external political or legal conditions: victims of very different regimes are similar in that they protect their persecutors and obstinately repeat that they betrayed themselves, their ideals, and their fellow-sufferers (Wingfield, 2008).

So, why do we say that trauma spreads further through the internal sense of helplessness, unworthiness, not-belonging, and dishonor? This somehow goes against justice and common sense. Shouldn't we say that trauma is even more devastatingly transmitted further by those who cause it in the first place; that is, by the executioners? This is a very difficult question, one that opens the door to the very core of trauma. In his memoirs of life in a Nazi concentration camp, Slovenian writer Boris Pahor and other survivors repeatedly ask the following question: "How can it be that none of the executioners at the trials defended themselves with a simple sentence: 'I'm sorry?'" (Pahor, 1997, p. 227). The answer is short and bitter: because they did not regret it. By executioners, we mean those rare individuals who have conceived or initiated crimes, although they were not necessarily involved in their implementation. For the implementation, they utilized a significant number of subordinate people. These executioners usually come from families in which their personal safety and dignity was constantly threatened and trampled, so much so that they were forever deprived of the opportunity to delve into their own personal experience of pain or pain in others. That is why we cannot expect them to show empathy for the victims or compassion for their own situation; not even mere understanding, because they only know the basic defense strategies such as denial, concealment, minimization, and attribution of their own problems to others (Gilligan, 1996).

Trauma, when this term is used in the strict sense, constitutes a threat to an individual's life, accompanied by feelings of intense fear, helplessness, and horror. This kind of trauma penetrates the wall of psychic defenses people use to protect themselves against the invasion of negative emotions, and promotes feelings of helplessness, dishonor, guilt, isolation, fear, helplessness, and pain. It has been found that when this invasion remains unhealed for a long time, as shown in the cases of Vietnam veterans in the U.S. who have been diagnosed with post-traumatic stress disorder (PTSD), the reason for this is that traumatic events arouse and further reinforce in one's internal experience feelings similar to those of non-secure attachment. Observing the effects of PTSD confirmed that lingering symptoms of the disorder were regularly present in soldiers whose lives—long before they went to fight in Vietnam—were plagued by a myriad of interpersonal problems and addictions, and who had to hide their failures or feelings of shame and dishonor in interpersonal relations and work behind the symptoms (Lansky, 1990). The war-induced traumatic experiences and their consequences in these cases had been used as an honorable exit from the feelings of dishonor and incompetence that had accompanied these individuals from childhood onwards.

Unlike the traditional, "Vietnam," "veteran," or simply masculine definition of trauma, by which trauma is merely external events that threaten our health or life, the new understanding of trauma emphasizes that a traumatic experience is primarily defined by our internal response to it. This aspect of trauma, which is the constant focus of current therapeutic work worldwide, is less visible, less famous, less heroic, and, needless to say, more shameful: the study of the psychological and interpersonal effects of trauma began with the trauma of rape and incest (Robb, 2006). The tragic side of apparently external traumatic events lies in the inner experience of these events, in which a series of perhaps half-forgotten and unresolved negative experiences from the family origin is awakened, which gives the current accident or incident completely different meaning. Because of this meaning an accident is not merely an accident that occurred in the present and for which one deserves all possible care and attention, but becomes a symbol of all past disasters and insecure ways of seeking help and assistance.

It is this deep inner feeling of powerlessness, loneliness, helplessness, and worthlessness that explains why victims cannot be compassionate to themselves and forgive themselves for becoming victims. First of all, victims no longer believe in compassion or that they have a right to it without having to earn it or fight for it in court or some other way. Second, victims believe that their trauma feelings are exactly what they have always deserved. Third, victims turn to their executioners because it is just like home, where—when they were helpless and defenseless—the only people they could turn for help were the ones who had done injustices to them. These were one and the same people, usually the parents. Fourth, because the termination of this forced loyalty to tormentors would also represent the disruption and mourning the loss of non-secure forms of attachment to parents and because such an exploration of the past means confrontation with shame, victims prefer to persist in relationships of imagined, conditional security and half-sincerity. Fifth, because they believe they are to blame for what happened to them, and because they persist in the non-secure relationships, victims soon find themselves in new traumatic circumstances. Sixth, the internalized trauma, given the fact that it is generally unrecognized and nonverbalized, has many and varied external consequences, consequences for mental and physical health, and consequences that appear through addictions, aggression, self-destructive behavior, and dysfunctional relationships. However, these behaviors do not reach and do not exhaust the essence of the trauma. In fact, these symptoms obscure the trauma and prolong the avoidance of its essence, because they discourage people from deepening their experience of themselves, others, and the world. This is how trauma is transferred to the next generation. Incompletely mourned violent deaths drive the children of victims to acts of vengeance or self-injury behavior (Walsh and McGoldrick, 1991).

Capacity for shame and grief

Trauma, as we have seen, destroys one's inner feeling of safety and thus destroys the feeling of belonging, self-efficacy, and, ultimately, of being lovable, which means that it reaches deep into one's perception of oneself, into who the person is and what is wrong with him/her that allowed this to happen. This is why victims cannot leave trauma behind, even when it is already long past. Given this weak image of themselves, victims cannot bear to explore their own feelings and experience of themselves. Most often, they will evade their own feelings of shame, helplessness, and vulnerability caused by trauma. In this case, their former dishonor will be mixed with new feelings of ashamedness, their former identity with the new identity, the identity of victims, and both together will shut the person between the walls of silence. This is why more or less covert disparagement is the worst kind of silencing that can be imposed on victims: "This happened to you because you're those kind of people, you already know why!" "You're counting bones!" "Thanks to you we're all trapped in the past!"

The first step out of the role of victim is disambiguation between the dishonor caused by the trauma and the other negative feelings about themselves that have deeper roots. The condition for this is the ability to recognize shame and get in touch with it in a secure relationship. Talking frankly, without anger and resentment, about one's own feelings of shame is the best way to get rid of these feelings, which will start migrating to the site of tormentors. The second step is to grieve. After restoring their dignity and their relationship with the world of safe and honest relationships, victims can start mourning everything the trauma irretrievably ruined for them: health, youth, childhood, innocence, the presence of their father, mother, brother, son, or daughter. This process of grieving is much more difficult when the death of someone close is sudden, murky, violent, premature, part of a mass killing, or takes place in a social environment that encourages denial, sealing, or silence, as was the case in Slovenia.

In Slovenian autobiographical literature from the Second World War there is a disturbing but incredibly sincere and profound example of how it is nevertheless possible to speak about even the worst traumas of war time. It is probably no coincidence that it comes from the pen of someone who was not fully immersed in the civil war, but was the victim of Fascist and Nazi persecution. Pahor's narrative *Necropolis*, which was written in 1966, has recently been read by other Europeans in translation. Why? The reason may be that, with regard to healing war traumas, the rest of Europe is not much better off than we are in Slovenia; it may be that we all lack a model of how to get out of black-and-white historiography and how to set up a convincing and effective treatment of trauma. And why is Pahor's *Necropolis* so persuasive?

In a non-evasive and vulnerable manner, the book describes the overwhelming fear that handcuffed prisoners in the Nazi Struthof concentration camp that led to their being completely frozen and unfeeling. They suffered fear, horror, threats of torture and annihilation, and total distress with no hope of a solution. But to Pahor this fear - and this is crucial - is no excuse for cowardice! Pahor says something like this: although we were all afraid every moment of our lives and trembled so much that we could hardly talk or think, this did not mean that we lost our inner compass; and even if we lost it for a moment, we still had room for initiative and solidarity, and this space returned our strength to us, because in this small island of self-respect and dignity we were not victims, even though we had every reason in the world for this. Pahor overcomes the trauma of the camp when he recognizes that he could be reproached that he survived because he ate the bread of dying fellow prisoners; more precisely, "because he counted on it." That is, he could be open to reproach not because he had simply eaten it, which would have been normal, but because he thought about the bread of his sick and dying fellow-sufferers even while he was helping them ("And we knew exactly whose portion would remain").

Why is this recognition that he had not been as brave as he would like to have been the key to overcoming the trauma? First, because it keeps initiative alive that is not characteristic of victims. It is typical of people who are struggling, take risks, and refuse to be helpless. Second, because this initiative reveals an attitude that comes not from the world of trauma, but from the world of the internal criteria of honesty, openness, recognition of shame, loyalty, and connectedness. Third, such a confession can only be made by someone who believes the confession will not ruin him and that people will accept him as he is. Pahor believes he can be sincere and still deserve empathy and compassion for the deeds of which he is ashamed and not proud of. He believes that he deserves empathy, even though he did not "earn" it by polishing his memories or faking amnesia, just as he did not "earn" it with heroic feats. This is the faith of a small child who cannot do otherwise but be sincere and lovable and is therefore unaffected by trauma. Despite the risk of annihilation the child feels he is worthy of love and empathy, even when he is not perfect. He thus confides in us, the readers, and leads us into a secure, confident world where honest conversation between people who support one another still exists.

In this light, we can more easily understand why in the early seventies only Boris Pahor was able to help Christian Socialist Edvard Kocbek do away with the false dichotomy, saying "Whoever is not for us supports collaboration," and hence the role of helpless victims, when he spoke openly of the postwar killings. From this one can learn the following lesson: as fear spreads, so too does honesty and sincerity. He who speaks honestly about his own trauma and does not wait for an apology from his tormentors opens the door to sincerity for all other victims; in fact, for all of us. All postwar generations in Europe lack this sincerity. If we are to avoid future traumas and injustices, we will have to sharply reduce the time it took Kocbek to confess: almost thirty years, and nearly five years of friendly persuasion by Pahor. The path of fear in our brains and the speed of a bullet are measured in milliseconds.

Literature

Erzar, T. and Kompan Erzar, K. 2011. *Teorija navezanosti.* Celje: Mohorjeva družba.

Gilligan, J. 1996. *Violence: Our Deadly Epidemic and Its Causes*. New York: Grosset/Putnam Books.

Herman, J. 1992. *Trauma and Recovery*. New York: Basic Books.

Lansky, M. 1990. The screening function of posttraumatic nightmares. In: *British Journal of Psychotherapy*, 7, pp. 384–400.

Pahor, B. 2010 [1967]. *Necropolis*. London: Dalkey Archive Press.

Robb, C. 2006. *This Changes Everything: The Relational Revolution in Psychology*. New York: Farrar, Straus and Giroux.

Walsh, F. and McGoldrick, M. (eds.). 1991. *Living Beyond Loss: Death in the Family*. New York: W.W. Norton.

Wingfield, R. 2008. The Shadow of Murder: Love and Hate in Times of Violence. In: Sarah Benamer and Kate White (eds.), *Trauma and Attachment*. London: Karnac Books.

THE HORIZONS OF RECONCILIATION AFTER TRAUMATIC EXPERIENCE

Barbara Simonič, Ljubljana

The age of trauma

Some describe our common era as an "age of trauma" (Rifkin, 2009: 423) because our everyday world seems to be severely threatened from all sides: by global diminution of natural resources, global warming, global terrorism, and global economic collapse. These are forms of collective trauma in that they threaten the basic framework with which we as members of our particular society have made sense out of our existence. On the other hand, more personal forms of traumatic events also exist. In addition to a wide range of collective traumatic events, like warfare, natural disasters, accidents, there is also violence inflicted by others, such as rejection or betrayal. This kind of trauma comes from another person and it is most frequently described as relational or interpersonal trauma (Kuczynska, 2010: 7–8).

Trauma is a psychophysical experience, even when the traumatic event causes no direct bodily harm. That traumatic events have an impact on the body as well as on the mind is well agreed-upon (Rothschild, 2000: 5). Trauma is a kind of wound. Coming from the Greek word "*trauma*" meaning a wound, it is regarded as referring to a psychological or bodily injury. Freud used the word to emphasize how the mind too can be pierced and wounded by events. Trauma is understood as an unusually intensive and unwanted experience that involves actual or felt danger to one's life or health and is evoked by direct contact of the individual with extreme, atypical life events (Kuczynska, 2010: 7). The DSM IV-TR (Diagnostic and Statistical Manual of Mental Disorders) refers to trauma as an experience of an event that involves actual or threatened death, serious injury to oneself or others, and a response involving intense fear, helplessness, or horror. Trauma is the unique individual experience of an event or enduring conditions in which the individual's ability to integrate his/her emotional experience is overwhelmed and the individual experiences a threat to his/her life, bodily integrity, or that of a caregiver or family. Trauma can be both physical and psychological. Even when the trauma is of a physical nature, the consequences are always also deeply psychological. Psychic response to trauma is an individual's response to an unexpected event, experienced intimately and forcefully. The individual experiences the event as extremely upsetting, overwhelming his internal resources, and resulting in feelings of danger, anxiety, and higher arousal (Briere and Scott, 2006: 4).

The number of events that could be a potential source of trauma is actually unlimited. The same event could be the source of significant trauma for one individual while not for another, all depending upon their psychophysical predisposition and vulnerability (Garland, 1998: 23). Potentially traumatic events could include not only natural disasters, events caused by humans, acts of terror and warfare, but also interpersonal traumas. Although the term suggests that it encompasses all traumatic events, the source of which is another human being, most researchers restrict the range of events under the heading of interpersonal trauma to ones where the perpetrator is another close person. The intentions of the perpetrator are either the desire to hurt the other and/or the desire to pursue his or her own goals, irrespective of harm and costs to other people. Examples of this kind of phenomenon may be assault, battery, mutilation, rape or sexual abuse (Kuczynska, 2010: 8).

Interpersonal trauma could occur in two ways. One type is simple acute trauma, where the perpetrator is a stranger, from whom security is not expected and who conducts a single attack (rape, beating, torture, war), or when there is a personal error, such as the lack of providing information about an upcoming natural disaster or terrorist attack. The second type is complex chronic trauma, where the perpetrator is a close, trusted person from whom safety, love, intimacy and support are expected, but they rather choose to intentionally and deliberately do hurtful things (Widera-Wysoczanska, 2010: 20). This is also referred to as relational trauma and it represents a specific category of psychological trauma involving an interpersonal loss within a relationship with a significant parent or caregiver. This loss may be signified by a break in trust through traumatic events, including various types of neglect and violence, which a person may be subjected to from early childhood and then on through youth and young adulthood, often up to the current moment of her/his life (Kuczynska and Widera-Wysoczanska, 2010: 1). This type is particularly taxing, often leaving deep wounds, because it often begins in childhood when the individual is particularly vulnerable for lack of fully developed coping mechanisms. Early interpersonal trauma has a negative impact upon the developing personality. Traumatized children are the most likely to go on to develop impairments in psychological functioning, specific psychiatric symptomology, and changes in brain functions. The impact of early interpersonal trauma is so pervasive the effects can transcend into latter stages, even after the trauma has stopped (Schore, 2003: 110–112).

Effects of trauma

Trauma affects the individual holistically. The aftermath of trauma can permeate all areas of a person's development and negatively impact their lives in the present and future. Complex chronic interpersonal trauma has especially deep effects. It occurs in connection with experiencing different types of abuse and negligence, and is most often present in a dysfunctional and pathological family environment. This type of trauma is *interpersonal* and is connected with a specific type of bond, mainly a dysfunctional one (Bowlby, 1973). It is the result of people who are close and important to the person wronged; moreover, the abuse inflicted deliberately and intentionally, is a traumatic event. The perpetrator hurts the individual by manipulating him/her, seducing, or imposing some other form of abuse (e.g. emotional, physical, sexual). When intimate relationships are severed through traumatic events we experience a loss of safety, trust, and value. By causing harm to the individual, the perpetrator evokes a feeling of betrayal and undermines trust in primary relationships. The second parent, caregiver or person on whom the child depends, who is a passive offender, does not offer protection and support. This situation causes a second injury: loss of basic confidence and a feeling of betrayal from the caregiver (betrayal trauma). The closer the relationship between perpetrator and the person wronged, the more serious its consequences can be (Widera-Wysoczanska, 2010: 18–19).

Trauma is undoubtedly a pivotal experience, challenging and fracturing not only an individual's feeling of self but also a society's sense of unity and community. Trauma can generate powerful emotions, such as fear, anger, mistrust and betrayal, which can in turn bind societies and communities together by generating a culture of resentment and anxiety. Rather than initiating a much needed process of healing after trauma, such reactions can easily generate a vicious cycle of ongoing trauma. It is present as fear of and intolerance towards difference, thus establishing new cycles of violence and hatred (Hutchison and Bleiker, 2008: 397). In this case, traumatized people may stay in various forms of trauma repetition. They may attempt to restore the lost illusions shattered by trauma through some form of collective beliefs that seek to bring back to life the illusory absolutisms that have been nullified. But there is also a more positive outcome that can be seen: a traumatized person may actually move toward a more authentic way of existing, in which existential vulnerabilities are embraced rather than disowned.

Trauma brings us face to face with our existential vulnerability and with death and loss as possibilities that define our existence and which loom as constant threats. Usually, trauma is highly disturbing, it makes a deep impact, it shatters one's sense of trust, and it can leave people feeling immobilized. Personal security is shaken and everybody's perspective on human life is shifted (Collins, 2007: 763). Traumatic experiences are imprinted deep into the body and soul, and as such they can be healed only through a deep and profound process, one marked with empathy and compassion. After surviving negative and hurtful traumatic life experiences we become different people - we change forever. We see life and ourselves in a different light. The destruction is severe. We feel that we will never be able to live again and that there is no reason to hope and love. Trauma brings feelings of depersonalization and also dehumanization; after such experiences, one doesn't feel to be the same person anymore, sometimes not even human. One has to become human again, a person again. This feeling can only be achieved through reconciliation with the self, the world and others.

In the case of relational/interpersonal trauma, these experiences also make victims feel that they can no longer live with the enemy, that they cannot talk to the enemy and can only think of getting revenge. The thought of any kind of contact and even possible reconciliation is not possible. There is a complete destruction of the medium of human relationship and an unbridgeable mistrust is incurred. What needs to take place to heal and restore relationships is a healing of the human heart, mind and soul of the individuals and groups that survived traumatic conflict (Puljek-Shank, 2007: 182).

Healing traumatic wounds and reconciliation

Healing trauma is in many ways a life-long experience. The decision to heal does not come naturally and it needs to become a work of intent for many years and for many generations to come. It is not natural since the natural reaction to the pain and hurt is either to strike back or to run away. Traumatic experience also teaches us that we cannot trust those who hurt us and therefore we are on guard and ready to strike back. In order to break the cycle of repetitive trauma one needs to take a risk and start a journey of healing and possible reconciliation, which is a matter of personal choice and it is a process that might last a lifetime. In order to deal with and heal our trauma we need to work through our traumatic experience. There are two ways of walking through trauma. The first one is to remember and repeat the story of traumatic experience in which the pain and suffering are locked and do not have a route for release from the persons' body, mind and soul. A person (or group) is trapped in this cycle, one that can go on for a long time, sometimes even forever. In this case the trauma creates negative energy that recycles itself within a person or group in a way that creates a violent and destructive eruption.

A second way of working on traumatic experience calls for the healing of trauma in a very holistic way. It requires serious work and dedication on the part of an individual (or group) and it becomes a *personal* choice to heal the trauma instead of repeating the trauma through generations. This personal decision stems from the desire to become human again, to be able to live in harmony with our selves and with others. Once the choice has been made it becomes clear that this will be a long process that might even last for years. This is the process of reconciliation (Puljek-Shank, 2007: 182–185).

But what does it really mean to be in the process of reconciliation? Reconciliation isn't forgetting, sugar-coating the pain and suffering, bypassing the truth, being nice to each other and pretending as if nothing happened. "Reconciliation is not about being cozy; it is not about pretending that things were other than they were. Reconciliation based on falsehood, on not facing up to reality, is not true reconciliation and will not last" (Tutu, 1998: 17). To facilitate reconciliation, this requires from us to hear the others pain and suffering, recognize the human in the others. As our finiteness and vulnerability for death and loss are fundamental to our existential constitution, so it is constitutive of our existence that we meet each other in the same darkness, deeply connected with one another in virtue of our common finiteness. This pushes us to start to see things in a different light, to start to see the situation from the other's perspective – this is possible through a universal capability such as empathy. This is when we start to develop a relationship and become connected with the other – also with our enemy. This is when we humanize our enemy and ourselves (Puljek-Shank, 2007: 195).

Competencies, such as empathy and compassion may be helpful in the process of healing trauma and reconciliation because they generate a social space. Empathy generally involves the ability to identify with (to at least some degree) the experiences and situation of the other. Empathy is a capacity, which in today's changing and frequently depersonalized world has great meaning. It often represents the "medicine" for social injury, which results from egoism and an egocentric view of the world. Especially in western and multi-cultured society, empathy is often promoted as a bridge that enables democratic dialogue with others. The capacity for empathy is universal and a natural capacity of each human being; as such, it is fundamental for a dialogical relationship at a deeper level (Simonič, 2010: 123–124). As such, empathy is a basis for reconstructing social relationships and communal bonds after mass violence and trauma. The respective reasoning behind this is that individuals and groups divided by conflict must be able to see the situation from the complex perspective of another. In so doing the suffering and trauma of others may 'resonate emotionally', thereby providing an understanding how another feels and why they may feel the things they do (Halpern and Weinstein, 2004: 579–582). Victims and perpetrators may be able to see each other as above all 'human'. This recognition may then lead to processes of re-humanization of victim and perpetrator and in turn inspire the agency needed to successfully embrace reconciliation. Feelings of empathy, and perhaps similarly, sympathy and compassion, may therefore prompt the shared understanding that is needed to take responsibility of, and in turn, resolve the conflict for the betterment of all (Hutchison and Bleiker, 2008: 395).

According to Edith Stein, empathetic experiences are central to being a person. She claims that empathy allows us to build up an understanding of the foreign person and his or her values, who then becomes for us a fully complex being, like ourselves. Empathic acts enable us to comprehend the other person and her values. The other has a living body, which belongs to his "I" as my living body belongs to my "I". In this way, others can be recognized as persons (Stein, 1989: 56–57). By recognizing that our enemy is after all a human being who deeply suffers and feels pain and hurt as we do, we recognize the human in the enemy. The very moment when this recognition transpires, both the enemy and we become human beings again. We gain this self-respect and dignity that all of us have lost. Having the strength for the first time to look the enemy in the eye forces us in many ways to look at ourselves, at our own responsibility, our own actions, prejudices and wrongs. This is the process when we take responsibility for what we have done to the other and the other takes responsibility for the wrongs done to us. We both end up owning the wrongs, naming them, and apologizing. This is the moment when both sides start to develop trust towards the other - that the same pain and suffering would not be done unto us again, that history will not repeat itself. We might be noticing that this enemy is suffering and hurting too. We are able to see this in our enemy because we were able to see our own pain and hurt. This is when we are able to feel compassion for the other. In this moment our enemy becomes human again - a beast no more. What needs to happen it is respect for the other (former enemy), respect that comes from deep within. With this respect we acknowledge that the other has the right to live life. And when we fully recognize the sacredness of life in the other, we at the same time recognize the equivalent within ourselves. This is the moment the door to making peace with the other opens (Puljek-Shank, 2007: 195–196).

The process of healing in the wake of trauma does of course inevitably take time. Reconciliation is thus a long-term project. But traumatic events, precisely because they disrupt existing patterns of identity and community, offer unique opportunities to initiate such a long-term process of healing (Hutchison and Bleiker,

2008: 397–398). We literally rise up from the ashes. During that time we became capable of hearing the enemy's story. This is the moment when we embark on the road of forgiveness and maybe realize that we would like to reconcile with the enemy. At the same time this moment represents a decision that trauma does not have control over our lives.

References

American Psychiatric Association 1994: *Diagnostic and Statistical Manual of Mental Disorders* (DSM – IV), Washington: American Psychiatric Association.

Bowlby, J. 1973. *Attachment and loss. Vol. 3, Loss, sadness and depression*, New York: Basic Books.

Briere, J., and Scott, C. 2006. *Principles of trauma therapy: A guide to symptoms, evaluation, and treatment*. Thousand Oaks: Sage Publications.

Collins, G. R. 2007. *Christian Counseling*, Nashville: Thomas Nelson.

Garland, C. 1998. Thinking about trauma. In: Garland, C. (Ed.), *Understanding Trauma*, pp. 9–31, London: Karnac.

Halpern, J., and Weinstein, H.M. 2004. Rehumanizing the Other: Empathy and Reconciliation. In: *Human Rights Quarterly* 26 (3), pp. 561–583.

Hutchison, E., and Bleiker, R. 2008. Emotional Reconciliation: Reconstituting Identity and Community after Trauma. In: *European Journal of Social Theory* 11(3), pp. 385–403.

Kuczynska, A. 2010. Individual and social aspects of trauma. In: Widera-Wysoczańska, A., and Kuczyńska, A. (Eds.), *Interpersonal Trauma and its Consequences in Adulthood*, pp. 7–14, New Castle: Cambridge Scholars Publishing.

Kuczynska, A., and Widera-Wysoczanska, A. 2010. Introduction. In: Widera-Wysoczańska, A., and Kuczyńska, A. (Eds.), *Interpersonal Trauma and its Consequences in Adulthood*, pp. 1–4, New Castle: Cambridge Scholars Publishing.

Puljek-Shank, A. 2007. Trauma and Reconciliation. In: Rill, H., Šmidling, T., and Bitoljanu, A. (Eds.), *20 Pieces of Encouragement for Awakening and Change: Peacebuilding in the Region of the Former Yugoslavia*, pp. 181–204, Belgrade–Sarajevo: Centre for Nonviolent Action.

Rifkin, J. 2009. *The Empathic Civilization*, New York: Tarcher Penguin.

Rothschild, B. 2000. *The Body remembers: The psychophysiology of Trauma and Trauma Treatment*, New York, London: W. W. Norton & Company.

Schore, A.N. 2003. Early Relational Trauma, Disorganized Attachment, and the Development of a Predisposition to Violence. In: Solomon, M.F., and Siegel, D.J. (Eds.), *Healing Trauma*, pp. 107–167, New York: W. W. Norton & Company.

Simonič, B. 2010. *Empatija*, Ljubljana: Brat Frančišek in Frančiškanski družinski inštitut.

Stein, E. 1989. *On the problem of Empathy*, Washington: ICS Publications.

Tutu, D. 1998. Chairperson's Foreword. In: *Truth and Reconciliation Commission of South Africa Report*, vol.1, Cape Town: Juta.

Widera-Wysoczańska, A. 2010. Interpersonal Trauma as Chronic and Complex. In: Widera-Wysoczańska, A., and Kuczyńska, A. (Eds.), *Interpersonal Trauma and its Consequences in Adulthood*, pp. 15–34, New Castle: Cambridge Scholars Publishing.

CIVIL SUITS FOR DIVORCE

Stanislav Slatinek, Ljubljana

In the traditional, healthy family spouses normally lived together – *convictus coniugalis* (can. 1151) – in unselfish and unconditional love. Divorces of marriages and failed marriages were very rare. Nowadays we witness the increasing decay of marital values. Divorces and separations are on the increase. Every marital divorce does not necessarily affect "(marital) bed, board and mutual cohabitation" (*communio tori, mensae et habitationis* – Demel 2004, 238). Spouses can agree to separate for some time for reasons of work, education, travel, health treatment etc. Despite this, the number of permanent divorces is increasing, which proves that partnership has become a real crisis area. The findings of the web dating service *Parship International* show that in Europe more than 50 % marriages end in divorce.[1] Sociologists already talk about "modern nomads" (Herman 2007, 52), who remain single after divorce or chose some new form of cohabitation. It is a new phenomenon of individualism which can in the near future completely annihilate family culture.

Since civil divorces today pose a major challenge for the state and the Church, I here wish to point to some basic solutions which the canon law of the Catholic Church offers to quarrelling spouses. First I want to recall the meeting of Pharisees and the Lord Jesus. To test him, they asked: "Is it lawful for a man to divorce his wife?" "What did Moses Command you?" he replied. They said: "Moses permitted a man to write a certificate of divorce and send her away." "It was because your hearts were hard that Moses wrote you this law," Jesus replied. "But at the beginning of creation God made them male and female. For this reason a man will leave his father and mother and be united to his wife, and the two will become one flesh. So they are no longer two, but one. Therefore what God has joined together, let man not separate." (Cf. Mr 10, 2–9) At this point nothing changed for civil societies. They still condone legal divorce. Every civil divorce is nowadays perceived as the final dissolution of matrimonial bond, while the Church tries to solve marital disputes in a different way. Thus it offers quarrelling

1 http://www.parship.com (15.7.2011)

spouses "divorce without dissolution of matrimonial bond" - *separatione manente vinculo* (can. 1152 – 1155). It is a divorce which means only conjugal marital life ceases, while the matrimonial bond is not disrupted (Hendriks 1999, 305). It is this kind of divorce I wish to speak about first, and then explain how forgiveness and reconciliation are essential for the existence of conjugal community.

1. Divorce without dissolution of matrimonial bond

The right to "divorce without dissolution of matrimonial bond" goes to those spouses who are baptised and have legitimate reasons to divorce. The most frequent reasons for divorce without dissolution of matrimonial bond are adultery and endangering mental and physical well-being of the spouse or children. Such acts endanger conjugal community and prevent marital life. They are utterly unjust acts towards the spouse and children which make family life impossible (Gramunt, Hervada, Wauck 1987, 96). In such cases only the innocent spouse has the legal right to separate from the adulterous or violent spouse. The wrongful spouse – adulterous or violent – can never claim the right to such divorce.

Now we have the canonical definition of marital divorce. The question arises: can we speak about the innocent and wrongful spouse in marital dispute at all? Are not both spouses in a certain dispute equally innocent and equally unjust? Already Jesus dealt with this dilemma when he said: "Why do you look at the speck of sawdust in your brother's eye and pay no attention to the plank in your own eye? How can you say to your brother, 'Brother, let me take the speck out of your eye,' when you yourself fail to see the plank in your own eye? You hypocrite, first take the plank out of your eye, and then you will see clearly to remove the speck from your brother's eye." (Lk 6, 41–42). The canon law tries to answer this complicated question when it deals with civil suits for divorce without dissolution of matrimonial bond.

When one of the spouses commits adultery, the other spouse (the one who does not) has the legal right to separate from the former. Here it is important (1) that he/she does not forgive the unjust, that is the adulterous spouse; (2) that he/she has not consented to adultery or caused it; and (3) did not commit adultery himself/herself. There has to be moral certainty about adultery, it has to be committed without coercion and with another person who is not one's spouse (Hendriks 1999, 307). Similar case is when one of the spouses is violent and endangers mental and physical well-being of his/her spouse or children. The spouse who is not violent or has not caused violence and is innocent has the right to separate if he/she finds living together unbearable.

Divorce without dissolution of matrimonial bond absolves the innocent spouse from some marital obligations. The spouse who is not guilty of divorce is thus absolved from the obligations derived from common marital life. By divorcing, the innocent spouse can find his/her table, bed and dwelling (D'Auria 2003, 373). Despite this, the innocent spouse is, together with the wrongful spouse, still obliged to provide necessary upkeep and education for their children. Thus divorced spouses are also obliged to care for one another in case of illness, disability or some other distress (375). Divorce without dissolution of matrimonial bond is never final, but always looks forward to uninterrupted marital union, to pacification, to renewal of conjugal life and to marital reconciliation.

2. Procedures for the divorce of spouses

It is not necessary to *go through statistics to* realise how alarming the situation is: more and more marriages are becoming battlefields. Marital divorces often happen due to insufferable conditions. Adultery and marital violence open doors to divorces without dissolution of matrimonial bond (Herman 2007, 46). The canon law offers quarrelling spouses three forms of divorce procedures. I will briefly present them.

a) Divorce of spouses by a decision

In most cases it is the local bishop who gives spouses the permission for divorce without dissolution of matrimonial bond. The general vicar or the bishop's vicar can permit divorce only with the bishop's special permission. When spouses ask their local bishop for divorce, general provisions of the canon law are observed (can. 1692–1696). The innocent spouse submits his/her request for divorce to the local bishop. The bishop carefully considers the request, and accepts it when he establishes legitimate reasons for divorce. Then he thoroughly questions the prosecuting spouse about the main reasons for divorce. The prosecuting spouse asking for divorce is bound to tell the bishop the whole truth and nothing but the truth about his/her marriage and should submit to bishop all the evidence which supports his/her demand for divorce. The conversation between the local bishop and the innocent spouse is intended primarily for marital mediation. The bishop at first tries to reconcile the quarrelling spouses and make them to restore their conjugal life (can. 1695). Only when he establishes that reconciliation between the spouses is not possible, he issues the decision which permits the prosecuting spouse to divorce from the wrongful spouse. The decision of the local bishop is a provisional measure which stimulates the prosecuting spouse to reconcile with the wrongful spouse as soon as possible. The decision is in regard to contents brief, clear and has a legal rationale. This legal document sets the rights and obligations of the spouses in the time of divorce. Before the decision is sent to the quarrelling spouses, the church prosecutor examines it. Despite their right to divorce, the spouses are obliged to reconcile and restore their matrimonial bond as soon as possible.

b) Divorce of spouses with judgment

Suits for divorce of spouses are always accepted by the bishop in the locality where the quarrelling spouses live. When suits are numerous, the bishop is helped by the judge. Divorce suit with the judge is usually carried out orally, except if one of the spouses or the church prosecutor demands a regular legal proceeding. After the judge examines the suit, he invites the quarrelling spouses to a hearing. The judge also do all what he can to reconcile the quarrelling spouses or at least made the innocent spouse to forgive the wrongful spouse, so the divorce will not become permanent. In order to gather as much reliable evidence as possible, the judge should hear also the suggested witnesses. When the judge tries all options and establishes that there are legitimate reasons for reasons for divorce, he passes the judgment orally, while in a regular legal proceeding the judgment is in written form. In case of a regular legal proceeding each spouse or the church prosecutor can appeal to the court of appeal (can. 1693 §2).

c) Divorce in cases when delay is dangerous

When living in the marriage becomes extremely dangerous, the innocent spouse can divorce by himself/herself. This right exists always when the marital life with a violent spouse becomes too dangerous for him/her or their children. When the wrongful spouse endangers physical or mental well-being of the innocent spouse[2] and their children to a degree when their lives are not safe or irreparable moral damage is being done, the innocent spouse can voluntarily discontinue their con-

2 For more on the violence against female spouses or partners see Juhant 2009, 136.

jugal life. He/she should as soon as possible inform his local bishop about this "decision" (*propria auctoritate* – can. 1153).

3. Forgiveness and reconciliation from the point of view of the canon law

Forgiveness and reconciliation of the quarrelling spouses are of utmost importance as they can be perceived as the process in which the quarrelling spouses are returning to their conjugal community. When anger, rage and resentments subside, it is highly recommendable that the innocent spouse, out of Christian love and for the sake of the family's well-being, does not deny his/her adulterous or violent spouse reconciliation and does not break up the conjugal life. Forgiveness is manifested by periods of kindness and dialogue. When the wrongful spouse confesses that he/she maltreated the innocent spouse and promises to improve, the process of reconciliation can begin. Reconciliation thus means that the wrongful spouse accepts the responsibility for his/her unjust deeds and that the innocent spouse responds with "spoken" or "tacit" forgiveness (Putz 2004, 231). Tacit forgiveness means that the innocent spouse consents to sexual intercourse with the wrongful spouse after he/she has learned about the crime of "adultery" or has been subjected to "violence".

The innocent spouse forgives the wrongful spouse if he/she lives with him/her for six months without complaining to the Church or civil authorities. He/she should particularly strive to forgive when the wrongful spouse repents; when he/she asks for forgiveness; when he/she returns to the innocent spouse, proposes to restore their conjugal community and promises to improve (Bianchi 2000, 150).

The bishop and the judge involved in the divorce procedure should also strive to make the quarrelling spouses reconcile. As therapists, they should always hope for a good outcome of the marital dispute (Maragnoli 187). It is their duty to make the quarrelling spouses to forgive and reconcile. They pay special attention to the innocent spouse so as to pave the path to the reconciliation. If the innocent spouse cannot forgive, he/she has the right to divorce, while the wrongful spouse should regret his/her unjust deeds and express willingness to restore the conjugal community. In order to facilitate the process of reconciliation, other people and family members are invited to participate in the procedure. The marital dispute in this way acquires a social dimension. It is expected that in this way the marital conflict will be solved much faster and better.

Forgiveness and reconciliation of the quarrelling spouses are essential also in order that the quarrelling spouses may receive from the spiritual goods of the Church, primarily from God's Word and the sacraments, help needed for their life. The wrongful spouse, who caused the divorce, should not be admitted to communion during the process of divorce (can. 915). Confessing and regretting the guilt is "an absolutely essential condition" (*conditio sine qua non*) to regain the right to enjoy the spiritual goods of the Church.

Reconciliation can be reached also without the process of divorce. The intervention of the innocent spouse is very important here. If the innocent spouse silently persists for six months with the adulterous spouse and does not expel him/her from their conjugal life, nor file a divorce suit (without dissolution of matrimonial bond), we can talk about reconciliation without divorce. The innocent spouse has thus as a reconciliatory partner out of "the Christian love" (*ex caritate christiana*) and for the sake of the family well-being renounced any revenge and the right to break up the marital life (Demel 2004, 240).

4. Forgiveness and reconciliation from the point of view of the Christian gospel

The Christian gospel considers forgiveness as the most important option for reaching reconciliation among people, especially when it comes to reconciliation of quarrelling spouses. Forgiveness is a very prolonged and difficult process. The only thing that can at this point help quarrelling spouses to make way for forgiveness and reconciliation is the gospel.

Centuries of experience show that rigorous justice is after all not the only way to rescue quarrelling spouses from the abyss of guilt. Whoever acknowledges only legal standards of justice practically does not see any possibility for forgiveness. If the innocent spouse thinks in this way, then he/she is completely convinced that the wrongful spouse should be punished, thus neglecting the fact that forgiveness is the best way to reconciliation (Juhant 2011, 42).

The Church thus tirelessly offers people reconciliation in Jesus Christ (John Paul II, 1997, 35). It is a force which can help the innocent spouse to forgive the unjust deeds of his/her spouse. Only the Christian gospel can bend human will and make man emotionally ripe for forgiveness. For this reason we can speak of the miraculous effects of the gospel, which can motivate the innocent spouse for an act of the moral order, such as forgiveness and reconciliation. The Christian gospel gives quarrelling spouses the grace to overcome the selfishness which manifests as anger, resentment, hatred and incessant mutual accusations.

The evangelical forgiveness and reconciliation are of great importance especially when acts of infidelity, adultery and marital violence occur. In such cases the innocent spouse often fails to recognise the value of forgiveness and reconciliation. And yet one has to give forgiveness and reconciliation their proper place. The gospel reminds us that Jesus' death on the cross means reconciliation forever. God's reconciliation embodied in Jesus again uplifts the adulterous or violent spouse, he/she recognises the sin and wants to convert.

The Christian gospel reveals the sin dwelling in human hearts. The Bible often describes adultery and marital violence as breaking of fidelity and love. The Bible describes how the sin of infidelity and violence often corrode the harmony of conjugal community. Jesus thoroughly unmasked these two sins by pledging total fidelity to the Father until death on the cross (Flp 2,8; Juhant 2010, 57). His fidelity provides adulterous and violent spouses with an opportunity for forgiveness and reconciliation. Jesus was the reconciliatory sacrifice for our sins and the sins of the entire world (Heb 7,27). Through Jesus adulterous and unfaithful spouses have merciful possibility to start anew. It is therefore extremely important that quarrelling spouses through Jesus receive strength for forgiveness and reconciliation.

The penance regarding to other's guilt is also important for reconciliation. People every moment, involuntary or intentionally, hurt others with their thoughts, words or deeds, especially in "interpersonal relationships" (Benedikt XVI, 2009, 64). This holds particularly true for people who are in a love relationship. Since we all sin, each spouse adds his/her own share of guilt to a marital dispute. Spouses can disentangle from this only if they are in penance sympathetic with one another (Krašovec 2000, 459). The surest option for sympathy in penance is that spouses willingly accept also marital suffering. If the innocent spouse is lenient towards the wrongful spouse, the latter will follow suit. Reconciliation is possible if the innocent spouse is willing to suffer and atone for the guilt of his/her spouse. Christ also focused his whole mission on voluntary sacrifice, and thus reached reconciliation for the entire humanity. When a spouse is ennobled by the Christian gospel, he/she is able to confess his/her own mistakes and atone for the mistakes of his/her spouse.

There is another reason why it comes to forgiveness – the fact of one's own imperfection. If the innocent spouse takes a stand that he/she is not obliged to forgive the unjust spouse for the damage done, this can mean that the innocent spouse is convinced in his/her own perfection. Such conceit can harden him/her so as to become incapable of forgiveness and loving coexistence (the Papal Biblical Commission 2009, 121). The awareness of one's own imperfection is thus extremely important for reaching marital reconciliation.

The present environment more than ever requires that we search the gospel of Jesus Christ and rediscover the real well of forgiveness and marital reconciliation. Many marriages are affected by intolerance and hostility as they lack forgiveness and reconciliation. The Church thus invites all Christians "to rediscover the grace of following Christ" (Benedict XVI, 2011, 102). Only fidelity to what God once and for all realised in the crucified and resurrected Jesus Christ will inspire (Christian) spouses to forgive and reconcile.

References

Benedikt XVI. 2009. *Ljubezen v resnici* (okrožnica). Cerkveni dokumenti 127. Ljubljana: Družina.

Benedikt XVI. 2011. *Gospodova beseda* (posinodalna apostolska spodbuda). Cerkveni dokumenti 131. Ljubljana: Družina.

Bianchi, P. 2000. Processi e procedimenti canonici per la separazione personale dei coniugi. *Quaderni di diritto Ecclesiale* 2, pp. 146–168.

D'Auria, A. 2003. *Il matrimonio nel diritto della Chiesa. Commento ai canoni 1055 – 1165 del Codice di Diritto Canonico*. Roma: LUP.

Demel, S. 2004. Ehescheidung. In: Stephan Hearing in Heribert Schmitz, ed. *Lexikon des Kirchenrechts*, pp. 237 – 240. Freiburg im Breisgau: Herder.

Gramunt, I. & Hervada, J. & Wauck, LeRoy A. 1987. *Canons and Commentaries on Marriage*. Collegeville, Minnesota: The Liturgical Press.

Hendriks, J. 1999. *Diritto matrimoniale. Commento ai canoni 1055 – 1165 del Codice di Diritto Canonico*. Milano: Ancora.

Herman, E. 2010. *Princip Noetove barke*. Maribor: Slomškova založba.

Janez Pavel II. 1997. *Zakrament pokore. Sedem govorov in apostolsko pismo*. Cerkveni dokumenti 70. Ljubljana: Družina.

Juhant, J. 2009. *Občutek pripadnosti*. Celje: Celjska Mohorjeva družba.

Juhant, J. 2010. On Living with: Dialogue as the Way to the Art of Personal and Common Life. In: Janez Juhant in Bojan Žalec (eds.), *Art of Life: Origins, Fundations and Perspectives*, pp. 49–59. Münster: LIT.

Juhant, J. 2011. Dialogue, Peace and Religion. In: *Bogoslovni vestnik* 71, 1, pp. 39–50.

Krašovec, J. 2000. *Med krivdo in spravo*. Ljubljana: Svetopisemska družba Slovenije.

Maragnoli, G. 2000. La separazione personale dei coniugi tra legge della Chiesa e legge dello Stato in Italia. In: *Quaderni di diritto Ecclesiale* 2, pp. 169–191.

Papeška biblična komisija. 2009. *Sveto pismo in morala. Svetopisemske osnove krščanskega delovanja*. Cerkveni dokumenti 124. Ljubljana: Družina.

Putz, G. 2004. Ehebruch. In: Stephan Hearing in Heribert Schmitz (eds.), *Lexikon des Kirchenrechts*, pp. 231–232. Freiburg im Breisgau: Herder.

ABSTRACTS

Felix Unger
Reconciliation: the prerequisite for the future in Europe

Author claims that reconciliation is a difficult process yet it is indispensible for perspective society. The prerequisite for reconciliation is tolerance, "the virtue of living together". Additionally he stresses the following conditions or positive factors of reconciliation: recognition that life has the highest value; justice: "Justice is an excellent and human basis ensuring coexsistence, freedom of people and therefore peace"; a cultivation of dialogue. Reconciliation is important as a positive factor for actually united Europe. He ends by establishing that after all reconciliation depends on us and on our living in truth.

Key words: *reconciliation, virtues, tolerance, life as the highest value, justice, united Europe, truth.*

Jože Trontelj
On the duty to learn from history

The past of humankind abounds with injustice and violence, often committed against large numbers of innocent people. Most of the victims were caught against their will between sides in various conflicts, which did not solve any of the problems that served as proclaimed reasons for war. During the intervals of peace, many became victims of paranoid measures put in place for the security of the state. On European soil, World War II and the three totalitarian systems are the darkest examples. The European Union was created in order to avoid similar senseless destruction, atrocities and suffering in the future. However, our fading memories of the horrible abuses may no longer guarantee the culture of peace, collaboration and democracy needed to avert the risk of repeated cycles of war and violence. Honest and passionate learning from history may be one of the few ways to avoid future disasters. On the other hand, enforced forgetting would be an enormous moral mistake with long-term, potentially severe consequences for society.

Key words: *World War II, totalitarian regimes, human rights violations in post-World War II Europe, learning from history, need for empathy.*

Jože Krašovec
Biblical foundations of reconciliation

Hebrew monotheism has several interdependent characteristics: God is the beginning and the end of everything so far created; consequently, mankind and Israel can prosper only if they preserve a vital link with God the Creator who acts as person. Because humans too are personal beings, their relationship to God and to their fellow men is based on sublime divine actions in the sacred history. Evil is not independent in origin; it could be generated only by created beings. God's offer to Israel has the binding force of a covenant, animated by the parent/child relationship or the one between spouses. The event of Creation and the basic link between God, humankind and the covenant people exclude the possibility of total separation. The interrelation of these presuppositions implies the distinctive biblical way to reconciliation. God is unconditionally bound to the chosen people and promises a final completion of salvation in reconciliation.

Key words: *God the Creator, God as person, covenant, sin, punishment, forgiveness, reconciliation.*

Stanko Gerjolj
Education for reconciliation on the example of conflict between Esau and Jacob

An example of resolving the conflict between the brothers Jacob and Esau is a true example of pedagogical dynamics of reconciliation process, which runs from reconciliation with a loved one through a reconciliation with itself and until the enforcement of a sovereign belonging to those closest to us and God. The key moment is reconciliation with itself, which is a prerequisite for all other dimensions of the reconciliation process.

Key words: *reconciliation, family, independence, belonging, God.*

Marcel V. Măcelaru
Babel from text to symbol: possibilities of reconciliation in the Hebrew Bible

The story of the Tower of Babel (Genesis 11) has been commonly interpreted as a clash between human pride and divine will, resulting in God's punishment upon humans in the form of confusing their speech and scattering them all over the earth. This essay argues that the divine action in the story should be viewed as positive and that the story itself, being an aetiology which explains the diversity of cultures in the world, is probably aiming at promoting peaceful cohabitation in spite of cultural differences. Such a message would have counteracted the ethno-religious exclusivism of post-exilic Judaism. This reading of the Tower of Babel story informs the discussion on reconciliation that frames it.

Key words: *Tower of Babel; cultural diversity; reconciliation in the Old Testament; aetiology; identity.*

Janez Juhant
Are victims necessary for the survival of mankind?

According to *Charta of human rights* all people should be integrated in a universal moral community. Every morality which excludes some persons or groups is not moralistic in accordance with the *Charta*. All racist and ideological images of man have been a forgery of people in order to sacrifice them. The consequences have been suffering and sacrifice of nations like Armenians, Ukrainians, Jews, Bosnians, Slovene and other class-enemies, Christians, and other mass victims. Because “the essential is against life”, we can say that the modern life is against the essence of man, because it deals mostly with his immediateness and austerities. Still today we are witnesses of mass-victims and unfinished processes of reconciliation. Those campaigns are covered by media and other mechanisms. We can paraphrase Girard: the old myths have been replaced by new (modern) ones. Because man is a limited being (“original sin”), we are all involved in victimisation and burdened with guilty. The Slovene revolutionary case is a horrible example of the implementation of modern machineries of victimisation. The processes of reconciliation here and over the world are going slowly and the “birth of humanism” and of empathy remains still an important task of moral consciousness of Slovenes and of whole humane race.

Key words: *man, human rights, moral universalism, reconciliation, victim, genocide.*

Wolfgang Palaver

Why the concern for victims requires forgiveness: Girardian reflections on monotheism, violence and reconciliation

Girard's mimetic anthropology helps us to understand the important difference between archaic religions and the Abrahamic revelation. Whereas archaic religions are siding with the persecutors scapegoating their victims the monotheistic traditions share the view of the victims who are rehabilitated. In this overcoming of the scapegoat mechanism roots our modern concern for victims. But this concern that is part of the best achievements of our modern world becomes – if it gets perverted – a dangerous weapon. Siding with victims can easily turn us into scapegoaters of the persecutors leading to a dangerous escalation of violence. The concern for victims must therefore be complemented by forgiveness enabling us to seek reconciliation. We can discover this connection between the rehabilitation of the victim and forgiveness at the heart of the Abrahamic revelation, especially in the New Testament.

Key words: *victim, reconciliation, forgiveness, violence, monotheism.*

Tadej Strehovec

Is it possible to establish a new type of national reconciliation on the basis of the old "symbolic" victims?

The Rene Girard theory of mimesis and mimetic violence could be the starting point in how to interpret the Slovenian history during and after the Second World War. The mass killings of thousands of innocent victims could be the result of mimetically violence in Slovenian society which should be revealed and addressed. The national reconciliation and forgiveness could be reached not only by the discovering the historical facts but also with the creation of new type symbolic places which can unite and heal the Slovenian society and common collective memory and unconsciousness. The establishment of the Garden of Peace or Slovenian version of Israeli Yad Washem museum could be one example of such symbolic place.

Key words: *national reconciliation, forgiveness, Second World War, Rene Girard, mimesis, mimetic violence, founding murder.*

Bojan Žalec
Reconciliation: a conceptual analysis

The author analyses the concept of reconciliation. He tries to shell out the conditions of reconciliation. His analysis involves the investigation of the connections between justice, punishment, inner motivation and transformation, reparation of relationships and forgiveness. Inner motivation for establishment of positive relationship and internal transformation of the parties involved in reconciliation are necessary conditions of true reconciliation. The author gives the following definition of reconciliation: Reconciliation is achieved when the harm done by injustice to positive relationship between individuals or groups is repaired or compensated in such a way that it no more hinders the establishing of positive relationship. Regarding justice he concludes that justice is an essential part of the process of reconciliation. On the other hand reconciliation is a positive factor, background or even a condition of (future) justice. Reconciliation is a relative, manifold (differentiate) and transitive concept. It is not true that forgiveness is a necessary condition of reconciliation as such.

Key words: *reconciliation, justice, reparation, inner transformation, positive relationship, forgiveness.*

Branko Klun
History and (in)justice. Levinas' advocacy of human singularity

According to Hegel, the history of the world is also the Last Judgement (die Weltgeschichte ist das Weltgericht). The totality of history represents the realisation of reason, justifing even human suffering and the death of the innocent from the perspective of its universal intelligibility. Levinas strongly opposes this view and advocates human singularity, which refuses every attempt to be subordinated to the impersonal judgement of history. It is here that he looks for the ethical meaning of every individual which transcends history and can only be experienced in an encounter with another person.

Key words: *Levinas, history, injustice, singularity, totality.*

Anton Jamnik
Reconciliation, an act of courage and inner freedom

Reconciliation is a process with its philosophical and theological foundations. They both complement each other, as it is of crucial importance to trust in the work of the Holy Spirit, along with human endeavours. It is the Holy Spirit who can truly liberate a human heart of all negative thoughts and hatred. Reconciliation does not imply forgetting about past events, it has to do with internal liberation which manifests itself in forgiveness, mutual respect and sincere wish to create new relations. In the words of Bl. John Paul II, reconciliation is a sign of internal strength, freedom and courage, but most of all it is the work of God. And so the human perspective of reconciliation, which is of equal importance, complements the theological perspective, which leads to a new level of life quality. Every human being in this world, in all its fragility, is in desperate need of forgiveness. This need presents itself in his humility to sincerely accept the forgiveness of both his fellow humans and God. At the same time, every human being is expected to exercise forgiveness, as this is the only way to stop the vicious circle of vengeance and hatred. Reconciliation happens on both personal and structural levels. If the latter are unfair, it is impossible to achieve new quality of relations within a society.

Key words: *reconciliation, courage, inner freedom, internal strength, God.*

Irena Avsenik Nabergoj
Forgiveness and reconciliation: From Joseph of Egypt to Shakespeare's Prospero and philosophical interpretations

The Bible is replete with moving narratives and statements about the greatness of divine and human forgiveness, mercy and reconciliation. In the Old Testament, the most well-known and popular is the narrative of Joseph in Egypt (Gen 37–50). We find the spirit of that story in resonant works from the antiquity on. Shakespeare's play *The Tempest*, written around 1610, is especially worthy of mention, even though it would be hard to claim that Shakespeare found inspiration for this play precisely in the story of Joseph. The similarity with the Joseph story is evident in all of the main circumstances and in development of event to the final act of reconciliation. Forgiveness and reconciliation became only recently important themes of philosophical discourse. Some philosophers present them as a secular virtue, some others are capable to penetrate to the last resorts of realisation of the ideal of forgiveness and reconciliation.

Key words: *forgiveness, reconciliation, literary representation, Shakespeare, The Tempest, mercy.*

Vojko Strahovnik
Guilt, shame and reconciliation in the context of humanity

Both guilt and shame uncover many very important aspects of morality, even though modern moral thought centres more on guilt than on shame. When considering the concept of reconciliation shame also plays a very central role. In the paper I defend an understanding of moral shame as an emotional response or attitude that has its relevance based on the criterion of humanity, which lies within us as a standard in a way that the criterion of humanity cannot merely be understood on the level of damage that others (i.e. victims) had suffered, but in a deeper sense, as the breach of humanity and overlooking the humanity in those others. Only such recognition of humanity enables genuine resolution and reconciliation.

Key words: *ethics, reconciliation, guilt, shame, humanity.*

Claudia Paganini
Can the media afford reconciliation?
Reconciliation as a principle of a minimalistic ethics

Today's debate about media ethics is no longer a discussion of scandals but is characterised by the conscious endeavour to place the ethics of its sub-areas on the solid ground of scientific reflection. The interdisciplinary orientation and the distinct character of its sub-areas have undoubtedly enriched the discussion but have also lead to the consequence that problems are addressed from diverging perspectives. In order to develop a media ethics which comprises the sub-areas of journalism, public relations, advertising, visual media communication, and new media we will first analyse the characteristics of the individual media sectors. We then intend to apply the findings of principlism to the media. In the same way as it has been done by Beauchamp and Childress in medical ethics, the attempt will be made to reconstruct a limited number of mid-range principles, which come to represent a so-called common morality. We will thus pose the question whether reconciliation could be one of these principles.

Key words: *media ethics, principlism, common morality, publicness, reconciliation.*

Corneliu Constantineanu

Reconciliation in a world of exclusion: the possibility of a radical novelty "in Christ"

The increasing tendencies towards intolerance, exclusion and various forms of conflict in our contemporary world, point to an urgent need to investigate and explicate the real possibilities for, and the meaning and significance of reconciliation. In the present paper I would like to explore the reality of the reconciliation of the world accomplished by God, in Christ, and, subsequently, the possibilities for reconciliation. I will examine in particular the paradigm shift which Apostle Paul makes vis-a-vis the classical understanding of reconciliation and the radical novelty he brings to the concept. This redefinition and new meaning Paul gives to the notion of reconciliation highlights also the new possibilities for reconciliation "in Christ".

Key words: *reconciliation, exclusion, victim, forgiveness, new creation, "in Christ".*

Wilhelm Guggenberger

Reconciliation and confession in the theology of Dietrich Bonhoeffer

Forgiveness and confession of guilt are indispensable preconditions of reconciliation. The German Lutheran theologian Dietrich Bonhoeffer estimated sincere acknowledgement of guilt to be one of the core characteristics of the church. Missing this recognition and confession the church cannot witness the grace of God in a proper way. Unreserved acknowledgement of guilt by the church is a vivid sign of God's unconditional forgiveness which is a fundamental Christian experience. Quite the witness of grace could enable other culprits to confess their own guilt and to foster the process of reconciliation by this. These insights have to be applied to mediation-activities of the churches in current conflicts.

Key words: *forgiveness, confession, grace, church, Bonhoeffer.*

Gunter Prüller-Jagenteufel, Vienna

"Restraining power" against evil and "scarring over" of guilt. Bonhoeferian remarks on "penultimate" steps toward reconciliation

Dietrich Bonhoeffer strongly emphasizes that forgiveness and reconciliation is an "ultimate" reality: a gift by God's grace. This ultimate reality, in traditional Lutheran terms called the justification of the sinner, can be realized already here and now, in the "penultimate" reality of our lives, if only partly and in a fragmented way. We experience only the beginning of the eschatological dynamic that characterizes our reality, even in the political and social area. So in order to build a peaceful future we have to rely on penultimate forms of forgiveness and reconciliation. Bonhoeffer calls this process the "scarring over" of guilt. Even if it is not yet fully forgiveness and reconciliation in the theological sense of the word, it is at least a start to build on. Therefore, it is the task of politics and also the churches to take the necessary steps in that direction.

Key words: *Dietrich Bonhoeffer, theology, christology, political ethics, reconciliation.*

Daniel G. Oprean

Reconciliation in church and society: church's ministry as God's reconciliation agency

The paper aims to demonstrate that reconciliation is a concept that should not be captive to its vertical dimension or in its close horizontal dimension, as an internal business of the churches. In the light of Christ's kenotic model of life and ministry the church needs a transformation of its life in such a way that she becomes God's reconciliation agency, an agency not of sterile talk about reconciliation, but rather of incarnated practice of reconciliation promoted in actions and for the society as a whole. By letting herself challenged and modeled by Christ' s perennial example the church could escape the trap of individualistic verticalisation or egocentric horizontalisation in regard to reconciliation and could become able to engage kenotically in actions of reconciliation, on the coordinates of education, social care and prophetic ministry in the world.

Key words: *reconciliation, church, society, kenosis, education, social care, prophetic ministry.*

Mari Jože Osredkar
Forgiveness allows a New Creation

The word “forgiveness” in Christian terms denotes the position or act by which a person pardons an offence and renounces any revenge for an injustice caused by another. Forgiveness has Biblical roots and achieves its most prominence in the texts of the New Testament. Herein Christ is exemplary in promoting God’s mercy. He invites all peoples to be compassionate and merciful as Our Heavenly Father. The Christian concept of forgiveness can be rephrased in the assertion: “forgiveness is the new creation”. Thus, a man, who does wrong, sins. This action deserves death. But life can well be maintained through an act of forgiveness. Forgiveness permits the continuation of life, an essential element of one being human. Life has been given to man as a gift from his inception, and that gift endures through man’s lifetime. In this way also, forgiveness too is a gift for a man in need of its restorative power. This concept of forgiveness is understandable in the context of “relational theology,” whose fundamental premise is that: “to live means to be in relationship with others.”

Key words: *forgiveness, sin, life, new Creation, relational theology.*

Drago K. Ocvirk
Jesus – neither a hand of reconciliation nor an apple of discord between Christians and Muslims

Jesus/Isa is an important figure for Christians and Muslims alike. The first are even called by his name, the second hold him for a Muhammad’s forerunner and *mahdi* – messiah. In the spirit of some kind of a generous and naive peacefulness some see in the figure of Jesus/Isa a meeting point where Christians and Muslims could unite and reconcile. But a serious examination of the Christian and Muslim narratives concerning Jesus/Isa indicates that there are in fact in them two completely different actors that cannot be reconciled and will remain a bone of contention as long as the members of both religions do not recognize those differences, admit them and thereby remit to others their otherness. The path to reconciliation at this level is not therefore the sameness at all cost, i.e. Jesus/Isa reduced to a common denominator, but a constant efforts to respect difference, uniqueness and specificity of the others and their constitutive narratives.

Key words: *Christian Jesus, Muslim Isa, forgiveness as admittance of otherness, respect of differences, reconciliation with contradictions, unity in diversity.*

Béla Mester
Reconciliation as a basis of establishing political communities: Athens after the thirty tyrants – Central Europe after its pocket-tyrants

This paper offers an analysis of the role of memory and oblivion in the process of the renewed narrative identity based on reconciliation of a political community. European culture has two opposite way to create a new narrative identity, based on a reconciliation process. The first one is based on sophisticated forms of *cultural memory*; the second one is rooted in the *taboo* of the public speech about the sins of the past. A paradigmatic instance of the later is Athens' general amnesty after the regime of *the thirty tyrants*. This paper will outline the main forms of the political identities based on the art of oblivion and art of memory. The main modern references will be Nietzsche's well-known essay on the history, and Jan Assmann's and Harald Weinrich's counter-theories about the cultural memory and oblivion. I will take a short glance to the cultural memory of the Central-European political communities, using Hungarian examples, in the last paragraph.

Key words: *art of memory, art of oblivion, cultural memory, Central-European political communities, political identity, reconciliation.*

Gábor Kovács
Recollection, forgetting, reconciliation – the hungarian case

It is beyond doubt that reconciliation is one of the most frequently used terms in Eastern-and South-Eastern-Europe. The cause of the repeated reference to this notion lies in the history of this region. Communism is a common heritage in this part of Europe. Historical recollection here has been burdened with the tragic experiences of genocides, massacres and deportations. Hungary is not an exception to the rule, but the problem, in the case of this country has been rooted deeper. The disintegration of the Greater Hungary, after the First World War, was a trauma for the national consciousness, which, using the term coined by István Bibó, the Hungarian political thinker, had evoked some kind of political hysteria lingering to our time. Hungary, after 1920, became a deeply divided national community with two parties opposing sharply to each other. On the one side were the westernizers (urbánusok) who wanted to complete a western-style modernization emulating western political and cultural models, on the other side were the Hungarian populists (népiek) who feared for the loss of 'Hungarian national character' and preferred a self-contained development. Communism, which, in a respect, brought with itself a low-standard modernization, made the situation more complicated. After the collapse of the communist regime, which ironically was mentioned as goulash-communism, it came soon to light that the bringing of the suppressed past from the social sub-consciousness to the social consciousness, is a necessary but not satisfactory precondition. After the political transformation of 1989 everyone can talk about the historical injuries which afflicted his/her family and everyone can construct his/her narrative concerning the past, but reconciliation seems to be much far away than it was ever. It came to light that reconciliation needs a delicate balance of recollection and forgetting, moreover a common set of basic values accepted by the whole national community.

Key words: *recollection, forgetting, reconciliation, Hungary, political hysteria.*

Jože Dežman
Slovenia and the criminal burden of Titoism

The reconciliation process in Slovenia is very dynamic and includes detabooization of numerous half-truths and lies of the Titoistic system of development and maintenance of revolutionary heritage. It is an intense public and political confrontation with the criminal legacy of the totalitarian regimes. Uncovering more than 600 concealed killing and burial sites, where around 100,000 prisoners of war and civilians were murdered by Titoism in the spring of 1945, after the end of the 2nd World War, is especially painful. More than one percent of the population of Slovenia was killed in those two months. Equally painful is facing the consequences of the discriminatory division of the population – a consequence of the segregation of the victims of war and the revolution and class war. The population of Slovenia was segregated according to ideological criteria. The process of sympathy with the victims and the condemnation of the crimes and the criminals is still ongoing. The Republic of Slovenia established a system of measures with the acts on denationalization, war burial sites and repatriations. Their effectiveness will be part of future research.

Key words: *reconciliation, transitional justice, truth, forgiveness, detabooization.*

Mitja Ferenc
Independent Slovenia and concealed mass graves

After reconciliation ceremony in Kočevski rog in July 1990 and after the establishment of independent country and democratic changes we expected that our new county will start to deal with question of mass murders that happened after Second World War and concealed graves that are related to those murders. Events that happened immediately after Word War II are one of the most traumatic in Slovenian history. But twenty years after mentioned reconciliation ceremony we observe that the graves of war losers and some civilians even 66 years after the end of the war are still not properly arranged. For immense majority it is not known where their bodies lie and they were not buried in decent and human manner. In Slovenia there is an agreement only on principal level that everyone who lost his life in the war or because of the war has the right to his name and his grave. On the other hand on practical level we deal with questions of reasonableness of graves arrangement, questions what will be written on the gravestone plaque and even with the reproaches that the past should be left alone because it supposedly does not concern young generations. All that causes pain, anger and sadness to people who, after decades of silence about fate of their relatives, gained some hope that they will get support at finding answers when the establishment of new country happened. All thoughts about reconciliation and unity of Slovenian people will be in vain if lack of concrete action of executive power will continue. As a nation we are for decades confronted with challenge to overpass this burden of past that is pushing us to the ground. Since 1990 there were many opportunities to do that, but they were not taken.

Key words: *concealed mass graves, extrajudicial executions, reconciliation, revolutionary violence, exhumation of mortal remains, Huda jama mine.*

Mark Kleyman

Urban development, grassroots authoritarianism and the problem of reconciliation in post-Soviet Russia

The current development of Russia provides the situation marked with a paradox. The spread of capitalism *tout court* is increasingly interlinked with the attempts to restore the main elements of the Soviet ideology and policies. For example, Stalin's practices in governance are often presented as an "effective management strategy". Therefore, the ideas of reconciliation and coping with the totalitarian past are often considered as "antipatriotic" ones. These tendencies might be considered as an outcome of grassroots authoritarianism that implies hostility toward any form of (O)otherness. As a result, there are still no widely accepted social norms that encourage individuals in maintaining, assisting and enhancing life. The paper provides an attempt to understand this situation, while we take into consideration the main trends of urbanization in Russia.

Key words: *Russia, urbanization, grassroots authoritarianism, reconciliation.*

Igor Bahovec

The meaning of culture for reconciliation: dialogue, memory and community

Divisions, disagreements and conflicts exist in most of human societies, looking either at a particular society - for example the neighbourhood, the nation -, or at relations between societies. Cultures are often strongly impressed by historical and existing divisions and conflicts. Divisions became part of the meanings, values, norms, ways of life, memory, etc.

In this paper we focus on the role of culture and community in reconciliation processes. We believe that a genuine reconciliation process should integrate all aspects of human life. Without this reconciliation cannot reach the deep level of human life needed for genuine co-existence and the more profound cooperation of previously hostile, conflicting or divided people, groups and cultures. Our specific aim is to clarify the Ubuntu (Southern African) way of reconciliation. We will focus mostly on the following elements of the process of reconciliation: community, dialog, memory, truth.

Key words: *culture, memory, dialog, truth, reconciliation, community, Ubuntu.*

Katarina Kompan Erzar and Tomaž Erzar
Healing the trauma of postwar killings in Slovenia

Because in the long term people can live only in secure relationships, dealing with the trauma of postwar killings in Slovenia is a matter of survival. Until we create the conditions for compassionate solidarity and mourning, as a society and as individuals we will be marked by broken relationships, suppressed despair, false courage, violence, and self-destructive behavior.

Key words: *post war killings, trauma, internalized shame, victimization, dignity.*

Barbara Simonič
The horizons of reconciliation after traumatic experience

We live in the age of trauma - a statement that holds true in the sense that our everyday world seems to be severely threatened from many sides, namely collective trauma, or personal and interpersonal traumatic experiences. When trauma happens it threatens us in many ways and leads to the feeling of dehumanization. But it doesn't end here: traumatized people try to find their way out from this impairment and often attempt to restore their former state at least in part. In doing so they often try to avoid painful feelings, and risk getting stuck in the vicious cycle of repeating some aspects of their trauma over and over again. On the other hand, there is a process that enables us to face existential vulnerability, anxiety and hatred, and it is possible only through reconciliation. Interpersonal competencies, such as empathy, compassion and sympathy, could be very helpful for healing emotionally traumatic wounds and for the process of re-humanizing the victim again.

Key words: *trauma, interpersonal trauma, emotions, empathy.*

Stanislav Slatinek
Civil suits for divorce

Divorces of spouses have become in our post-modern society very frequent phenomena. The canon law enables believers "to divorce without dissolving matrimonial bond". By such divorce, spouses cease to live together, while their marriage remains uninterrupted. This right goes to a believer in the Catholic Church when such divorce is justifiable. The most frequent reason for a separation with a matrimonial bond still existing is adultery or infidelity. Other legitimate reason is endangering mental and physical well-being of one's spouse and children. The spouses are nevertheless bound to strive for reconciliation. Reconciliation manifests in marital sexual intercourse. This is the extremely prolonged and difficult process which calls for confessing (one's wrongdoings) and forgiving one another. At this point only the gospel can help a believer.

Key words: *marriage, divorce, adultery, infidelity, violence, reconciliation, forgiveness.*

THE AUTHORS

Prof.Dr.Dr.h.c. Felix Unger
President
European Academy of Sciences and Arts
St.-Peter-Bezirk 10
5020 Salzburg
Austria
www.euro-acad.eu

Professor Jože Trontelj
President of Slovene Academy of Sciences and Arts

Professor Jože Krašovec
Member of Slovene Academy of Sciences and Arts and of European Academy of Sciences and Arts
Faculty of Theology, University of Ljubljana
Poljanska c. 4
SI-1001 Ljubljana

Professor Stanko Gerjolj
Dean of the Faculty of Theology, University of Ljubljana, Slovenia
E-mail: stanko.gerjolj@teof.uni-lj.si

Marcel V. Măcelaru, DPhil (Oxon)
Title/Position: Associate Professor of Hebrew Bible and Old Testament Studies & Executive Dean
Institution: Evanđeoski Teološki Fakultet, Osijek, Croatia
Email: marcel.macelaru@evtos.hr

Professor Janez Juhant
Ph.D., Faculty of Theology, University of Ljubljana, Slovenia
E-mail: janez.juhant@guest.arnes.si

Professor Wolfgang Palaver
University of Innsbruck

Tadej Strehovec
Assistant, Faculty of Theology, University of Ljubljana
Mail: Tržaška 85, 1000 Ljubljana, Slovenia
E-mail: tadej.strehovec@teof.uni-lj.si

Bojan Žalec
Asssociate Professor of Philosophy, the Head of the Institute of Philosophy and Ethics at the Faculty of Theology, University of Ljubljana
Mail: Faculty of Theology, Poljanska c. 4, SI-1001 Ljubljana
E-mail: bojan.zalec@teof.uni-lj.si

Branko Klun
Associate Professor of Philosophy, Faculty of Theology, University of Ljubljana,
E-mail: branko.klun@teof.uni-lj.si

Anton Jamnik
Th.D., Bishop, Assistant Prof., Faculty of Theology, University of Ljubljana, Slovenia
E-mail: anton.jamnik@guest.arnes.si

Irena Avsenik Nabergoj
Associate Professor, Faculty of Theology, University of Ljubljana
Mail: Glavarjeva 47, SI-1000 Ljubljana, Slovenia
E-mail: irena.avseniknabergoj@teof.uni-lj.si

Vojko Strahovnik
Faculty of Theology, University of Ljubljana
vojko.strahovnik@guest.arnes.si
Vojko Strahovnik is research associate at Faculty of Theology, University of Ljubljana and Assistant Professor and Head of chair for legal theory and ethics and public policy at the Faculty of Government and European Studies, Kranj.

Claudia Paganini
Univ.-Ass. Mag. Dr. Claudia Paganini
Institut für Christliche Philosophie
Karl-Rahner-Platz 1 A-6020 Innsbruck
Tel.: +43/650/3926340 *Fax:* +43/512/507-2736
E-mail: claudia.paganini@uibk.ac.at

Corneliu Constantineanu
Associate Professor, The Head of Pentecostal Theological Institute in Bucharest, Romania
E-mail: corneliu_c@yahoo.com

Dr. Wilhelm Guggenberger
Assistant Professor at the Institute of Systematic Theology, Catholic Theological Faculty of the University of Innsbruck, Austria.
Teaching Christian Social Ethics, Member of the Research Programme "Religion - Violence - Communication - World Order"
Dean of Studies at the Theological Faculty
Address:
Institut für Systematische Theologie
Karl Rahner-Platz 1, 6020 Innsbruck
wilhelm.guggenberger@uibk.ac.at

Gunter Prüller-Jagenteufel
Address:
Dr. Gunter Prüller-Jagenteufel
Associate Professor for Moral Theology at the Catholic Theological Faculty of the University of Vienna;
Schenkenstraße 8-10, 1010 Wien
e-mail: gunter.prueller-jagenteufel@univie.ac.at
The author is vice-president of the Austrian Section of the European Society of Catholic Theology and a member of the International Bonhoeffer Society.

Daniel G. Oprean
Evangelical Theological Seminary, Osijek, Croatia
E-mail: daniaoprean@gmail.com

Mari Jože Osredkar PhD
Affiliation address (institution): *Teološka fakulteta, Poljanska 4, SI-1000 Ljubljana*
Address for mail correspondence: Černetova 20, SI-1000 Ljubljana
E-mail address: mari.osredkar.ofm@siol.net

Professor Drago K. Ocvirk
Faculty of Theology, University of Ljubljana, Slovenia
Drago K. Ocvirk is a Professor of Christian fundamental theology, missiology and world religions at the Faculty of Theology, University of Ljubljana. He also lectures regularly at Holy Name of Mary Seminary at Tenaru, near Honiara, in Solomon Islands. He is the Chairman of the Institute for Religious Studies, Ecumenism and Dialog at the University of Ljubljana.
E-mail: drago.ocvirk@guest.arnes.si

Béla Mester, PhD
Senior Research Fellow, Institute for Philosophical Research of the Hungarian Academy of Sciences, Budapest, Hungary
Associate Professor, College of Nyíregyháza, Hungary
E-mail: mester@webmail.phil-inst.hu

Gábor Kovács, Senior Research Fellow, Institute for Philosophical Research of the Hungarian Academy of Sciences, Budapest, Hungary
gbrkvcs3@gmail.com

Jože Dežman
Acting Manager of the Archives of the Republic of Slovenia
Mail: Arhiv Republike Slovenije, Zvezdarska 1, 1000 Ljubljana
E-mail: jdmemores@gmail.com

Mitja Ferenc
PhD, Associate Professor, Department of History, University of Ljubljana, Faculty of Arts, SI-1000 Ljubljana, Aškerčeva 2, e- mail: ferenc.mitja@guest.arnes.si

Mark Kleyman
Affiliations address (Institution):
Department of Philosophy,
Ivanovo State University of Chemistry and Technology,
Prospekt Engelsa 7,
RUS-153000 Ivanovo,
RUSSIA
E-mail address: mark.kleyman2712@gmail.com
Area of research interests: social psychology, community psychology, urban anthropology, urban studies.

Igor Bahovec, Ph.D. in Sociology, is an Assistant Professor at the Faculty of Theology, University of Ljubljana. His *research interests include religion* and (postmodern) culture, person, civil society/community, intermediary institutions and social capital, intercultural dialog.
E-mail: igor.bahovec@guest.arnes.si

Katarina K. Erzar & Tomaž Erzar
Assisistant Prof./Assoc. Prof., Faculty of Theology, University of Ljubljana, Slovenia;
Franciscan Family Institute
E-mail: tomaz.erzar@guest.arnes.si
lia-katarina.kompan@guest.arnes.si

Barbara Simonič
Faculty of Theology; Franciscan Family Institute
Poljanska cesta 4, 1000 Ljubljana
barbara.simonic1@guest.arnes.si
Dr. Barbara Simonič is assistant professor at Faculty of Theology (Marital and Family Studies) and Marital and Family Therapist at Franciscan Family Institute.

Stanislav Slatinek
Assistant Prof., Faculty of Theology, University of Ljubljana, Slovenia
E-mail: stanislav.slatinek@guest.arnes.si

Theologie Ost – West
Europäische Perspektiven
hrsg. von Prof. Dr. Janez Juhant (Universität Ljubljana) und Prof. Dr. Albert Franz (Universität Dresden)

Janez Juhant; Bojan Žalec (Eds.)
Art of Life
Origins, Foundations and Perspectives.
With contributions of Ulrich Beck, Wilhelm Schmid, Santiago Sia, Karl M. Woschitz and others

All civilizations have cultivated some kind of *ars vivendi*, and also our own (present) is no exception. At one hand the present society more deeply than ever interferes with secrets of life. Yet at the other hand, there are signs of non-mastering the life, the escape in the opposite direction, to non-life. There are even sings of turning to death. The former Pope John Paul II spoke about our culture as a culture of death. How can we consider the art of life as a challenge for solving difficult problems of man's life in the time being?

Bd. 14, 2010, 360 S., 19,90 €, br.,
ISBN 978-3-643-90043-2

Janez Juhant; Bojan Žalec (Eds.)
Humanity after Selfish Prometheus
Chances of Dialogue and Ethics in a Technicized World

Neither any technological development nor any institutional mechanisms (economical, legal, political etc.) can compensate the lack of ethical persons. Reaching sustainable development and life of quality is possible only on the basis of view which is not trapped, flat and reducing, on the basis of an effort, which ca – founded on temperance and humility (in relation to the nature, self, others and (O)other) - (co)create cooperation, higher order synthesis and synergy of the crafts that are the conditio sine qua non of survival, harmonious world and (decent) existence of a human (as a human) in it.

Bd. 15, 2011, 304 S., 19,90 €, br.,
ISBN 978-3-643-90075-3

LIT Verlag Berlin – Münster – Wien – Zürich – London
Auslieferung Deutschland / Österreich / Schweiz: siehe Impressumsseite